FIFTY MAJOR PHILOSOPHERS:
A REFERENCE GUIDE

FIFTY MAJOR PHILOSOPHERS
A REFERENCE GUIDE

DIANÉ COLLINSON

CROOM HELM
London • New York • Sydney

© Diané Collinson 1987
Croom Helm Ltd, Provident House, Burrell Row,
Beckenham, Kent BR3 1AT
Croom Helm Australia, 44-50 Waterloo Road,
North Ryde 2113, New South Wales

British Library Cataloguing in Publication Data

Collinson, Diané
  Fifty major philosophers: a reference guide.
  1. Philosophy — Dictionaries
  I. Title
  103′.21   B41
  ISBN 0-7099-3466-1

Library of Congress Cataloging-in-Publication Data

Collinson, Diane, 1930–
  Fifty major philosophers.

  Includes bibliographies and index.
  1. Philosophy — History. 2. Philosophers — Biography.
I. Title.
B72.C59 1987   109′.2′2 [B]   87-8929
ISBN 0-7099-3466-1

Typeset in Times Roman by Leaper & Gard Ltd, Bristol, England
Printed and bound in Great Britain by Mackays of Chatham Ltd, Kent

Contents

Preface

For each philosopher treated in this book I have provided the following: a short statement describing the main thrust of his philosophy; information about his life; and concise expositions of one or two aspects of his thought, along with mention, where appropriate, of its connection with the thought of other philosophers. I have selected for exposition those aspects of an individual's philosophy which I take to be especially important, interesting, and characteristic of his work. My aim has been to enable the reader briefly to share something of the point of view of each philosopher. No living philosopher is included in the book.

At the end of each essay I have provided information that can launch the interested reader into further and more detailed study. First, there are notes to which the numbers in the text refer; second, a list of other philosophers treated in the book whose thought relates in one way or another to that of the philosopher in hand; third, details of the philosopher's principal writings; fourth, a list of books suitable for further reading.

At the end of the book there is a short glossary of philosophical terms. It contains brief explanations of technical or semi-technical terms that occur a number of times in the book. For the most part it has been possible to give a brief explanation of such a term with its first use, but it was not feasible to repeat the explanation for every subsequent use. Subsequent or unexplained uses therefore appear in bold print in order to indicate that there is a glossary entry for the term or for a cognate of it. The term does not appear in bold print on the occasion of its being briefly explained in the text. The glossary entries should not be taken to be either clear-cut definitions or complete explanations of the terms they describe. They are meant to provide only a first foothold for a reader not familiar with the philosophical terrain.

Accommodating fifty philosophers between two covers has involved presenting a good deal of information in a closely packed way. By choosing to expound just one or two aspects of each philosopher's work I have sought to avoid offering material that is too condensed to be readily understood. By supplying the appendices, already mentioned, to each essay I have tried to provide the means of augmenting and developing what I have written. I have thought of each essay as providing guidance towards the main routes of further study; that is, as embodying references and indications which, if pursued, will help the enquiring reader to enjoy the sort of critical understanding and appreciation that each of these fifty philosophers deserves.

Diané Collinson

The Philosophers

Thales of Miletus
about 624-546 BC

Western philosophy is said to have begun in the sixth century BC at Miletus on the Ionian seaboard of Asia Minor. Ionia was the meeting place of East and West; it was also the land of Homer. The first Milesian philosophers, Thales, Anaximander and Anaximenes, were open not only to oriental influences and the Homeric tradition but to the mathematics of Egypt and Babylon and to the ideas and information that flowed along the trade routes passing through Ionia.

What we know of Thales of Miletus has come to us through the reports of others, for nothing of his own writing has survived. He seems to have been, in the characteristically Greek manner, extremely capable in a number of ways. He probably travelled to Egypt to learn astronomy, geometry and practical skills to do with the measuring and management of land and water. According to Herodotus he predicted an eclipse of the sun that occurred in 585 BC. His knowledge of geometry enabled him to navigate ships and to measure pyramids by reference to the shadows they cast at certain times of day. Herodotus relates the story of how Thales overcame the problem of getting an army across an unbridged river by diverting the flow of water to run behind the army's encampment until the channel in front of it was shallow enough to be forded. He seems, too, to have been politically astute and is reported to have advised the Ionians to set up a single deliberative chamber at Teos in the middle of Ionia and to regard the other cities as demes or lesser townships. He features in the history of mathematics as the originator of geometrical proof. According to Proclus,[1] Thales produced a number of propositions which, although not presented in correct logical sequence, were nevertheless related to each other in the **deductive** way that came to be required for geometrical proof.

But it was not these wide-ranging achievements that earned Thales the title of philosopher; rather, it was his attempt to provide a rational description and explanation of the world. This rational project significantly distinguishes his thought from earlier, mythologically based accounts of the world. Thales asked the question: What is the source of all things? The answer he gave was: water. He maintained, according to those who wrote about him,[2] that everything comes into being from water and that the earth floats on water like a log. Aristotle discusses this view in his *Metaphysics*. He points out that Thales does not seem to consider that the water on which the earth rests must itself rest on something. He suggests that Thales arrives at the supposition that water is the primary substance, maintaining its own nature while other things come into being from it, through observing that everything is nourished by moisture and that seeds and sperm are moist.

We have to remember that Thales' ideas, as well as those of the other Milesians, may have been shaped for us by the outlook and understanding of those who reported them. It has been suggested that Aristotle, who at three hundred years' remove could have known about Thales only indirectly, may not have fully comprehended what he meant. Thales, it is argued, would have subscribed to the then popular conception of the world and its surrounding water as stretching downwards limitlessly, so that for him there would have been no troublesome question such as that raised by Aristotle about its ultimate support. That the earth rested on water was an Egyptian belief as well as part of the Homeric tradition and it would be a small move from thinking of it as the support of all things to thinking of it as the source of all things. But the details of Thales' thoughts about the relationship of water to everything else are unknown and Aristotle may, to some extent, have made his own inferences from Thales' broad conception. What is noteworthy is that Thales apparently substantiated his cosmogony, that is, his theory of the universe, by observation of the natural world rather than by reference to mythology and proverbs.

Thales' second major claim about the nature of the universe was that 'all things are full of gods'. His exact meaning is not entirely clear but he is widely taken to have meant that some kind of vital force permeates the world; that all things are in some sense besouled or partake of a common and unifying vitality. Whether he propounded a relationship between water and the 'gods in all things' is not known, but it would be difficult to deny a relationship of some sort between them, given the **premiss** that water is the source of *everything*.

Thales' view of the nature of the world may seem at first to be more like a theory in the natural sciences than philosophy. Its philosophical content and importance are explained with superb lucidity by Nietzsche:

> Greek Philosophy seems to begin with a preposterous fancy, with the proposition that *water* is the origin and mother-womb of all things. Is it really necessary to stop there and become serious? Yes, and for three reasons: Firstly, because the proposition does enunciate something about the origin of things; secondly, because it does so without figure and fable; thirdly and lastly, because in it is contained, although only in the chrysalis state, the idea — Everything is one. The first-mentioned reason leaves Thales still in the company of religious and superstitious people; the second, however, takes him out of this company and shows him to us as a natural philosopher; but by virtue of the third, Thales becomes the first Greek philosopher.[3]

Notes

1. Proclus took his information from a *History of geometry* written by Eudemus, who attributed several theorems to Thales, maintaining that he must have employed them to solve certain practical problems in navigation. See G.S. Kirk, J.E. Raven and M. Schofield, *The presocratic philosophers*, 2nd edn (Cambridge University Press, Cambridge, 1983), pp. 2 and 85-6.
2. Plato, Aristotle, Theophrastus, Simplicius, Diogenes and Eudemus were the major reporters of Thales's ideas. See Kirk, Raven and Schofield, *The presocratic philosophers*, pp. 1-6 and 76-99.
3. Fredrich Nietzsche, *Early Greek Philosophy*, trans. Oscar Levy (Russell and Russell, New York, 1964), p. 86.

See also in this book

Anaximander, Anaximenes, Pythagoras.

Thales' writings

A *Nautical star-guide* was ascribed by some to Thales; others said the *Star-guide* was written by Phokos of Samos. Various other writings were attributed to Thales but none of the attributions is certain.

Further reading

Text

Diels, H. (ed.) (1964) *Die Fragmente der Vorsokratiker*, 11th edn (Weidmann, Zurich). These are the presocratic texts in Greek.
Freeman, K. (ed.) *Ancilla to the pre-Socratic philosophers*, a complete translation of the fragments in Diels (Harvard University Press, Cambridge, Mass., 1983).
Kirk, G.S., Raven, J.E., Schofield, M. *The presocratic philosophers*, 2nd edn (Cambridge University Press, Cambridge, 1983). This is the book I have used for textual references.

General

Barnes, J. *The pre-Socratics* (2 vols, Routledge and Kegan Paul, London, 1979; 1-vol. edn, 1982)
Dicks, D.R. 'Thales', *Classical Quarterly* vol. 9 (1959), pp. 294-309
Emlyn-Jones, C. *The Ionians and Hellenism* (Routledge and Kegan Paul, London, 1980)
Guthrie, W.K.C. *A history of Greek philosophy* (6 vols, Cambridge University Press, Cambridge, 1962-81; paperback edition, vols IV and V, 1986)
Stokes, M.C. *One and many in presocratic philosophy* (University Press of America, Lanham, distr. by Eurospan, London, 1986)
Taylor, A.E. *Aristotle on his predecessors* (Open Court, La Salle, Ill., 1977)

Anaximander
about 610-546 BC

Anaximander is thought to have been only a few years younger than Thales. Theophrastus describes him as Thales' 'successor and pupil'. Like Thales, Anaximander seems to have been a mixture of astrologer, geologist, mathematician and physicist as well as a philosopher. He probably introduced the gnomon (the shadow-casting rod of the sundial) into Greece. And it was he who, according to Agathemerus, 'first dared to draw the inhabited world on a tablet'.[1] One fragment remains of the book, *Concerning nature*, that he is said to have written. According to all reports it was a very large work, offering a **cosmogony**, accounts of the heavenly bodies and of the development of living organisms, studies of natural history, biology, meteorology and astronomy, geography and maps of the world, and dissertations upon every aspect of human and animal life. He set the example of intellectual prowess for the many brilliant thinkers who succeeded him.

Anaximander maintained that the original world-forming stuff is *apeiron*, a substance that is without boundary, limit or definition. By this he may have meant that *apeiron* was spatially infinite or that it was indefinite in the sense that it was unlike any one kind of matter in the physical universe; or he may have meant both. He described *apeiron* as surrounding everything boundlessly and as being that from which all the heavens and all the worlds in them come into being: earth, air, fire and water are somehow generated from the indefinite substance. Things are constantly in motion and what has its birth from the infinite returns to it at death. Anaximander seems to have believed that some kind of ultimate balance or state of justice is maintained between all things, probably through interactions between the cosmic opposites of hot and cold, dry and wet. A passage from Plutarch indicates some of the details of this cosmogony:

He [Anaximander] says that that which is productive from the eternal of hot and cold was separated off at the coming-to-be of this world, and that a kind of sphere of flame from this was formed round the air surrounding the earth, like bark round a tree. When this was broken off and shut off in certain circles, the sun and the moon and the stars were formed.[2]

Anaximander believed that the earth was cylindrical in shape, its depth being one-third of its width so that it was like the drum of a column. It was, he suggested, 'held up by nothing, but remaining on account of its similar distance from all things'. He conjectured very shrewdly about the origins of the human race, maintaining that the first living creatures were born in moisture enclosed in thorny barks and that humankind appeared later in the development of organic life. He argued that this must have been so and that human beings were produced from creatures of another sort because, whereas most other creatures are self-supporting, human beings need prolonged nursing and could not have survived if their present form had been their original one.

The extant fragment of Anaximander's writing occurs as part of an account of his views given by Simplicius:

And the source of coming-to-be for existing things is that into which destruction, too, happens, 'according to necessity; for they pay penalty and retribution to each other for their injustice according to the assessment of Time', as he describes it in these rather poetical terms.[3]

Commentators agree that the last clause in that passage indicates that the phrase preceding it is a direct quotation of Anaximander's words. But there is little agreement over the actual meaning of the fragment and its reported context. One interesting speculation is that in the metaphor of paying penalties for injustice Anaximander offers an underlying **metaphysical** principle that

5

explains the surface appearances of things. For the implication may be that the changes and conflicts, the give and take that we observe occurring everywhere in nature, are parts of a process of exploration and reparation which, in the long run, maintains an equilibrium or state of 'justice' in the whole. This view is consistent with Anaximander's other reported remarks that the *apeiron* 'is both principle and element' and 'steers all things'. Moreover, the interaction of opposites features importantly in accounts of his natural philosophy, although the details of how Anaximander himself understood such interactions are not known.

Perhaps we should not make too much of Anaximander as a metaphysician. There is no doubt that it was his amazingly comprehensive natural philosophy rather than his metaphysical views that commanded widespread acclaim and respect, established his reputation as an intellectual giant and set a standard of intellectual achievement. Nevertheless it is interesting to speculate about the metaphysical implications of his ideas and especially to savour the excitement, so often engendered in us by these early philosophers, of conjecturing in adventurous, innocent and primitive ways, as most of us do in childhood, about the origins and essential nature of the cosmos.

Notes

1. G.S. Kirk, J.E. Raven and M. Schofield, *The presocratic Philosophers*, 2nd edn (Cambridge University Press, Cambridge, 1983), p. 104.
2. Ibid., p. 131.
3. Ibid., p. 118.

See also in this book

Thales, Anaximenes, Heraclitus.

Anaximander's writings

Books on nature and on the stars are ascribed to Anaximander but there is no certainty that these ascriptions are correct.

Further reading

Text

Diels, H. (ed.) *Die Fragmente der Vorsokratiker*, 11th edn (Weidmann, Zurich, 1964). These are the presocratic texts in Greek.
Freeman, K. (ed.) *Ancilla to the pre-Socratic philosophers*, a complete translation of the fragments in Diels (Harvard University Press, Cambridge, Mass., 1983)
Kirk, G.S., Raven, J.E., Schofield, M. *The presocratic philosophers*, 2nd edn (Cambridge University Press, Cambridge, 1983). This is the book I have used for textual references.

General

Barnes, J. *The pre-Socratics* (2 vols, Routledge and Kegan Paul, London, 1979; 1-vol. edn, 1982)
Emlyn-Jones, C. *The Ionians and Hellenism* (Routledge and Kegan Paul, London, 1980)
Guthrie, W.K.C. *A History of Greek philosophy* (6 vols, Cambridge University Press, Cambridge, 1962-81; paperback edition, vols IV and V, 1986)
Kahn, C.H. *Anaximander and the origins of Greek cosmology* (Columbia University Press, New York, 1960)
Stokes, M.C. *One and many in presocratic philosophy* (University Press of America, Lanham, distr. by Eurospan, London 1986)
Taylor, A.E. *Aristotle on his predecessors* (Open Court, La Salle, Ill., 1977)

Anaximenes
about 585-528 BC

Anaximenes was the third of the trio of philosophers known as the Milesians. He is thought to have flourished around 540 BC and Diogenes Laertius recorded, in his *Lives of Famous Philosophers*, probably compiled in the third century AD, that he was a pupil of Anaximander.

Like Anaximander, Anaximenes maintained that the first principle of all things was infinite. But, unlike Anaximander, he was prepared to specify what that first principle was, namely air. Theophrastus, a pupil of Aristotle, reports Anaximenes as believing that other material substances were derived from air through processes of rarefaction and densification:

Being made finer it [air] becomes fire, being made thicker it becomes wind, then cloud, then (when thickened still more) water, then earth, then stones; and the rest comes into being from those. He, too, makes motion eternal, and says that change, also, comes about through it.[1]

The one extant sentence of Anaximenes' writing is: 'As our soul, being air, holds us together and controls us, so does wind [*or* breath] and air enclose the whole world.'[2]

Although Anaximander rather than Anaximenes is often regarded as the high point of Milesian philosophy, it is arguable that Anaximenes was in some ways the more advanced thinker. Certainly his account is an advance on Thales', since it specifies how earth, fire and water might come from his primary material, air. But it is also an advance on Anaximander's account in that it avoids postulating an indefinite substance as the primary one. Moreover, it appeals to common sense rather than mythology because it is based on observations of natural processes; at the same time it is rooted in the traditional belief that air is the source of life.

Anaximenes taught that the earth was flat and rode upon air, that the stars 'are implanted like nails in the crystalline' and that the heavenly bodies move around the earth 'just as if a felt cap turns round our head'.[3] He explains the occurrence of earthquakes by reference to the earth's alternating between dry and wet conditions. When the earth dries out, it 'breaks asunder and is shaken by the peaks that are thus broken off and fall in'.[4] Rain, he maintains, is produced when the air thickens to form clouds which are then compressed so that moisture is squeezed from them. Hail is the result of the coalescence of the descending water and snow falls when wind is mixed in with the moisture. Aetius reports him as saying that the sun 'is flat like a leaf' and that all the heavenly bodies are fiery but have earthly bodies among them.[5] Anaximenes not only endeavours to provide natural explanations for all phenomena but he also, through his conception of air as holding together both human souls and the world itself, seems to suggest an organic unity that embraces every-

thing that exists, including human beings.

Although the Milesians mark, for Western philosophy, the advent of scientific and rational thought, the move from myth to reason was not sudden. Myth and reason interacted, influencing each other, so that traditional beliefs about elements such as air and water were gradually transformed by increasingly rational reflection and awareness of the natural world. The shift in attitude was from explaining the world by reference to gods or strange powers to explaining it by reference to a natural order of causes and regularities. The Milesians were scientists in that they observed the world and developed theories from their observations. But they were philosophers as well because their main concern was not just to say what the world is but how it came to exist at all; they wanted not only to describe phenomena but to discover their ultimate source.

Notes

1. G.S. Kirk, J.E. Raven and M. Schofield, *The pre-Socratic philosophers*, 2nd edn (Cambridge University Press, Cambridge, 1983), p. 145.
2. Ibid., pp. 158-9.
3. Ibid., pp. 154-5.
4. Ibid., p. 158.
5. Ibid., p. 154.

See also in this book

Thales, Anaximander.

Anaximenes' writings

From a passing remark about his use of plain and economical language it has been inferred that Anaximenes wrote a book.

Further reading

Text

Diels, H. (ed) *Die Fragmente der Vorsokratiker*, 11th edn (Weidmann, Zurich, 1964). These are the pre-Socratic texts in Greek.
Freeman, K. (ed.) *Ancilla to the pre-Socratic philosophers*, a complete translation of the fragments in Diels (Harvard University Press, Cambridge, Mass., 1983)
Kirk, G.S., Raven, J.E. Schofield, M. *The pre-Socratic philosophers*, 2nd edn (Cambridge University Press,

Cambridge, 1983). This is the book I have used for textual references.

General

Barnes, J. *The pre-Socratics* (2 vols, Routledge and Kegan Paul, London, 1979; 1-vol. edn, 1982)

Coxon, A.H. 'Anaximenes' in N.G. Hammond and H.H. Scullard (eds), *Oxford classical dictionary* (Oxford University Press, Oxford, 1970)

Emlyn-Jones, C. *The Ionians and Hellenism* (Routledge and Kegan Paul, London, 1980)

Guthrie, W.K.C. *A History of Greek philosophy* (6 vols, Cambridge University Press, Cambridge, 1962-81; paperback edition, vols IV and V, 1986)

Stokes, M.C. *One and many in presocratic philosophy* Cambridge, Mass., (University Press of America, Lanham, distr. by Eurospan, London 1986)

Taylor, A.E. *Aristotle on his predecessors* (Open Court, La Salle, Ill., 1977)

Pythagoras
about 571-496 BC

Pythagoras was a mathematician and a mystic. He was probably born at Samos, an island off the coast of Ionia, but spent much of his life at Croton in southern Italy where he founded and led a community of scholars who were his disciples and who are reported to have loved him for the inspiration of his society. The way of life of this Pythagorean community involved secrecy and public silence concerning its practices. In spite of this, most of our information about it is derived from reports of what its members did and said. The accuracy of such reports is questionable but one of them, it has been remarked, shines like a ray of light through the clouds. It was written by Dicaearchus, a pupil of Aristotle:

> What [Pythagoras] used to teach his associates, no one can tell with certainty; for they observed no ordinary silence. His most universally celebrated opinions, however, were that the soul is immortal; then that it migrates into other sorts of living creature; and in addition that after certain periods what has happened once happens again, and nothing is absolutely new; and that one should consider all animate things as akin.[1]

The doctrine of the transmigration of souls is called 'metempsychosis'. If the soul is immortal and if it migrates between persons and other sorts of living creatures then certain things follow. It follows, for example, that in killing and eating creatures we may be killing our own kind, even our former friends and relatives. Because of this the Pythagoreans developed an elaborate set of prescriptions concerning the killing and eating of creatures as well as a range of prohibitions designed to establish and maintain purity of soul. A few examples will best convey the flavour of Pythagorean religious thought:

> Abstain from beans.
> Do not touch a white cock.
> Do not look in a mirror beside a light.
> Do not stir the fire with iron.
> When the pot is removed from the fire, do not leave its mark in the ashes.
> When rising from bed, roll the bedclothes together and smooth out the impress of your body.
> Do not let swallows share your roof.
> Be not possessed by irrepressible mirth.[2]

Like the Milesians, who were his philosophical predecessors and contemporaries, Pythagoras produced a **cosmogony**. But the focus of his cosmogony and of all his thought is very different from that of the Milesians, largely because of his preoccupation with mathematics and his intellectual mysticism. Where the Milesians asked questions about the origins and workings of the Cosmos, Pythagoras pondered on religion and on the human soul and its salvation. Where the Milesians observed physical phenomena, Pythagoras engaged in studies of arithmetic and geometry. It is these mathematical studies that unite the strands of his philosophy and which inform every aspect of his thought.

Aristotle tells us that Pythagoras believed that numbers rather than elements such as air and water were the principles of all things:

> such and such a modification of numbers

being justice, another being soul and reason, another being opportunity — and similarly almost all other things being numerically expressible ... they supposed ... the whole heaven to be a musical scale and a number ... Evidently, then, these thinkers also consider that number is the principle both as matter for things and as forming their modifications and their permanent states, and hold that the elements of number are the even and the odd, and of these the former is unlimited and the latter limited.[3]

Aristotle also describes the Pythagorean Table of Opposites. The table gives ten principles which are the contrarieties thought to govern human affairs: limit and unlimit, odd and even, one and plurality, right and left, male and female, resting and moving, straight and curved, light and darkness, good and bad, square and oblong.

Number, for Pythagoras, is both the matter and the meaning of the Cosmos. He held that even and odd together produce unity and that unity produces number, which is the source of all things. As Aristotle informs us, definite numbers were assigned to things by the Pythagoreans. Marriage, for instance, was five because five is the sum of three, the first masculine number, and two, the first feminine number. Numbers also determined shapes of things. One is a point, two a line, three a surface and four a solid. Numbers were represented by geometrical patterns made from the appropriate quantity of dots. Thus there were 'square' or 'oblong' numbers, depending on how the dots were arranged. Ten was a sacred number and a diagram, the Tetraktys, shows that ten is the sum of the first four integers, one, two, three and four:

If we think of points, lines and surfaces as the units from which everything in nature is formed and of each of these units as repre-senting a number, it is possible to see how Pythagoras conceived of number as the source of everything. He thought that the heavens were like a musical scale, that the stars produced harmonies and that souls at their best must be harmonious with the heavens. That musical scales can be expressed numerically was another reason for regarding number as fundamental and originating in the Cosmos. Curiously, the Pythagoreans believed that neither the earth, which they thought was spherical, nor the sun was the centre of the universe. They said that both earth and sun revolved around a central fire and that the world breathes in air from the Unlimit by which it is surrounded.

The Pythagorean study of number and its relationship with the physical universe, and especially its relationship with music and astronomy, produced a strange blend of mysticism and real mathematical development. On the mystical side numbers were seen as sublime and as dictating hierarchy and ritual for the religious life and the purification of the soul. On the purely mathematical side Pythagorean geometry covered several of Euclid's books, including, of course, 'Pythagoras' Theorem', which proved that the square on the hypotenuse of a right-angled triangle is equal to the sum of the squares on the sides enclosing the right angle. Pythagoras is also believed to have proved that the side and the diagonal of a square are incommensurable, a discovery which made the early Greeks abandon concepts of number and measurements in their geometry. There is a story of doubtful accreditation that relates that Hippasus, a Pythagorean, was put to sea and drowned because he had disclosed to the uninitiated the fact that some geometrical quantities could not be expressed as whole numbers.[4] Proclus, in his book on Euclid written in the fifth century AD, remarked that Pythagoras and his followers turned the study of geometry into a liberal education by transforming a mass of arithmetical and geometrical material into an orderly **deductive** system. Certainly Plato, over a century later, was profoundly influenced by both the mathematics and the disquisitions on the soul that were developed by the Pythagoreans in the sixth century BC.

Notes

1. Quoted in J. Barnes, *The pre-Socratics* (2 vols, Routledge and Kegan Paul, London 1979), vol. 1, pp. 102-3.
2. These and other prohibitions are discussed in J.S. Kirk, J.E. Raven and M. Schofield, *The presocratic philosophers*, 2nd edn (Cambridge University Press, Cambridge, 1983), pp. 230-1.
3. Quoted in Kirk, Raven and Schofield, *The pre-socratic philosophers*, pp. 329, 330.
4. Pythagorean mathematics is discussed in W.W. Rouse Ball, *A short account of the history of mathematics* (Dover Publications, New York, 1960), pp. 19-28.

See also in this book

Thales, Anaximander, Anaximenes, Plato.

Pythagoras' writings

There are no extant writings attributable to Pythagoras. There is a huge quantity of reportage of his beliefs, ideas and teaching and there are several biographies of him.

Further reading

Text

Diels, H. (ed.) *Die Fragmente der Vorsokratiker*, 11th edn (Weidmann, Zurich, 1964). These are the pre-Socratic texts in Greek.
Freeman, K. (ed.) *Ancilla to the pre-Socratic philosophers*, a complete translation of the fragments in Diels (Harvard University Press, Cambridge, Mass., 1983)
Kirk, G.S., Raven, J.E., Schofield, M. *The presocratic philosophers*, 2nd edn (Cambridge University Press, Cambridge, 1983). This is the book I have used for textual references.

General

Barnes, J. *The pre-Socratics* (2 vols, Routledge and Kegan Paul, London, 1979; 1-vol. edn, 1982)
Emlyn-Jones, C. *The Ionians and Hellenism* (Routledge and Kegan Paul, London, 1980)
Gorman, P. *Pythagoras: a life* (Routledge and Kegan Paul, London, 1979)
Guthrie, W.K.C. *A history of Greek philosophy* (6 vols, Cambridge University Press, Cambridge, 1962-81; paperback edition, vols IV and V, 1986)
Maziarz, E.A. and Greenwood, T. *Greek mathematical philosophy* (Frederick Ungar, New York 1968)
Raven, J.E. *Pythagoreans and Eleatics* (Cambridge University Press, Cambridge, 1948)
Stokes, M.C. *One and many in presocratic philosophy* (University Press of America, Lanham, distr. by Eurospan, London, 1986)
Taylor, A.E. *Aristotle on his predecessors* (Open Court, La Salle, Ill., 1977)

Heraclitus of Ephesus
flourished 504-501 BC

Diogenes Laertius tells us that Heraclitus was exceptionally haughty and supercilious and that he eventually became a misanthrope who lived in the mountains and fed on grasses and plants. But all that is known for certain about him is that he came of an aristocratic family, spent most of his life in Ephesus and was not generally liked by his fellow citizens. About one hundred fragments of his writings are extant. They are mostly epigrams and cryptic remarks dealing with the cosmos and the soul.

He maintained that the world was not created but had always existed and, like his predecessors and all other pre-Socratic thinkers, he brooded over the fact that change is incessant and universal. Flux, fire and cosmic unity are his main themes. He wrote: 'This world-order ... always was and is and shall be: an ever-living fire, kindling in measures and going out in measures.'[1] He argues that coherence and stability persist within and indeed because of the process of continual change. Wisdom consists in recognition of this underlying coherence and unity of all things: 'Things taken together are wholes and not wholes, something which is being brought together and brought apart, which is in tune and out of tune; out of all things there comes a unity, and out of a unity all things.'[2]

Heraclitus calls this underlying structural coherence 'the Logos'. He says: 'Listening not to me but to the Logos it is wise to agree that all things are one.'[3] Perception of the fundamental unity is wise in that it sees beyond the conflict of the world of appearances. It recognises, for example, that it is disease that makes health good and weariness that reveals the benefits of rest. Opposites, Heraclitus points out, may be related in a variety of ways. A path regarded from one point of view may be seen as the way up; from another as the way down. Salt water may be an evil for humankind but good for fish. Moreover, pairs of opposites may form unities and pluralities and may link up with other pairs and other complex unities. Yet all such variations occur within a total unity and if we recognise that all opposites and changes are generated by the Logos then we will see that all things ultimately are divine. Thus Heraclitus says that 'to god all things are beautiful and good and just, but men have supposed some things to be unjust, others just.'[4] Sometimes he speaks of the unified totality as if it were god, immanent in all things: 'God is day, night, winter, summer, war, peace, satiety, hunger ...; he undergoes alteration in the way that fire, when it is mixed with spices, is named according to the scent of each of them.'[5]

He believed that fire is the archetypal form of matter and that the world is 'an ever-living fire', parts of which, in accordance with the principle of the Logos, are continually being extinguished and then rekindled. Even water becomes fire and fire changes to earth and water: 'All things are an equal exchange for fire and fire for all things, as goods are for gold and gold for goods.'[6] Perhaps in those words there is an echo of Anaximander's remark about things paying 'penalty and retribution to each other for their injustice.'[7] Both philosophers seem to have had intuitions of a fundamental equilibrium in the universe. For Heraclitus fire was not only the prime matter of the universe but its form as well. It was the Logos incarnate, the material enactment of the principle of change and flux. He sometimes describes its balanced give and take as 'the indicated way', that is, the way things are and have to be in the world we have. He points out that if the conflict ceased it would be because some factions had overcome others and that would mean that the world as we know it would have ceased to be. He believed that souls are

fire, too, and that human life is as much a part of the eternal flux as anything else, and he stipulates that 'a dry soul is wisest and best.'[8] This is rather surprising since it is difficult to reconcile the superiority of the dry over the wet soul with the previously mentioned view that everything, ultimately, is divine. But perhaps we have to think of soul as essentially having the character of dryness, even though it will relate to and take its meaning from its opposite, wetness. Certainly, we think of soul as light, ethereal, incorporeal, and as the principle of life, and this is consistent with Heraclitus' remark 'For souls it is death to become water.'[9] He thought that virtuous souls do not become water when their bodies die but eventually become part of the cosmic fire. He believed that sleeping, waking and dying are connected with degrees of fieriness in the soul. The soul of a sleeping person is partly detached from the world fire because the senses, which in the waking state are in direct contact with the world fire, are lulled and in abeyance when one is asleep. In sleep the individual soul maintains contact only by breathing, the mind becomes forgetful and reason ebbs. But on waking, contact with the Logos is regained and reason is restored.

Heraclitus' ideas strike us as sharply different from those of the Milesians. His vision is a somewhat mystical one. He is difficult to interpret but at the same time appeals to many of our intuitions; thus he exerts a fascination. The flavour of his oracular thought is best imparted by dwelling on some of his aphoristic remarks, many of which are germanely provocative to a philosophic cast of mind.

Thunderbolt steers all things.
The real constitution of things is accustomed to hide itself.
The path up and down is one and the same.
Evil witnesses are eyes and ears for men, if they have souls that do not understand their language.

11

Human disposition does not have true judgement, but divine disposition does.

An unapparent connection is stronger than an apparent one.

War is the father of all and the king of all, and some he shows as gods, others as men; some he makes slaves, others free.[10]

Notes

1. G.S. Kirk, J.E. Raven and M. Schofield, *The presocratic philosophers*, 2nd edn (Cambridge University Press, Cambridge, 1983), p. 198.
2. Ibid., p. 190.
3. Ibid., p. 187.
4. Ibid., p. 191, note.
5. Ibid., p. 190.
6. Ibid., p. 198.
7. See *Anaximander* in this book, p. 5.
8. Kirk, Raven and Schofield, *The presocratic philosophers*, p. 203.
9. Ibid.
10. Ibid., ch. 6.

See also in this book

Thales, Anaximander, Anaximenes, Pythagoras.

Heraclitus' writings

Diogenes Laertius, writing in the third century AD, reported that Heraclitus wrote a three-part book called *On nature*. Recent commentators have pointed out that the aphoristic character of the fragments of his work that have survived does not support the idea that they come from a continuous piece of writing.

Further reading

Text

Diels, H. (ed.) *Die Fragmente der Vorsokratiker*, 11th edn (Weidmann, Zurich, 1964). These are the pre-Socratic texts in Greek.
Freeman, K. (ed.) *Ancilla to the pre-Socratic philosophers*, a complete translation of the fragments in Diels (Harvard University Press, Cambridge, Mass., 1983)
Kirk, G.S., Raven, J.E., Schofield, M. *The presocratic philosophers*, 2nd edn (Cambridge University Press, Cambridge, 1983). This is the book I have used for textual references.

General

Barnes, J. *The pre-Socratics* (2 vols, Routledge and Kegan Paul, London, 1979; 1-vol. end, 1982)
Emlyn-Jones, C. *The Ionians and Hellenism* (Routledge and Kegan Paul, London, 1980)
Guthrie, W.K.C. *A history of Greek philosophy* (6 vols, Cambridge University Press, Cambridge, 1962-81; paperback edition, vols IV and V, 1986)
Kahn, C.H. *The art and thought of Heraclitus* (Cambridge University Press, Cambridge, 1981)
Kirk, G.S. *Heraclitus: the cosmic fragments* (Cambridge University Press, Cambridge, 1954)
Stokes, M.C. *One and many in presocratic philosophy* (University Press of America, Lanham, distr. by Eurospan, London, 1986)

Parmenides
flourished 501-492 BC

Parmenides was born towards the end of the sixth century BC. He was a citizen of Elea in southern Italy and is said to have made excellent laws for the city. He was a major figure in pre-Socratic philosophy and the most prominent member of the group of thinkers who became known as the Eleatic school. He wrote his thoughts in verse, in the form of a revelation from a divine source. Fragments of his poem, some 150 lines, are preserved in the writings of Simplicius. The poem has a prologue and two main themes: 'The Way of Truth' and 'The Way of Seeming, or Opinion'.

Commentators have agreed that it is extremely difficult both to translate and understand Parmenides' poem. In 'The Way of Truth' he declares that:

There still remains just one account of a way, that it is. On this way there are very many signs, that being uncreated and imperishable it is, whole and of a single kind and unshaken and perfect. It never was nor will be, since it is now, all together, one, continuous. For what birth will you seek for it? How and whence did it grow? I shall not allow you to say nor to think from not being: for it is not to be said nor thought that it is not ...[1]

Parmenidean reality is therefore an uncreated and timeless plenum. It is invisible, motionless, the same everywhere, and 'it is perfected, like the bulk of a ball well-rounded on every side, equally balanced in every direction from the centre'.[2] Its unchanging immobility is in sharp contrast to the Pythagorean view that reality consists of changing opposites and is unbounded. 'The Way of Truth' deals with matters that are apprehended by reason, that is, with the subjects listed in the left-hand column of the Pythagorean Table of Opposites.[3] 'The Way of Seeing' deals with the senses and Parmenides introduces it with the following statement: 'Here I end my trustworthy discourse and thought concerning truth; henceforth learn the beliefs of mortal men, listening to the deceitful ordering of my words.'[4]

The error of those who travel the 'Way of Seeing' is to dwell upon opposites. The fundamental pair of opposites is dark and light. All others are derivable from that pair. Parmenides thoroughly condemns any reliance on the senses and describes in detail the errors of their use, explaining that he gives us 'the whole ordering of these ... so no thought of mortal man shall ever outstrip you',[5] meaning thereby that if we are told of all the possibilities of error we shall be less easily deceived by plausible instances of it.

In spite of the obscurity and difficulty of much of Parmenides' writing there are several extremely interesting aspects to his philosophy. For a start, his distinction between reason and the senses has been and still is a fundamental one in Western philosophy. Then, 'The Way of Truth' has been described as one of the first attempts to reason from language and logic to the life of the world; certainly it manifests and perhaps inaugurated, philosophical problems about discrepancies between what may be argued through reason and what is perceived through the senses. Moreover, Parmenides has been described as 'the father of **idealism**' in that the reality of 'The Way of Truth' can be seen as a non-material reality. But careful reading of his words does not support this. He asserted the bounded materiality of That which Is. He is a monistic **materialist** rather than an idealist. He did not claim that reality was thought, but that it could be truly apprehended only by thought.

Notes

1. See G.S. Kirk, J.E. Raven and M. Schofield, *The presocratic philosophers*, 2nd edn (Cambridge University Press, Cambridge, 1983), pp. 248-9.
2. Ibid., p. 252.
3. See *Pythagoras* in this book, esp. p. 9.
4. Kirk, Raven and Schofield, *The presocratic philosophers*, p. 254.
5. Ibid., p. 256.

See also in this book

Thales, Anaximander, Anaximenes, Pythagoras, Zeno, Plato.

Parmenides' writings

Simplicius transcribed extracts from Parmenides' poem into his own works because, Diogenes reported, 'of the scarceness of the treatise'. Sextus Empiricus preserved the proem, or prologue, to the poem.

Further reading

Text

Diels, H. (ed.) *Die Fragmente der Vorsokratiker*, 11th edn (Weidmann, Zurich, 1964). These are the pre-Socratic texts in Greek.
Freeman, K. (ed.) *Ancilla to the pre-Socratic philosophers* a complete translation of the fragments in Diels (Harvard University Press, Cambridge, Mass., 1983)
Kirk, G.S., Raven, J.E. and Schofield, M. *The presocractic philosophers*, 2nd edn (Cambridge University Press, Cambridge, 1983). This is the book I have used for textual references.

General

Barnes, J. *The pre-Socratics* (2 vols, Routledge and Kegan Paul, London, 1979; 1-vol. edn, 1982)
Emlyn-Jones, C. *The Ionians and Hellenism* (Routledge and Kegan Paul, London, 1980)
Guthrie, W.K.C. *A history of Greek philosophy* (6 vols, Cambridge University Press, Cambridge, 1962-81; paperback edn of vols IV and V, 1986). Parmenides is treated in vol. II.
Taran, L. *Parmenides* (Princeton University Press, Princeton, 1965)

Zeno of Elea
flourished 464 BC (or perhaps later)

Zeno is best known for his paradoxes. He was a pupil and follower of Parmenides, the most prominent of the Eleatics, who maintained that reality is one, unchanging and motionless, and that it is properly apprehended by reason rather than by the senses. According to Proclus, Zeno produced about forty 'paradoxes' or 'attacks'. About eight of them survive. The most important are two against plurality and four against motion. They support the Parmenidean contention that change and motion are illusions based on sense experience and are against the pluralism asserted by the Pythagoreans. In his dialogue, *Parmenides*, Plato makes Zeno say:

> these writings of mine were meant to be some protection to the arguments of Parmenides against those who attack him ... My writing is an answer to the partisans of the many and it returns their attack with interest, with a view to showing that the hypothesis of the many, if examined sufficiently in detail, leads to even more ridiculous results than the hypothesis of the One.[1]

One of Zeno's arguments against plurality is along the following lines: A continuum such as a segment of time can be subdivided into shorter parts. This process of subdivision can either go on *ad infinitum* or it cannot. If it can go on, then we have an infinite number of parts making up a finite segment of time. If it cannot go on, then we have a segment of time that cannot be divided. Both these alternatives are unacceptable. How can an infinite number of subdivisions comprise a finite segment of time? Can there be a segment of time that is not divisible?

The story of Achilles and the tortoise is Zeno's most famous paradox. It is meant to show that motion is impossible. Suppose a race run over 100 metres in which the tortoise is given a 50-metre start on Achilles. It is impossible for Achilles to overtake the tortoise; for by the time Achilles reaches the tortoise's starting point, S, the tortoise has moved on to S_1, and by the time Achilles arrives at S_1, the tortoise has advanced to S_2, and so on. Thus Achilles never catches up with the tortoise. The distance between them will diminish *ad infinitum* as they move from point to point but it will never disappear.[2]

In both those paradoxes reasoning seems to come into conflict with experience of what takes place in the world. Zeno's four most discussed paradoxes have been resolved in terms of the **differential calculus** and their resolutions are to be found in Bertrand Russell's *Our knowledge of the external world*.[3] Russell remarks that: 'Having invented four arguments, all immeasurably subtle and profound, the grossness of subsequent philosophers pronounced him to be a mere ingenious juggler, and his arguments to be one and all sophisms.' But Zeno, as Russell recognised, should not be thought of as a mere inventor of puzzles. In recent years diligent attention has been given to his arguments. He is, by and large, accorded high respect. The problem the paradoxes expose is a profound, perennial one: how to relate appearance to reality, sense to reason. Nevertheless, his method and style are redolent of logic-chopping and fast debate rather than of a deep philosophical commitment to Parmenidean oneness. Jonathan Barnes's assessment of him is shrewd:

> Zeno was not profound: he was clever. Some profundities did fall from his pen; but so, too, did some trifling fallacies. And that is what we should expect from an eristic disputant. If we meet a deep argument, we may rejoice; if we are dazzled by a superficial glitter, we are not bound to search for a nugget of philosophical gold. Fair metal and base, in roughly equal proportions, make the Zenonian alloy.[4]

Notes

1. Plato, *Parmenides*, 128b.
2. For an interesting discussion see 'Achilles and the Tortoise' in Gilbert Ryle, *Dilemmas* (Oxford University Press, Oxford, 1954), pp. 36-53.
3. Bertrand Russell, *Our knowledge of the external world* (Allen and Unwin, London, 1956), ch. 6.
4. Jonathan Barnes, *The pre-Socratics* (Routledge and Kegan Paul, London, 1979), vol. I, pp. 236-7.

See also in this book

Parmenides, Plato.

Zeno's writings

Zeno's work is known only through the reportage of others, chiefly Proclus, Simplicius and Plato.

Further reading

Text

Diels, H. (ed.) *Die Fragmente der Vorsokratiker*, 11th edn (Weidmann, Zurich, 1964). These are the pre-Socratic texts in Greek.

Freeman, K. (ed.) *Ancilla to the pre-Socratic philosophers*, a complete translation of the fragments in Diels (Harvard University Press, Cambridge, Mass., 1983)

Kirk, G.S., Raven, J.E., Schofield, M. *The presocratic philosophers*, 2nd edn (Cambridge University Press, Cambridge, 1983)

General

Barnes, J. *The pre-Socratics* (2 vols, Routledge and Kegan Paul, London, 1979; 1-vol. edn, 1982)

Emlyn-Jones, C. *The Ionians and Hellenism* (Routledge and Kegan Paul, London, 1980)

Guthrie, W.K.C. *A history of Greek philosophy* (6 vols, Cambridge University Press, Cambridge, 1962-81; paperback edition, vols IV and V, 1986)

Heath, T.L. *Mathematics in Aristotle* (Clarendon Press, Oxford, 1949)

—— *History of Greek mathematics* (2 vols, Dover Publications, London, 1981)

Lee, H.D.P. *Zeno of Elea* (Cambridge University Press, Cambridge, 1936)

Stokes, M.C. *One and many in presocratic philosophy* (University Press of America, Lanham, distr. by Eurospan, London, 1986)

Vlastos, G. 'Zeno of Elea' in P. Edwards, (ed), *Encyclopaedia of Philosophy* (Collier-Macmillan, New York, 1967)

Socrates   469-399 BC

Socrates' name is probably the most widely known in Western culture. His fame does not derive from his writings for he left none. Most of our knowledge of him comes from dialogues written by Plato, who was deeply influenced by him and developed his ideas in such a way that it is impossible to see exactly where Socrates' thought ends and Plato's begins. Nevertheless, certain key ideas and a particular approach and method are attributable to Socrates even though they are presented in Plato's words. His chief philo-sophical method was that of *elenchus*: an eliciting and questioning of beliefs in order to establish truths and reveal inconsistencies.

Socrates was an Athenian. He lived in Athens when that city was at the height of its glory under the rule of Pericles. He was taught the **cosmological** philosophy of the time and engaged in many public debates, chiefly with the Sophists, who were purveyors of practical wisdom, teachers of oratory and arguers of any issue the Athenian citizens might wish to air. Socrates became famous for his elenctic questioning of these teachers and for his confounding of their sometimes glib arguments. His deep and enduring interest was in human and ethical matters and it was to these that he dedicated himself after the Oracle at Delphi, in response to questioning from Chaerephon, a friend of Socrates, decreed that no man living was wiser than Socrates. Thereafter he sought, in Plato's words in the *Apology*, 'to persuade every man ... that he must look to himself, and seek virtue and wisdom before he looks to his private interests, and look to the State before he looks to the interests of the State; and that this should be the order that he observes'.[1]

Socrates' personal and social moral integrity was apparently complete, and it cost him his life. In 406 BC, when he was a member of the Committee of the Senate, he courageously refused to be party to a demand that eight commanders who were to be impeached for negligence of duty should be tried together. It would have been contrary to Athenian law to try them thus. Two years later he refused to conspire with a usurping group called The Thirty to act against prominent citizens. The Thirty then fell from power but in 400 BC Socrates was brought to trial by the restored democratic regime and was accused of not worshipping the gods of the state, of introducing unfamiliar religious practices and of corrupting the young. The penalty for these offences was death.

Socrates' accusers probably assumed that

he would voluntarily exile himself from Athens and so avoid the charges. But he chose to stand trial and conduct his own defence. He was found guilty and then, in accordance with Athenian law, was given the opportunity to propose his own suitably substantial punishment. This he would not do. Instead he suggested he be given daily free meals, and an irritated jury then voted for the death sentence. During the month that elapsed between sentence and execution an escape was arranged for Socrates by his friends. Again he refused the way out, insisting that it would go against his sense of duty and his principles to evade what Athens decreed. He spent the last day of his life discussing the immortality of the soul with two friends, Cebes and Simmias. His death was brought about by drinking hemlock.

Aristotle wrote that 'two things may properly be ascribed to Socrates: **inductive** reasoning and definition by **universals**'.[2] Zenophon, in his *Memoirs of Socrates*, lists some of the terms for which definitions were sought: 'What was pious, what impious; what honourable, what base; what just, what unjust; what wisdom, what folly; what courage, what cowardice; what a state or political community;' and so on.[3] In the Platonic dialogue *Laches*, Socrates asks: 'What is Courage?' He deals with the ensuing discussion in his characteristic elenctic style. The young man, Laches, to whom the question is addressed, replies by saying that 'courage is not running away in battle'. Socrates then points out that it is not a particular example of courage that is being asked for but the identification of some quality of property common to all courageous acts and which entitles them to be called courageous. This kind of tactic is typical of the Socratic search for definitions. If in the course of a discussion a common property was discovered then the definition was attempted, though not always successfully. However, Socrates always seemed to assume that definitions were possible and that, properly construed, they provided

knowledge. This assumption is consistent with the view developed later by Plato that the perfect **Forms** of all things existed independently of their imperfect physical examples and could be known by the exercise of intellect and reason. It is not nowadays assumed that definitions of the kind Socrates sought are possible for everything.

Socrates' shift of philosophical attention away from physics was an influential one that set philosophical thought in new directions. In the *Phaedo*, when talking to Cebes, he relates that while studying the physical sciences he came across a passage in Anaxagoras which said that Mind was the cause of all things. It delighted him, he said, that Mind or intelligence should be regarded as primary since he was sure that Mind would arrange all things for the best and for the common good. So he quickly read all Anaxagoras' books, hoping to learn what was good and bad. But he continues:

> How high were my hopes, and how quickly were they lost to me! As I proceeded, I found my philosopher altogether forsaking mind and making no appeal to any other principle of order, but having recourse to air, and ether, and water and many other eccentricities.[4]

Socrates' consistent aim was to learn how to live virtuously. He argued that each one of us seeks our own good but that we can be mistaken about or ignorant of what constitutes that good. However, since we do seek only our good then once we infallibly know that good we cannot do evil: all wrongdoing is therefore error, knowledge is virtue, and no one knowingly does evil. The **premisses** and ramifications of this **argument** have furnished material for ethical debate ever since it was first given formulation in the dialogues of Plato.

Notes

1. Plato, *Apology*, 30 A.
2. Aristotle, *Metaphysics*, 13, 4, 1078, B 17-32.

3. Zenophon, *Memoirs of Socrates*, 1.
4. Plato, *Phaedo*, 98 B, 98 C.

See also in this book

Plato, Aristotle.

Some writings about Socrates

Socrates features in the following Dialogues of Plato: *Charmides, Laches, Hippias Major, Euthydemus, Protagoras, Gorgias, Meno, Apology, Crito, Phaedo, Phaedrus, The Symposium, The Republic, Theaetetus, Parmenides, Epistles.* A number of these are published as Penguin Classics, the four Dialogues, *Euthyphro, The Apology, Crito* and *Phaedo*, appearing together in one volume called *The last days of Socrates*.

The Greek text of Plato's Dialogues, with English translations facing, is published in Loeb Classical Library (Heinemann, London, 1921-29, repr. 1967).

Ferguson, J. *Socrates: A source book* (Macmillan, London, 1970)

Further reading

Dover, K.J. *Greek popular morality in the time of Plato and Aristotle* (Oxford University Press, Oxford, 1974)
Guthrie, W.K.C. *History of Greek philosophy*, (6 vols, Cambridge University Press, Cambridge, 1962-81; paperback edition, vols IV and V, 1986), vol. III, part 2, and vols IV and V
Huby, P. *Greek ethics* (Macmillan, London and New York, 1967)
—— 'Socrates and Plato' in D.J. O'Connor (ed.), *A critical history of Western philosophy* (The Free Press, New York, 1964; Macmillan, London, 1985)
Santas, G. *Socrates* (Routledge and Kegan Paul, London, 1979)
Taylor, A.E. *Socrates* (Peter Davies, London, 1932; Greenwood Press, London, 1976)
Vlastos, G. (ed.) *The philosophy of Socrates* (Anchor Books, New York, 1971)

Democritus of Abdera
about 460 BC-371 BC

Democritus' name is associated with atomism, a doctrine he expounded and elaborated but which was probably first articulated by Leucippus. Some fragments of Democritus' writing have survived and from all accounts he was a highly prolific author. He wrote on ethics, physics, mathematics, music, literature, language and technical subjects.

Atomism is generally regarded as a response to problems generated by the ideas of the Eleatic School. The Eleatics had argued that reality was one, whole, motionless, uncreated and limited, and that not-being was impossible. A major difficulty of such an account is in trying to show how a fundamental reality of the kind described can be the source of the experienced world of change, motion, generation and perishing. Atomism as propounded by Leucippus and Democritus avoided the difficulty by producing a different account of reality. It maintained that not-being, or the void, was as real as being; not-being was simply a non-corporeal reality, while being was corporeal reality. Atomism further argued that not-being must exist since it was necessary for motion and that being and not-being together were the source of everything. The atoms that moved in the void were infinite in number and varied in size and shape. Each was indivisible yet capable of connecting with other atoms to form larger entities: the visible bodies of the sensible world. Simplicius described Democritus' view in the following way:

these atoms move in the infinite void, separate one from the other and differing in shapes, sizes, positions and arrangement; overtaking each other they collide, and some are shaken away in any chance direction, while others, becoming intertwined one with another according to the congruity of their shapes, sizes, positions and arrangements, stay together and so effect the coming into being of compound bodies.[1]

Democritus worked out the consequences of atomism in considerable detail. Since everything consisted fundamentally of atoms moving in the void, sense perception and thought must be explicable by reference to that fundamental condition. Briefly, Democritus explained different senses by reference to the different shapes, interactions and amassings of atoms. He held that soul and fire atoms were spherical and that the sphere

17

was the most mobile and penetrative of the shapes, but he did not make clear how the spherical atoms would combine together to compose a mind. Perhaps this was not a problem for Democritus since the general belief at the time was that soul was the life of the whole body and was not concentrated in one particular part of it. However, the attempt to pursue the consequences of atomism produced deeply interesting questions about perception and knowledge. For instance, Theophrastus reported that Democritus explained sight by saying that the visual image 'does not arise directly in the pupil, but the air between the eye and the object of sight is contracted and stamped by the object seen and the seer; for from everything there is always a sort of effluence proceeding'.[2] Thus, what we actually see, according to Democritus, depends on the particular concatenation of atoms in the object and in the seer. There is, in experience, no unvarying knowledge available independently of particular individual dispositions and no knowledge of the fundamental reality of the atoms and the void. Democritus distinguished between what he called 'obscure knowledge' obtained by the senses and 'genuine knowledge' which, were it attainable, would be knowledge of atoms and the void. It is difficult to see how 'genuine knowledge' might be achieved. For since soul atoms functioned in the same way as all other atoms, that is, by collision and formation into groups, they would appear to be subject to just the same kind of idiosyncratic or individual interpretations as sense perceptions.

In spite of this and other criticisable aspects of Democritus' views, atomism was highly important in the development of Greek philosophy and has been widely influential in succeeding centuries. Modern atomic theory, although quite distinct from it in many ways, acknowledges the parenthood of Greek atomism. There are, moreover, interesting connections to be traced between the atomism of Democritus and the logical atomism propounded by Bertrand Russell in

the early twentieth century. Both Democritus and Russell assert that reality is fundamentally plural, but Democritus bases his account on a conception of indivisible physical atoms, whereas Russell bases his on indivisible logical atoms.[3]

Notes

1. J.S. Kirk, J.E. Raven and M. Schofield, *The presocratic philosophers* (Cambridge University Press, Cambridge, 1983), p. 426.
2. Ibid., p. 428.
3. See *Russell* in this book, pp. 134-8.

See also in this book

Parmenides.

Democritus' writings

Democritus is thought to have written a book called *The Little World-system* as well as numerous other works which were listed in order by Thrasylus.

Further reading

Text

Diels, H. (ed.) *Die Fragmente der Vorsokratiker*, 11th edn (Weidmann, Zurich, 1964). These are the pre-Socratic texts in Greek.
Freeman, K. (ed.) *Ancilla to the pre-Socratic philosophers*, a complete translation of the fragments in Diels (Harvard University Press, Cambridge, Mass., 1983)
Kirk, G.S., Raven, J.E., Schofield, M. *The presocratic philosophers*, 2nd edn (Cambridge University Press, Cambridge, 1983). This is the book I have used for textual references.

General

Barnes, J. *The pre-Socratics* (2 vols, Routledge and Kegan Paul, London, 1979; 1-vol. edn, 1982)
Emlyn-Jones, C. *The Ionians and Hellenism* (Routledge and Kegan Paul, London, 1980)
Furley, D.J. *Two studies in Greek atomists* (Princeton University Press, Princeton, 1967)
Guthrie, W.K.C. *A history of Greek philosophy* (6 vols, Cambridge University Press, Cambridge, 1962-81; paperback edition, vols IV and V, 1986)
Stokes, M.C. *One and many in presocratic philosophy* (University Press of America, Lanham, distr. by Eurospan, London 1986)

Plato   427-347 BC

Plato is widely regarded as occupying the high peak of Greek philosophy. He was

Socrates' pupil and Aristotle's teacher. As a young man he became an enthusiastic admirer of Socrates and later wrote the philosophical dialogues through which Socrates is now known to us. Much of his own philosophy is a development of Socratic themes. In particular he extended Socrates' search for the definitions of concepts such as justice, courage and pity into a full-blown theory about the nature of reality. This is his Theory of Ideas, or Forms, in which he posits the existence of a realm of perfect Forms that are eternal, unchanging and able to be known by the intellect, of which the ever-changing world of material objects is an imitation. His most famous work is the *Republic*, a dialogue in which Socrates and others discuss the nature of justice, its importance in the ideal state and the qualities required in the rulers and citizens of such a state. Plato was abundantly gifted and extremely versatile. He was a master of poetry and drama as well as prose and might well have risen, if he had so chosen, to eminence as an Athenian statesman and politician. He wrote with literary as well as philosophical brilliance on a wide range of topics in **metaphysics**, ethics, **epistemology**, politics, psychology, mathematics, education, theology and the arts.

Plato was born into an aristocratic family in the city state of Athens at a time of great ferment and change. The city was at war with neighbouring Sparta and at the same time was experiencing considerable political, moral and social conflict within itself. Relatives of Plato were influentially involved in superseding the ruling party but, once in power proved, according to Plato himself, to be far more tyrannical than those they ousted. They tried to connect Socrates with their activities and thereby instigated the sequence of events that led to his trial by a subsequent government and his death in prison. In a letter describing these events Plato wrote: 'When I observed all this — and some other matters of similar importance — I withdrew in disgust from the abuses of those days.'[1]

There is much uncertainty about the details of Plato's life. Accounts of it given by his biographers and those who referred to him in their writings vary considerably. He was about thirty when Socrates died. Soon after, he embarked along with other followers of Socrates on travels to Egypt and then to Sicily where he probably had discussions with Pythagoreans and became deeply interested in philosophical matters. When he returned to Athens, around 385 BC, he founded his own school of research and teaching, the Academy. In his sixties he was invited to return to Syracuse to tutor its young ruler, Dionysius II. But once again Plato found he was dangerously close to a highly charged political situation, the intrigues of which continued for several years. Several attempts to tutor Dionysius were made but all failed and eventually Dion, the man who had first invited Plato to try to humanise the tyrannical young king, was assassinated. The whole protracted and devious episode must have been a bitter experience for the author of the *Republic*.

Plato's writings fall roughly into three main groups. The first consists of early dialogues having largely to do with the pursuit of moral excellence and with the definitions of virtues and qualities such as courage and piety. The middle group, which includes the *Republic*, shows the development of important Platonic doctrines: the Theory of Forms, the theory of knowledge that is linked to it, and Plato's account of the human soul and its destiny. The third group of writings has a somewhat different character. Several of these dialogues show a concern with logical issues and a method of **dialectic** called Collection and Division which shows how the relationships between the Ideas or Forms may be elucidated by analysing a Form of wide generality, such as Virtue, into its different subdivisions. To this group of dialogues belong the *Laws*, the *Statesman* and the *Philebus*, works of a more technical kind and written in a more austere style. In what follows I shall outline the main features of the Theory of Forms and a famous section of the *Republic.*

The Theory of Forms is not presented in any systematic way in Plato's writings. Expositions, developments and critical examinations of it occur in a number of dialogues. In his discussions Plato sometimes uses the Greek word 'idea', though it did not mean 'something seen mentally' as it does nowadays, and sometimes the word 'eidos', meaning 'form'. Both words relate to the verb 'idein', 'to see'. Commentators have pointed out that both 'idea' and 'eidos' may be translated as 'shape'. The belief in a world of perfect or ideal Forms grew from the recognition of the ever-changing and imperfect nature of sensible objects and the realisation that it is possible to formulate perfect conceptions of at least some things, and particularly of geometrical figures such as circles, triangles and so on. Such considerations led Plato to posit the existence of a realm of perfect Forms, non-corporeal, eternal and wholly real, of which the world of material objects apprised by the senses was an imitation. In a recollection of Plato, Diogenes Laertius brings out the difference between the two worlds in the following way:

> Plato was speaking of his forms and using the words 'tableness' and 'cupness'. Diogenes said "Plato, I can see a table and a cup; I can't see tableness and cupness." "Precisely," said Plato. "To see a table and a cup you need eyes, and you have those. To see tableness and cupness you need intelligence, and you don't have that."[2]

From the distinction between the intelligible and the sensible worlds Plato derived a complex theory of knowledge which is unfolded by means of a series of **analogies** or illustrations in the later books of the *Republic.* Through the character of Socrates, Plato had argued in the earlier books that the just ruler of a state is one who has philosophical knowledge of the Good. In a famous passage he says: 'Unless philosophers become kings of states or else those who are now called kings and rulers become real or adequate philosophers ... there can be no respite from evil either for states or, I believe, for the human race.'[3]

He therefore sets out the kind of education that can produce a just ruler. It is extremely rigorous and culminates in knowledge of the Form of Good. It is seen as a kind of ascent from a shadowy and imperfect grasp of things in which the senses sometimes suffer illusions and believe shadows to be real things and sometimes perceive particular material objects, to a higher and illumined understanding, achieved by reasoning, of more general natures and concepts and, eventually, to a directly **intuitive knowledge** of Forms themselves. In *Republic* Book VI we are given an idea of the stages of this ascent by the analogy of the Divided Line. We have to suppose a vertical line on which four segments are marked. The two lower segments represent the visible world, the two higher the intelligible world. The very lowest segment relates to what Plato calls 'shadows and reflections', the one above it to 'the whole class of natural or manufactured things'.[4] The lower segment of the intelligible world is concerned with reasoning about the objects of the visible world; the upper segment then uses the conclusions of that reasoning to discover first principles, without any resort to the objects of the sensible world. Plato's famous allegory of the Cave, in *Republic* Book VII, vividly illustrates the ascent to knowledge in a way that relates not just to the education of the rulers of a state but to the intellectual development of any person. In the dialogue Socrates asks his hearers to imagine what it would be like to live in a large cave with a single opening to the light and to be chained there in such a way that one's back is always to the light at the entrance. Out in the open, on the slope rising away from the cave entrance, a fire burns, and between the fire and the cave entrance is a parapet and path along which people pass, talking as they go, and who are screened by the parapet in such a way that only the things they carry high up, models and artefacts of all kinds, show over the top of the parapet. Because of the fire, the shadows of these objects are cast on to the back wall of the cave and are seen by the chained prisoners, who cannot look outwards. Such prisoners, Socrates says, never having seen the world outside, would have experienced only the shadow life and the reflected sound of the voices of the passers by. They would therefore take the shadows and echoes to be reality.

Socrates then asks his hearers to imagine what would happen if a prisoner were set free and forced first to go to the entrance of the cave, next to look at the actual objects moving along the parapet path, and then to look at the fire. 'Would he not', he asks, 'be perplexed and believe the objects now shown him to be not so real as what he formerly saw?'[5] They agree that the prisoner would not think them as real as the shadows he was used to, and that the light of the fire would make his eyes ache so that he would try to turn back to the cave. But Socrates urges them to suppose further that the released prisoner is then dragged up the difficult and rocky ascent into full sunlight so that he is thoroughly dazzled and has gradually to accustom himself to looking at everything by first observing objects at night by the light of the moon and stars. 'Last of all', Socrates says, 'he would be able to look at the sun and contemplate its nature, not as it appears when reflected in water or any alien medium, but as it is in itself in its own domain.'[6]

The allegory is plain. The prisoner who is turned to the light progresses from a belief in the reality of shadows to beliefs or opinions about the particular material objects in the sensible world. He is then forced further out into this sensible world and ascends to higher levels by reasoning about what he finds, and thereby reaching conclusions that count as knowledge. Eventually he is able to look at the sun itself, the source of all illumination and the symbol of Good itself. The whole

process of education for rulers, or Guardians, as Socrates calls them, takes fifteen years. The lynchpin of all its components is a dialectic which, for Plato, was a discussion carried on by means of questions and answers which sought only to reveal truth, never to score debating points. In Epistle VII it is described in the following way:

after practising detailed comparisons of names and definitions and visual and other sense-perceptions, after scrutinising them in benevolent disputation by the use of question and answer without jealousy, at last in a flash understanding of each blazes up, and the mind, as it exerts all its powers to the limit of human capacity, is flooded with light.[1]

The generation and his own rejection of the Theory of Forms was succinctly described by Aristotle when he wrote that 'Socrates provided the starting point for this theory ... by his definitions, but he did not separate the definitions from the particular objects; and was right in refraining from doing so.'[7] But in spite of Aristotle's rejection of it, both the theory and Platonism in general became profoundly influential. In the centuries after his death Plato's philosophy was taken over by **Neo-Platonists** and especially by Plotinus,[8] whose reorganisation of Plato's thought became the basis of Platonism for several centuries. Augustine absorbed several Platonic themes which were then perpetuated through his writings. In the twelfth and thirteenth centuries further translations of Plato's work appeared, although at that time they were overshadowed by the massive presence of Aristotelianism at its most dominant. By the fifteenth century, as part of a reaction to **scholasticism** and Aristotle, a new wave of Neo-Platonism was advancing, especially in Italy where an intensive study of Greek culture and the splendours of antiquity had begun. Humanists such as Colet, Erasmus and Thomas More brought these ideas to England where, in the seventeenth century, they were given a new impetus in the work of the Cambridge Platonists, Benjamin Whichcote, Henry More and Ralph Cudworth.

Plato's influence on philosophy and culture in general is rivalled only by Aristotle's. The thought of both is woven not only into Christian theology but into many of our ways of thinking and talking about the world.

Notes

1. Plato, *Epistle VII*.
2. Diogenes Laertius, *The lives and opinions of eminent philosophers*, trans. C.D. Yonge (Bohn, London, 1853), vol. 1, Book III.
3. Plato, *Republic*, 473 c 11.
4. Ibid., 510a 8.
5. Ibid., 515d 5.
6. Ibid., 516b 4.
7. Aristotle, *Works*, 13, 9, 1086 B 2.
8. See *Plotinus* in this book, pp. 26-8.

See also in this book

Socrates, Aristotle, Plotinus, Augustine.

Plato's major writings

Apology, Crito, Euthyphro, Laches, Ion, Progavoras, Republic, Gorgias, Meno, Hippias I and II, Symposium, Phaedo, Phaedrus, Theatetus, Parmenides, Philebus, Laws. Plato's *Works* in 12 volumes with English translation are published in the Loeb Classical Library (Heinemann, London, 1921-9, repr. 1967).

Further Reading

Annas, J. *An introduction to Plato's Republic* (Clarendon Press, Oxford, 1981)
Guthrie, W.C.K. *History of Greek philosophy* (6 vols, Cambridge University Press, Cambridge, 1962-81) vol. III
Huby, P.M. 'Socrates and Plato' in D.J. O'Connor (ed.), *A critical history of Western philosophy* (The Free Press, New York, 1964; Macmillan, London, 1985)
Irwin, T. *Plato's moral theory* (Clarendon Press, Oxford, 1977)
Raven, J.E. *Plato's thought in the making* (Cambridge University Press, Cambridge, 1965)
Rowe, C. *Plato* (Harvester Press, Brighton, 1986)
Strauss, L. *Studies in Platonic political philosophy* (University of Chicago Press, Chicago, 1983)

Aristotle   384-322 BC

Although Aristotle lived and worked nearly two and a half thousand years ago his thought, like Plato's, is still a vital and indeed constitutive part of Western culture. He was Plato's pupil but not his uncritical disciple. He took the whole of objective knowledge for his field of study and attempted a systematic delineation and exposition of the particular sciences. He also gave an account of what he called First Philosophy: the science of being, which, because it dealt with being itself, underlay all the particular sciences and was therefore primary. He wrote extensively on logic, physics, natural history, psychology, politics, ethics and the arts. The treatises and lecture notes he prepared for teaching have survived and are contained in about twelve volumes. They are written in a rather severe academic style. Regrettably, the books and dialogues he wrote for general reading are lost but, from remarks made by those who read them, we know that they possessed a literary style and, according to Cicero, a 'golden eloquence' that were much admired.

Aristotle was born in Stagira in northern Greece. At the age of 18 he enrolled in Plato's Academy and stayed there until Plato's death in 347 BC. He then went to Assos in Asia Minor and for the next five years worked with a small group of scholars on philosophical and biological topics, spending the last two years of this time at Mitylene in Lesbos. In 342 BC he was invited to return to Macedonia as tutor to the boy who was to become Alexander the Great. He left Macedonia in 335 BC, returned to Athens and there founded his own school, the Lyceum, where he taught for twelve years. When Alexander the Great died in 323 BC there was strong feeling in Athens against Macedonia, and Aristotle, because of his Macedonian connections, became the object of hostility. He was indicted with impiety but, remembering the fate of Socrates, he left Athens and went to Chalcis in order, it is said, to prevent the Athenians 'sinning a second time against philosophy'. He died at Chalcis a year later at the age of 62.

Aristotle founded a system of logic which was the basis of logical studies until the nineteenth century. He regarded logic as a kind of general tool for the study and acquisition of knowledge of all kinds and his writings on the subject are known as the *Organon*, meaning instrument or tool. The central feature of his logic is the syllogism, defined by him as a 'discourse in which, certain things being stated, something other than what is stated follows of necessity from their being so'. The most usual form of syllogism consists of three propositions, two of which are the premisses and one the conclusion of an **argument**. A typical syllogism runs as follows:

All men are mortal.
Socrates is a man.
Therefore Socrates is mortal.

If the premisses in a syllogism are true and if its form, or pattern, is **valid**, then the conclusion of the syllogism is and must be true. The valid syllogism that has true premisses therefore constitutes a proof of what its conclusion states. The example above exhibits the form of syllogism and propositions most used in Aristotelian logic, but there are other forms. Aristotle lists ten Categories or Predicaments which are the ten different ways in which the subject of a proposition, for example 'all men' in the first premiss of the syllogism above, may relate to its predicate, for example 'are mortal' in the same premiss. The proposition 'All men are mortal' belongs to the Category of Quality since it tells us what 'all men' are *like*, namely 'mortal'. The proposition 'Socrates is a man' belongs to the Category of Substance; it tells us what Socrates *is*. The other Categories are those of Quantity, Relation, Place, Time, Position, State, Action and Passivity.

A much-discussed question about Aristotle's logic is: What is its subject-matter? Is Aristotle describing thought processes, or giving a grammatical analysis of language, or providing a theory of the relationships between actual things? Some commentators

consider that what he does is a blend of all three. The debate is an absorbing one, well worth the attention of anyone seeking a full understanding of the nature and development of logic.

The chief concern of Aristotle's First Philosophy is substance. He wrote:

If there is no substance other than those which are formed by nature, natural science will be the first science; but if there is an immoveable substance, the science of this must be prior and must be first philosophy, and universal in this way, because it is first. And it will belong to this to consider being *qua* being — both what it is and the attributes which belong to it *qua* being.[1]

In its primary sense substance is that which bears or supports qualities; it is that to which predicates may be ascribed. In its secondary sense it refers to particular *kinds* of substances, as it does in the Categories where to assert that 'Socrates is a man' is to say that Socrates is a substance of a certain kind, namely *man*kind. Aristotle pursues his analysis by deploying two pairs of concepts, Matter and Form, and Potentiality and Actuality, and by developing a doctrine of Four Causes. He points out that any individual thing has two aspects, Matter and Form. In the case of an individual wooden table its matter, the wood, is one aspect and its form, the structure that organises the wood into a table, is the other. This distinction is a relative one, for the wood that is seen as matter in relation to the table has already been 'formed' as wood from even more basic constituents which, in Aristotelian physics, are further analysed into earth, air, fire and water. Aristotle does not allow us to go on to assume that those four elements are ultimately reducible to something such as matter itself. He regards the four elements as the most basic forms of Matter and the notion of a prime and undifferentiated Matter as an invention of thought.

If we now think of the imposition of Form

on Matter as a temporal process we can see it under the aspect of the other of Aristotle's pairs of terms: Potentiality and Actuality. Consider, for example, the process in which Matter and Form are involved when a dandelion plant develops from a seed. The dandelion is, for Aristotle, the actuality of what its seed potentially is, just as an acorn is potentially what an oak tree actually is. If we now add to this perspective the doctrine of Causes, we have the framework of Aristotle's philosophical account of the nature of reality and his answer to questions about how orderly changes take place in the world. He specifies four kinds of Causes which together explain why and how something is what it is: a Material Cause, the matter composing it; a Formal Cause, the pattern or law that determines its development; an Efficient Cause, the agent or initiator of the process; and a Final Cause, its end or result. In the case, again, of the dandelion, its Material Cause is its seed; its Formal Cause is the law or pattern of development peculiar to dandelions; its Efficient Cause is the parent plant that produced the seed; its Final Cause is that condition of completeness characteristic of the mature dandelion. It is important to understand that the Greek word *aitia* used by Aristotle and translated for us as 'cause' does not have exactly the same meaning as is nowadays given to the word. The Greek *aitia* refers to what is 'responsible' for something, and thus has a broader meaning than our modern 'cause'; one that is able to encompass the different sense of the Four Causes.

Aristotle's views on knowledge are best understood by relating them to Plato's. Plato had argued that knowledge, as distinct from belief or opinion, is possible only of what is real, unchanging and eternal; that the world apprehended by the senses is always changing and so cannot be known; and that knowledge is therefore possible only of the non-sensory world of Ideas, or **Forms**, that is apprehended by the intellect. Mathematical knowledge is the paradigm here: a perfect triangle or perfect circle may be known to

the intellect as a concept or definition but cannot be an object for the senses.[2]

Aristotle wishes to maintain, like Plato, that the ultimately real is knowable and that what is knowable is unchanging. But he argues forcefully against Plato's doctrine of Forms, rejecting the claim that there is a distinct and wholly real world of perfect Forms or Ideas which can be intellectually apprehended. He maintains that the **essences** of particular material things do not exist separately from those things and that the existence of material things does not have to be explained by the existence of Forms. One important objection he makes to Plato's view is that if we allow that the essence of an object is something separate from that object then that essence is also a something which could be said to have its own separate essence, and so on infinitely. However, Aristotle's own account of how knowledge of reality is possible is not very convincing and, it is sometimes remarked, is not really dissimilar from Plato's. He believed that all the propositions of the sciences were **necessarily** and universally true and so were deduced from necessarily true premisses. But this immediately raises a problem of infinite regress, in that the necessarily true premisses will require a like proof of their necessary truth, and so on. In the *Posterior analytics* Aristotle therefore reflects on how we can know 'the immediate primary premisses' of a science. He says that sense experience of things, repeated many times, eventually allows a **universal** to form in the mind and that the universal is recognised as such by the intellect. Thus, knowledge of reality, for Aristotle, seems to be achieved by a process of **induction** which is given the seal of certainty by an intellectual **intuition** of the correctness of its conclusions. What is especially of note in this is that the universal, although it is not seen as separate from individual things, plays much the same part in Aristotle's theory of knowledge as the Form or Idea did in Plato's.

Aristotle's concept of God was importantly influential in the later development of a rational Christian philosophy and theology and it was consistent with his and the general Greek veneration of reason and intellect. In his *Physics* Aristotle had argued that everything is in motion and that it is impossible to conceive of either a beginning or end of motion; there must therefore be an eternal mover producing the eternal motion and this mover must itself be unmoved since, if it were not, a mover would have to be sought for it. God is therefore the Unmoved Mover. He is eternal, non-material, unchanging and perfect; he must be actuality without potentiality, for potentiality involves change and is less than perfect. The Unmoved Mover is also a Person, since intelligence is the essence of being a person, but his thought is of thought itself and he is supremely happy in his perfect knowledge of all things. Aristotle's God does not produce the motion of everything in any kind of physical way but does so in virtue of being the Final Cause of the universe, the ultimate good towards which everything moves. It was this concept of an independent, eternal and intellectual Unmoved Mover that had, in later centuries, to be reconciled by such thinkers as Augustine, Thomas Aquinas, Duns Scotus and William of Ockham with the Christian conception of a God of love, possessed of will and capable of incarnation as well as of communication with the beings he creates.

Aristotle's doctrine of the soul, although unclear at one or two crucial points, is as fascinating to modern readers as it was to his contemporaries. Plato had taught that soul and body were distinct entities, that the soul is immortal and that it inhabited a body temporarily. Aristotle regarded the human person as a unified being and a part of nature. For him the *psyche*, or soul, is the animating force in a body. He speaks of it as 'the form of the body' and as 'the first grade of actuality of a natural body having life potentially in it'. It is the Efficient, the Formal and the Final Cause of the body and it does not survive the death of the body. He dismisses doubts about the unity of body and soul as meaningless and says, 'it is as meaningless as to ask whether the wax and the shape given to it by the stamp are one'.[3] He maintained that corresponding with the vegetative activities of a living thing was a vegetative aspect of the soul; a sensitive aspect as well in creatures having senses and, in the case of humankind, mind also, which is 'the part of the soul with which the soul knows and thinks'. But whereas in the case of the vegetative and the sensitive there are physical counterparts to or manifestations of the soul's activity, in the case of mind there is no such physical manifestation. Aristotle says that mind 'before it thinks is not actually any real thing': we have to think of thoughts as imposing form on mind, as 'in-forming' it. He distinguishes between passive and active mind. The mind is passive in receiving or being 'in-formed' by thought, but mind can be active and generative as well. Of this activity Aristotle says: 'this is a sort of positive state like light; for in a sense light makes potential colours into actual colours. Mind in this sense of it is separable, impassable and unmixed.'[4]

Aristotle has now posited the existence of an aspect of soul that is almost divine in its attributes. Commentators have pointed out that in doing so he lapses from his customary commonsense and empirical approach, or that he is unable to free himself entirely from the Platonism of his early education. But there is another way of reflecting on what has been seen either as an inconsistency in analysis or a failure of independent thought. Aristotle could not accept Plato's sharply dualistic account of a person as comprising some kind of uneasy partnership of soul and body; but nor was he satisfied by the prospect, suggested by so much of his own approach, of entirely assimilating human mental capacities to what is physical and sensory. He might, for the sake of consistency and comprehensiveness, have propounded a straightforward physicalism, but in fact he persisted in a sensitive fidelity to the complex and enigmatic notion that human beings have of their own nature. The philosophical problem that he tried to deal with, that concerning the relationship of body to mind, is with us still.

The scope of Aristotle's work is immense. It ranges from the charting of planets to the classification of fishes; from study of the winds, the seas and the weather to the analysis of dramatic tragedy; from morals and politics to geometry and number. Aristotle's influence has been immeasurable. After his death his pupil, Theophrastus, succeeded him as head of the Lyceum and immediately began to spread his master's doctrines. In the third century AD, Plotinus took what he wanted from Aristotelian teaching and incorporated it into his own Neo-Platonism. In the Middle Ages Aristotle's logic was carefully studied in Europe, but it wasn't until the thirteenth century that a new and very powerful burgeoning of interest in his work was brought about by the rendering into Latin of Arabic versions of it, along with a number of Islamic commentaries. Thomas Aquinas then became the foremost disseminator of Aristotle's thought. He accorded it scholarly treatment of a profoundly perceptive kind. Others were less scrupulous, adapting and distorting Aristotle's ideas to their own ends and sometimes transmogrifying them beyond recognition. As the physical sciences developed and instruments of measurement became more refined, many of Aristotle's scientific observations were shown to be faulty and from the sixteenth century onwards his astronomy as well as parts of his other sciences gradually came to be discredited. The potency of his philosophy, of his **metaphysics**, logic, politics, ethics and aesthetics, remains unimpaired. He was widely known as 'The Philosopher' well into the eighteenth century.

Notes

1. Aristotle, *Metaphysics*, VI, I, 1026a 27ff.
2. See *Plato* in this book, pp. 18-22.

3. Aristotle, *De anima*, 412 B6.
4. Ibid., 430a 14-25.

See also in this book

Plato, Plotinus, Augustine, Aquinas, Duns Scotus, Ockham, Galileo, Hobbes.

Aristotle's major writings

Organon (Logic), *De anima* (On the soul), *Metaphysics*, *Nicomachean ethics*, *Eudemian ethics*, *Politics*, *The art of poetry*. Aristotle's *Works* with English translations are published in the Loeb Classical Library (Heinemann, London, 1926-65). His writings are published in English in W.D. Ross (ed.), *The works of Aristotle translated into English* (12 vols, Oxford University Press, Oxford, 1908-52).

Further reading

Ackrill, J.L. *Aristotle the philosopher* (Oxford University Press, Oxford, 1981)
Barnes, J. *Aristotle* (Past Masters, Oxford University Press, Oxford, 1983)
Heath, T.L. *Mathematics in Aristotle* (Clarendon Press, Oxford, 1949)
O'Connor, D.J. 'Aristotle' in D.J. O'Connor (ed.), *A critical history of Western philosophy* (The Free Press, New York, 1964; Macmillan, London, 1985)
Taylor, A.E. *Aristotle* (Dover Publications, distr. Constable, London, 1965)
—— *Aristotle on his predecessors* (Open Court, La Salle, Ill., 1977)

Plotinus   205-270 AD

Plotinus' philosophy derives from Plato's and he is chief among a group of philosophers flourishing in the first four centuries AD and known generally as the **Neo-Platonists**. He was born in Egypt, studied at Alexandria and taught at Rome, where he was especially favoured by the Emperor Gallienius, who had a penchant for philosophy.

Plotinus' writings were disorderly and difficult to understand. After his death they were edited by his disciple and pupil, Porphyry, who arranged them into the Enneads: six groups of writing, each of which has nine parts. Porphyry also identified three periods in Plotinus' work and allocated the writings, independently of their arrangement in the Enneads, appropriately to those periods: before Porphyry was Plotinus' student; the time of his studentship; and after his studentship. It is by no means certain that Porphyry's presentation is strictly chronological. In his writing, Plotinus tends to move back and forth between his ideas, reworking and developing them in a fairly random fashion. But everything he does contributes to what turns out to be a close-knit **metaphysical** system, the dominant themes of which are the One, the Intellectual Principle, and Soul. Soul is central in his philosophy. It is the concept through which we can delineate the status and scope of the human person within reality as a whole.

In Plotinus' system the ultimate reality is the One. It is ineffable and indescribable, the ultimate unknowable that is 'beyond existence' and yet its source. Below the One in the hierarchy of reality is the Intellectual Principle. This Principle embraces all intelligible **Forms** and Thought itself. It, in turn, stands above Soul which nevertheless has the capacity to contemplate and come to know the Forms of the Intellectual Principle. Plotinus uses the term 'Soul' to refer both to the world Soul and individual souls. A soul is closely related to the body it inhabits but is superior to the body. It is responsible for sensation, perception and knowledge. As in Plato, it is the pilot or guide of the body. The body that obeys the soul achieves a harmony with the higher elements of reality and approaches a state of union with reality as a whole. A soul dominated by body loses its unity as it becomes dispersed among the individual physical things which command its attention.

For Plotinus, as for Plato, the One is also the Good. Human virtue and its pursuit consist in general in the contemplation of and participation in the higher levels of reality. The aim is towards an intellectual condition in which souls

> have Truth for mother, nurse, real being, nourishment; they see all things, not those that are born and die, but those that have real being; and they see themselves in

others. For them all things are transparent, and there is nothing dark and impenetrable.[1]

The ultimate mystical state is beyond good and evil. In it all sense of individuation, of being a subject contemplating an object, is lost. Plotinus says: 'The vision is confounded with the object seen, and that which was before object becomes to him the state of seeing, and he forgets all else.'[2]

Since everything is ultimately the One, Plotinus has to face the problem of accounting for the presence of evil. He does this by equating change, multiplicity and plurality, and the gradual diminishing of the shining lightness of the One to the disintegrated heaviness of matter, with the dilution of the perfect to the less perfect. This gradation, he argues, is necessary because it is the best and fullest expression of the One. Thus, reality seen as a whole is the best possible world, although some individual parts of it are less than perfect. Moreover, within the total unity it is always possible, he maintains, for the less perfect to achieve an excellence peculiar to it. Matter, for instance, although of low status, is the necessary stuff for receiving Forms from a higher level and a felicitous embodiment of a Form is efficacious in raising a soul to higher realms.[3]

Like Plato, Aristotle and numerous other philosophers, Plotinus saw the highest human condition in the overcoming of our sensual and physical nature and the cultivation of a contemplative and intellectual understanding of an underlying reality. Some commentators have concluded from this that Plotinus rejected the everyday world of ordinary experience. But such a rejection would not be consistent with his philosophy. Although he advocated a discipline striving to ascend to higher levels of understanding, he also maintained that the lower levels could provide appropriate instantiations of the higher Forms, presenting us not only with glimpses of a means of access to the higher possibilities, but with distinct, individual aesthetic experiences, each of which has a place within the ordered hierarchy of the whole. However, whereas Plato placed a moral obligation on the philosopher who attained to the supreme vision to return and foster the aspirations of those still struggling at lower levels, Plotinus simply urges all to strive upwards towards the ultimate mystical participation in the One. The means to this ecstatic absorption into pure being are the intellectual knowledge of Forms and all kinds of aesthetic participation. He likens the ultimate state of mystical contemplation to the total engrossment of someone who is reading a book so absorbedly that she or he is no longer aware of the activity of reading. In such a condition one's whole consciousness is possessed by the object of contemplation in such a way that there is no longer a gap between the knowing subject and the known object. Plotinus regarded this as a state in which desire is fulfilled.

Notes

1. Plotinus, *Enneads*, III, 8 [30] 11.
2. Ibid., III, 8 [30] 8.
3. Plotinus' conception of a Form is similar to but not identical with Plato's. For example, Plotinus thought that there were Forms of individuals; Plato did not think so.

See also in this book

Plato.

Plotinus' writings

All Plotinus' works were written between 253 and 267 AD. They have survived only in the arrangement of them made by Porphyry into the *Enneads*.
Plotinus: The Enneads, ed. S. MacKenna and B.S. Page, 3rd edn (Faber and Faber, London, 1962)
For a selection see *The essential Plotinus*, trans. E. O'Brien (Hackett, Indianapolis, Indiana, 1964)

Further reading

Brehier, E. *The philosophy of Plotinus*, trans. J. Thomas (University of Chicago Press, Chicago, 1958)
Merlan, P. 'Plotinus' in P. Edwards (ed.), *Encyclopaedia of philosophy* (Collier-Macmillan, London and New York, 1964)

Augustine of Hippo
354-430 AD

Augustine expounded a Christian philosophy that sought to combine faith and reason. He said: 'Understanding is the reward of faith. Seek therefore not to understand in order that you may believe, but to believe in order that you may understand.'[1] Faith was therefore primary for him in that he saw it as the prerequisite for a Christian philosophy. But faith alone, he held, is simply a kind of blind assent. It must be consolidated and made intelligible by means of reason. His best known works are the *Confessions* and the *City of God*. In the *Confessions* he writes of his early life, his repentance and conversion, and discusses questions about time and the presence of evil in the world. In the *City of God* his main themes are the human will, the relationship between theology and reason, and the division of history into two 'cities', one formed by self-love, the other by the love of God. His mature thought owes a good deal to the influence of Plato and **Neo-Platonism**.

Augustine was born at Thagaste in north Africa at a time when the Roman Empire was being destroyed by the barbarian invasions. His mother, Monica, was a Christian; his father was not. Augustine's education was completed at Carthage where he taught for some years before moving to Rome and then Milan. In Carthage he lived, according to the *Confessions*, a life of debauchery, 'seduced and seducing, deceived and deceiving in divers lusts',[2] but at the same time experiencing a restless longing for truth and religious understanding. For a while he espoused Manichaeism, a religious doctrine that maintained that human life is a struggle between good and evil, God and matter, and which advocated a life of asceticism in order to free oneself from evil powers. But Manichaeism did not satisfy him and when his continuing search for truth brought him in contact with a form of Christianity that had embraced Neo-Platonic philosophy he decided to enter the

Christian Church. He returned to north Africa and after living for two years within a monastic community was ordained and became assistant to Valerius, the Bishop of Hippo, eventually succeeding him in the bishopric. Thereafter he lived with his clergy and preached, wrote and travelled in pursuit of his duties until his death in 430.

Augustine used philosophy in the service of theology, adopting Platonic and Neo-Platonic ideas and shaping them to his own approach. Like Plato, he thought of the soul as inhabiting and deploying the body. He said, 'Man is, as far as we can see, a rational soul making use of a mortal and material body.'[3] At the same time, because of his Christian conviction that God creates each soul when a human being comes into existence, he could not endorse Plato's view of the soul as being in exile from its real home during its habitation of a human body. He held that all knowledge is the product of the rational soul but that it may be of two kinds of objects: objects of sense and objects known independently of sense experience, the latter being perceived by the mind 'through itself'. In the case of sensory knowledge he thinks of the mind as using the bodily senses as instruments for obtaining knowledge and thus of perception as fundamentally an activity of mind; for the mind at its highest intellectual level is able, he says, to judge and interpret the information it is made aware of through the senses. The objects known by the mind through itself rather than through the senses are known directly and therefore more clearly and readily and the direct understanding of them is analogous to the sense of sight. He says, 'Reason is the mind's sight, whereby it perceives truth through itself, without the intermediary of the body.'[4] This whole theory of the way in which the mind knows and understands is redolent of Platonism. For Augustine, as for Plato, the highest intellectual activity results in an illumination of the mind and a recognition of certain ultimate and eternal truths which are latent in all human minds. These truths, he maintained, furnish us with standards against which we make our judgements of how things should be, and in apprehending them 'we behold by a perception of the mind the pattern which governs our being and our activities, whether in ourselves or in regard to other things, according to the rule of truth and right reason'.[5] In all this he seems to be struggling to establish the human being as a unity, but fails to recognise the while that any such unity is precluded by the framework of Platonism that he has adopted for his ideas.

When Augustine considers human nature he finds it extremely complex. His central concern is with the moral life and with the way in which philosophy, understood as the search for wisdom, can secure the happiness for which God created humanity. As always, he starts from tenets of faith, from belief in revelation, the bestowal of grace by God and the presence of God in all things. He distinguishes between the nature of non-rational entities that simply fulfil their natural propensities and rational beings whose nature has a duality in that it possesses not only a range of natural propensities but also the ability to choose which propensities to follow and which to restrain. He uses the word 'loves' to describe all human urges that prompt us to both actions and passions, including the actions that are freely chosen. Only a 'love' that is fulfilled as the result of a free choice can be subject to praise or blame, and the life of virtue is one in which a person is able to evaluate and order 'loves' in accordance with their true worth. That worth is understood when a person comes to know the truths latent in the human mind, since they are the basis of God's law which, Augustine says:

> while always remaining in him fixed and unalterable, is transcribed into the souls of the wise, in such a manner that they know that their lives are the better and the more sublime in proportion to the degree of

29

perfection of their contemplating it by their minds and keeping it in their lives.[6]

The understanding and enactment of God's law is the achievement of philosophic wisdom.

In Augustine's scheme of things evil is not anything attributable to God who created everything that is but is a lack of being, a deficiency of full existence. Taking evil to be a lack or negation of being provided an answer to the question of how there can be evil in a world created by a God who is entirely good. It also provided a forceful objection to the Manichaean claim that evil was generated from matter. Augustine thought that evil came about through the ability of the free human will to choose among 'loves', that Adam first transgressed in choosing and that humankind has subsequently borne the burden of his sin and required the mediation of Christ for its redemption.

Augustine's philosophical reflections on the nature of time are of enduring philosophical interest. In a famous passage in chapter XIV of the *Confessions* he says: 'What then is time? If no one asks me, I know what it is. If I wish to explain it to him who asks me, I do not know.' When he does try to explain what time is, he finds he produces **paradoxes**. He argues, for example, that we measure time in many ways yet, if we think carefully about the nature of time, it does not seem to be anything that can be measured since past time does not exist once it is past, future time does not exist since it has not yet come and present time becomes past time as soon as it comes into existence. Time is a kind of extendedness, but he cannot say *what* it is that is extended. We measure the motion of a body but, Augustine asks, 'could I measure the motion of a body — how long it takes, how long it is in motion from this place to that — unless I could measure the time in which it is moving?'[7] He seems to be coming to the conclusion that we use time to measure time and this, of course,

brings him no nearer to being able to say what time is. He eventually decides that it is 'a certain kind of extension' and that what we measure when we measure time are impressions or memories in the mind. Addressing his mind, he says:

In you, as I have said, I measure the periods of time. I measure as time present the impressions that things make on you as they pass by — I do not measure the things themselves which have passed by and left their impression on you. This is what I measure when I measure periods of time. Either, then, these are the periods of time or else I do not measure time at all.[8]

Augustine thus finds a resolution of the difficulty of the non-existence of past and future time by allowing that impressions, memories and expectations can exist now in the mind. To speak, for example, of a long time in the past is to speak of a long present memory of some past time. When we speak of future times we are speaking of our mental expectations.

Numerous criticisms may be made of Augustine's reflections on time. Particularly questionable, I think, are some of the ways in which he analyses our commonsense remarks about time, according them a rather naive face value which permits a rapid proliferation of difficulties. However, this kind of approach has merits because its often swift collapse into paradox and absurdity stimulates criticism and the pursuit of fresh lines of investigation. It certainly contributes to the at once passionate and innocent intensity of Augustine's search for truth and beatitude. Moreover, this tendency in his work to provoke new questions and further enquiry meant that it had an enduring liveliness and interest so that it became a potent factor in mediaeval religious thinking and in the Reformation. In the twentieth century Augustine's views on language have been the starting point for Wittgenstein's reflections on language and meaning in his *Philosophical investigations*.[9]

Notes

1. Augustine, *In Iohannis Evangelium tractatus*, xxix, 6.
2. Augustine, *Confessions*, Book IV, Ch. 1.
3. Augustine, *De moribus ecclesiae*, i. 27.52.
4. Augustine, *De immortalitate animae*, 6.10.
5. Augustine, *De Trinitate*, ix, 7.12.
6. Ausustine, *Epistola* 120.3; *De ordine*, ii. 8.25.
7. Augustine, *Confessions*, Ch. XXVI.
8. Ibid. Ch. XXVIII.
9. L. Wittgenstein, *Philosophical investigations*, trans. G.E.M. Anscombe (Basil Blackwell, Oxford, 1968), pp. 1, 2, 3ff.

See also in this book

Plato, Aristotle, Plotinus.

Augustine's major writings

Confessions (Penguin, Harmondsworth, 1972)
City of God (Penguin, Harmondsworth, 1972)
Augustine's works in Latin are in Migne's *Patrologia Latina*, vols 32-46. They are in English translation in *The works of Augustinus Aurelius, Bishop of Hippo*, ed. M. Dods (T. and T. Clarke, Edinburgh, 1871-76 and 1953-5). A range of his writings is available in *Augustine of Hippo: later works*, trans. J. Burnaby (SCM Press, London, 1955).

Further reading

Bonner, G. *St. Augustine of Hippo: life and controversies* (SCM Press, London, 1963)
Brown, P. *Augustine of Hippo: a biography* (Faber and Faber, London, 1967)
Gilson, E. *The Christian philosophy of Saint Augustine*, trans. L.E.M. Lynch (Victor Gollancz, London, 1961)
Leff, G. *Medieval thought* (Penguin, Harmondsworth, 1958)
McEvoy, J. 'St. Augustine's account of time and Wittgenstein's criticisms', *Review of Metaphysics*, 37, pp. 547-78
Marenbon, J. *Early mediaeval philosophy (480-1150): an introduction* (Routledge and Kegan Paul, London, 1983)
Markus, R.A. 'Augustine' in D.J. O'Connor (ed.), *A critical history of Western philosophy* (The Free Press, New York, 1964; Macmillan, London, 1985)
Marrou, H.I. *Saint Augustine and his influence through the ages* (Longman's, London, 1958)
O'Meara, J.J. *The young Augustine* (Longman, London, 1954 and 1980)

Moses Maimonides (Moses Ben Maimon) 1135-1204

Maimonides was an extremely influential Jewish philosopher. His *Guide of the per-plexed*, one of the great works of medieval philosophy, seeks largely to reconcile Aristotelianism with Judaism and to prove the existence of God from Aristotelian principles. His thought owes something to that of Avicenna (980-1037), the Islamic philosopher who studied Aristotle and Neo-Platonism, and to Averroes (1126-98), another Islamic philosopher renowned for his Aristotelian scholarship.

Maimonides in turn was carefully studied by Thomas Aquinas and by Jewish and Muslim philosophers. Echoes of his work are found in Spinoza's *Ethics* and he was admired by Leibniz and by Moses Mendelssohn. He departed from Aristotle's views in several respects but most radically in maintaining that God created matter as well as form out of nothing.

Maimonides was born in Cordova when that part of Spain was Muslim. His family left there in 1148 and after much travelling settled in north Africa for a while. In 1165 Maimonides moved to Old Cairo where he remained for the rest of his life, becoming a court physician and leader of the Jewish community. He wrote in Arabic on a broad range of topics: legal doctrine, ethics, religious belief, medicine, logic and philosophy. His *Guide of the perplexed* is something known as *Guide for the wanderer* since the Arabic word translated as 'the perplexed' or 'the wanderer' refers to an indecisive mental state that hovers between different beliefs. The *Guide* was written for those who are to some extent knowledgeable in philosophy and theology but who are confused by the conflicting claims of science and faith. It has a curious characteristic deliberately imposed on it by Maimonides, who shared Averroes' conviction that the religious faith of ordinary people would be seriously undermined if they became acquainted with simplified and uncritical accounts of Aristotelian views. That characteristic is a certain kind of disorder. When writing the *Guide* Maimonides deliberately refrained from presenting Aristotelianism in its own orderly and systematic way, thus impeding any ready comprehension of it: a reader not intellectually astute would not perceive the full force of Aristotle's arguments, while those who were astute could grasp them properly only by a careful process of reconstruction of the disorganised material. Maimonides tells us that he even includes contradictory statements in the *Guide* and it has been suggested that part of his intention in all this was to indicate that where reasoning comes to an end faith can take over. He says:

> The object of this treatise is to enlighten a religious man who has been trained to believe in the truth of our holy law, who conscientiously fulfils his moral and religious duties, and at the same time has been successful in his philosophical studies.[1]

When Maimonides considers the reconciliation of the Jewish Law with science, or philosophy, he discusses the idea that allegorical or figurative speech is used in the Scriptures because the understanding of many people is severely limited. He admits that allegory will not satisfy anyone with a strongly philosophical cast of mind but that those steeped in the religious tradition as well as trained in philosophy should recognise the need for both kinds of approach rather than reject one in favour of the other. Faith would be banished if every religious topic was required to be understood in literal terms. Knowledge of God, he insisted, is not to be sought by struggling to formulate literal descriptions of the divine being but by reflecting instead on his negative attributes. God could not be known by likening him to his creatures, for his being has nothing in common with other beings; thus, negative ascriptions would successfully nullify false ideas about his nature and properties.

Maimonides' account of God's intellect does not seem to be consistent with the above claims. Like Aristotle, he maintains that God is pure intellect and asserts also that the human intellect has a resemblance to God's. These remarks run counter to the view that only negative ascriptions may be made to God and to the view that God's attributes are entirely different from those of his creatures. Perhaps Maimonides is at work here to challenge the philosopher-believer to whom the *Guide* is addressed.

A major difficulty in the reconciliation of philosophy with faith is produced by the juxtaposing of Aristotle's view that the world is the logically **necessary** consequence of the divine Intellect and exists eternally, with the religious account of a creation brought about by God's exercise of his will. Maimonides tackles the difficulty by arguing, first, that the Aristotelian account does not succeed in proving the eternal and necessary existence of things and, second, that it is unacceptable because it is contrary to what is proclaimed by the Law and the prophets. His discussion of the matter is finely balanced for he does not assert a superior or supra-rational knowledge on the part of prophets. When he analyses the capabilities of people who become prophets he emphasises the need for intellectual ability of a very high order. Imagination is required as well but it is intellect that, for Maimonides, is primary and which enables a prophet to partake of what he calls the Active Intellect. Prophecy in its profoundest and most compelling exercise involves intellectual activity similar in kind to philosophical activity.

Maimonides was a significant and subtle thinker in his own right. He is equally important when seen as a disseminator of Aristotelianism and as an element in the development of medieval **scholasticism**. He posed many of the problems that were to dominate Western philosophy in the thirteenth century and his enquiries into the relationship between faith and philosophy, reason and revelation, contributed influentially to a debate that grew and flourished for nearly two hundred years after his death.

Notes

1. Maimonides, *Guide of the perplexed*, Introduction to the First Part.

See also in this book

Aristotle, Aquinas, Duns Scotus, Ockham, Spinoza.

Maimonides' major writings

Commentary on the Mishnah (1168)
The guide of the perplexed (c. 1190), trans. Schlomo Pines with an Introduction by Leo Strauss (University of Chicago Press, Chicago and London, 1963)
Treatise on resurrection (1911)

Further reading and selections

Weiss, R. and Butterworth, C. *Ethical writings of Maimonides* (Dover Publications, Constable, London, 1984)
Twersky, I., *A Maimonides reader* (Behrman House, New York, 1972)
Russell, H.M. and Winberg, J. (trans.) *The Book of Knowledge: from the Mishnah Torah of Maimonides* (Royal College of Physicians, Edinburgh, 1981)
The Chicago University Press edition of *The Guide of the perplexed* contains excellent introductions by the editor and the translator.

St Thomas Aquinas
1225-1274

The philosophy of Thomas Aquinas, 'the angelic doctor', is closely interwoven with his theology. Aquinas wanted to establish a harmonious coexistence between faith and reason by showing, first, that tenets of faith do not contradict the conclusions of philosophy and, second, that they neither derive from nor form the grounds of philosophical arguments. He was largely responsible for the incorporation of the philosophy of Aristotle into Christian doctrine and Western culture. He wrote prodigiously and his two best-known works, the *Summa contra Gentiles* and the *Summa theologiae*, are both of encyclopaedic proportions. As its title implies, the *Summa contra Gentiles* (Summary against the Gentiles) was meant for non-Christians. It treats of the nature and works of God, human wisdom and happiness, and of the compatibility of faith with reason. The *Summa theologiae* (Summary of theology) consists entirely of questions and their answers presented in the form of lengthy articles. It deals with reason and revelation as means to knowledge of God, offers five proofs of God's existence, analyses God's nature and properties and discusses the grace through which the human intellect can apprehend the deity. Three years after his death, in spite of some quibbling on the part of ecclesiastical authorities concerning his theological views, Thomas was canonised by Pope John XII.

Thomas is thought to have been born early in 1225 at the castle of Roccasecca near Naples. He was the seventh son of the Count of Aquino. At the age of five he was sent to be educated at the Benedictine abbey of Monte Cassino and in due course went to the University of Naples where he read Aristotle and studied the seven liberal arts: logic, rhetoric, arithmetic, geometry, grammar, music and astronomy. At the age of 19 he angered his family, who expected him to become a Benedictine monk, by joining the less acceptable brotherhood of Dominican friars. To help him escape his family's displeasure the Dominicans despatched him to Paris, but on the way he was kidnapped by his brothers and was kept at home for over a year. He refused to give up his allegiance to the Dominicans and was eventually allowed to return to them and resume his formal studies. In 1252 he went to the University of Paris to give a series of lectures to qualify him for a Mastership. He became a professor at Paris at the age of 30 and returned to Italy in 1259 to teach at various institutions and to serve the Popes at Orvieto, Viterbo and Rome. In 1269 he returned to Paris but gave up teaching four years later because of failing health. He died on 7 March 1274 at a Cistercian monastery near Fossanova, having been unable to recover from a head injury sustained as he was travelling to Lyons a few weeks earlier.

Although Aquinas was a highly original thinker, his philosophy is grounded in that of

Aristotle.[1] He uses the Aristotelian distinctions between form and matter, substance and accident, actuality and potentiality, as a framework for his ideas. The distinction between actuality and potentiality is between what something actually is and what it is possible for it to be. Thus a piece of coal may, at a particular time, be actually black, cold, shiny and hard, and potentially grey, hot, powdery and soft, since it can be heated and become ash. The distinction between substance and accident is made clear through the same example. To heat a lump of coal to the point at which it is merely warm is to bring about an accidental change in it but to burn it fiercely so that it turns to ash is to effect a change of substance. In an accidental change the substance remains the same; in a substantial change it becomes another kind of substance. The changes take place by means of changes in forms: accidental forms are involved in accidental changes such as the change in the coal from cold to warm; substantial forms are involved in changes of substance, such as the change from coal to ash.

Aquinas uses the term 'matter' for anything capable of substantial change and he believed that everything terrestrial partakes of both matter and form. Angels, he held, are non-corporeal but each angel has its own form and is differentiated from all other angels by that particular form, whereas human beings, being composed of both matter and form, are differentiated from each other by being different parcels of matter.

Aristotle had maintained that it is the form of something that actualises it or makes it what it is, but Aquinas develops a more elaborate **metaphysic** of being in which he argues that it is the act of coming into existence rather than the actualisation of a form that has supreme significance. He distinguishes between the essence and the existence of a thing. Briefly, the essence of something may be thought of as its definition and this definition may be known and understood without knowing whether the thing does or does not actually exist. Thus the actual existence of something is distinct from its definition. Aquinas says:

> every essence or quiddity can be understood without its act of existing being understood. I can understand what a man or phoenix is and yet not know whether or not it exists in the nature of things. Therefore, it is evident that the act of existing is other than essence or quiddity.[2]

The distinction between essence and existence does not apply to God. Aquinas argues that God, unlike other beings, cannot be caused by anything external to himself and so his existence must be caused by his own essence. He says, 'His essence is nothing other than His act of existing ... by its very purity, His act of existing is distinct from every other act of existing.' God is individuated from all other existents by pure goodness and possesses all perfections without qualification, and 'all these perfections belong to Him according to His simple act of existing'.[3] Aquinas' remarks on the identity of existence and essence in God are not easy to understand. Commentators have worked to bring clarity and coherence to his account but not with complete success.[4]

In all his work of analysis, definition and classification we see Aquinas intent on the task of elucidating the nature of things and giving an account of the most ultimate grounds of existence and the reasons for everything being as it is. Following Aristotle, who described philosophy as 'a science which considers What Is simply in its character of Being, and the properties which it has as such', he starts from ordinary human experience of things and reasons to large principles. Into this structure he incorporates the Christian dimension, carefully separating truths arrived at through reasoning from those he believes can be imparted only through revelation or divine authority.

Aquinas is probably best known for his Five Ways to God. He does not think that the existence of God is self-evident and he derives the proofs he offers in the Five Ways from statements of facts about ordinary experience. This does not mean that he is attempting to vindicate a **hypothesis** by adducing evidence for it; rather, he offers a philosophical argument, asserting that since we have a world which comes into being, decays and passes away, then it follows that such changes require the existence of an efficient cause that is beyond them. The first proof invites us to consider the changes that take place in the world, arguing that anything that moves is moved by something else, that an infinite series without beginning is impossible, and that we therefore have to arrive at the concept of an unmoved mover. The second proof looks at actual causes of changes, arguing that there must be a first cause which is God since no other cause could be the cause of itself. The third proof argues that the fact that some beings come into existence and perish shows that they are **contingent** rather than **necessary** beings and that a necessary being must be postulated as the source of the existence of contingent beings. In the fourth proof Aquinas points out that we judge some things to be better than others and maintains that such degrees of perfection imply the existence of a best, a truest, a supreme being which is the cause of all relative perfections and is itself pure perfection. The fifth proof concerns the way in which natural bodies appear to operate towards some good end or purpose and from this it is argued that there must be an intelligent being by whom everything is given an end that relates to things as a whole.

Commentators have pointed out that the observations from which the five proofs begin are acceptable to most people but that it is not always easy to see how Aquinas moves from the observations to the conclusions about God's existence. They remind us, too, that in criticising Aquinas we should preserve a historical sense, remembering, for example, that Aquinas did not have the same understanding as we have of the notion of

infinity and that he did not distinguish sharply between causal relationships and logical entailment. It has further been pointed out that even if Aquinas' five proofs were shown to be logically in order and were accepted as proofs of the existence of a prime mover, they do not provide proof of the existence of a God having the attributes ascribed to the God of Christianity. Aquinas manages to extract Christian attributes such as wisdom and goodness from the notion of a necessary being but his logical procedures are complicated and are vulnerable to critical scrutiny. Nevertheless, the method and procedure of the Five Ways clearly reveal Aquinas at work to fulfil his aim of showing that faith and reason arrive at the same knowledge even though they work in different ways.

Aquinas followed Aristotle in regarding the human soul as the form of the human body. He said of the soul that it is the first principle of life in living things; it is what makes a living thing alive. He believed that the soul and body together are one **substance** in which two components can be distinguished and that the body without the soul is not strictly a body at all but an aggregate of material things. He maintained that each human soul is created by God and does not exist prior to the existence of the body. If the soul is regarded as that which animates a body then it follows that all living things are besouled. In a plant it is a *vegetative* soul that is responsible for its growth and nourishment. Animals have *sensitive* souls since they are capable of sensation, and human beings have *rational* souls in virtue of their further capacity for rational activity. As with his enquiry into the existence and nature of God, Aquinas develops his account of the human soul by arguing from ordinary sense experience towards metaphysical conclusions. In the human being there are activities that go beyond matter. The mind can conceive of or know other than purely material things and this suggests that it is not itself entirely material. There are direct physical counterparts of vegetative and sensitive soul activities and human beings are of course capable of these activities but in so far as the rational soul is engaged in understanding concepts or reflecting about logic, mathematics, metaphysics and God, its activities have no bodily counterpart. This means that there is some part or aspect of the human soul that does not require concomitant bodily activity and which is therefore immaterial and capable of surviving the death of the body. Human beings are between, on the one hand, God and the angels and, on the other, the animal world; but Aquinas specifically rejects the Platonic view that the soul *is* the human being and that it simply makes use of a body. For Aquinas it is the body and soul together that constitute the human person and the body is as much the essence of a person as the soul is. The moral life of a person consists in seeking direct knowledge of God and its achievement is joy through the possession of truth. The intellect is the power by which knowledge is attained and the will is the power of choice, but the will cannot make a choice until the intellect descries means to an end perceived as good in some way. The will necessarily strives towards what the intellect perceives as good and the act of choice is the choice of a means to achieving that good. Of course, this does not mean that a person necessarily chooses the best but that he or she always chooses what is seen as in some way a good. Even if one knows that one has not made a morally good choice, or does some action one knows to be wrong, it is, according to Aquinas, not the evil as such that one desires but something in the deed that appears good and desirable.

Aquinas held that human beings are able to act freely. Free acts are those done out of reason and will and the whole nature of liberty depends upon the mode of knowledge. Animals, Aquinas says, 'do not judge of their own judgements, but follow the judgement imprinted on them by God'. He continues:

Man, however, judging about his actions through his power of reason, can judge concerning his choice insofar as he can know the nature of the end and of the means to the end, and, likewise, the relation and order of the one to the other. Man, therefore, is his own cause, not only in moving but also in judging. Hence he has free choice, as one is speaking of the free judgements as to whether to act or not.[5]

The importance of Aquinas' work and the influence it exerted can scarcely be overestimated. He brought together Christianity and Aristotelianism and showed that philosophy and theology could coexist and support one another. The discovery and dissemination of the thought of Aristotle was in itself an achievement of supreme significance and at the same time the complexity and interrelatedness of Aquinas' own works inspired an abundance of fresh thought, criticism, discussion and new developments in philosophy and theology for centuries after his death. That inspiration is at work still.

Notes

1. See *Aristotle* in this book, pp. 22-6.
2. Thomas Aquinas, *On being and essence*, V, trans. Robert P. Goodwin, in *Selected writings of St. Thomas Aquinas* (Library of Liberal Arts, Bobbs-Merrill, Indianapolis and New York, 1965), p. 54.
3. Ibid., p. 58.
4. For discussions of the difficulties of Aquinas' account of existence and essence see, for example, F.C. Copleston, *Aquinas* (Penguin, Harmondsworth, 1955), Ch. 2, pp. 96-104; and A. Kenny, *Aquinas* (Past Masters Series, Oxford University Press, Oxford, 1980), Ch. 2, pp. 49-60.
5. Thomas Aquinas, *On free choice*, Article I, in Goodwin, *Selected writings*, p. 123.

See also in this book

Plato, Aristotle, Duns Scotus, Ockham.

Thomas Aquinas' major writings

Aquinas' works in Latin are in the Parma edition in 25 volumes, reprinted in New York in 1948.
Summa contra Gentiles (Summary against the Gentiles),

trans. A. Pegis *et al.* as *On the truth of the Catholic faith* (Random House, New York, 1955-7)
Summa theologiae (Summary of theology), trans. in 61 volumes (Eyre and Spottiswood, London, 1963-80)
De ente et essentia (On being and essence) in A. Pegis, (ed.), *Basic writings of St Thomas Aquinas*, 2 vols (Random House, New York, 1945)
De veritate (On truth) in Pegis, *Basic writings of St Thomas Aquinas*, 2 vols (Random House, New York, 1945)
See also Robert P. Goodwin (trans.), *Selected writings of St Thomas Aquinas*, cited in note 2 above.

Further reading

Copleston, F.C. *Aquinas* (Penguin, Harmondsworth, 1955)
Kenny, A. *Aquinas* (Past Masters, Oxford University Press, Oxford, 1980)
O'Connor, D.J. *Aquinas and natural law* (Macmillan, London, 1967)
Weisheipl, J. *Friar Thomas d'Aquino* (Blackwell, Oxford, 1974)

John Duns Scotus
c. 1265-1308

John Duns Scotus was an original and critical thinker. The mainsprings of his thought were the philosophical theology of Thomas Aquinas and the Augustinian tradition. He is important as a philosopher largely because he reacted against both these influences. He saw will rather than intellect as primary in the concept of God and he sharply separated matters of faith from matters of reason. He died early, leaving his writings in disarray. Many of them were added to or completed by his pupils and the task of sorting the authentic from the inauthentic or the doubtful has been a difficult one that has generated, and still generates, lively debate. Duns Scotus is often known as 'the subtle Doctor', no doubt in recognition of his shrewd reasoning and his perception of fine distinctions.

Records of Duns Scotus' life are scant. He was born either at Maxton or near Duns in Scotland. He entered the Franciscan order and studied at Oxford and then at Paris, where he duly followed the usual course of writing commentaries on Peter Lombard's *Four books of sentences*, a highly organised collection of questions about various and conflicting theological pronouncements. The

four sets of sentences, compiled in the twelfth century, had become the standard textbook for any theological student aspiring to a mastership. Duns Scotus' *Commentaries on the sentences* have titles taken from his two places of study. They are known respectively as *Opus Oxoniense* and *Reportata Parisiensia*. Commentaries were always in dialectical form; that is, they assessed the arguments ranged for and against particular views or claims and sought resolutions of what was at issue. Scotus' *Opus Oxoniense* is generally regarded as his most important work. He died at Cologne, having achieved a considerable written output in a life of around forty years.

As a Franciscan friar Duns Scotus was well steeped in the Augustinian tradition and Augustine's belief that knowledge of God was attained by illumination. He knew the work of Thomas Aquinas equally well and was entirely familiar with Aquinas' Aristotelianism and with his view that reason confirms and complements religious truth acquired through revelation. He rejected Augustine's doctrine of illumination and much of Aquinas' Aristotelian conception of God, as well as the latter's account of the relation between faith and reason. His own views have been described as 'a counterblast to Thomism'.[1]

Duns Scotus distinguishes sharply between theology and philosophy. Theology treats of God and the attributes of God, but theological truths, he maintains, are not susceptible of the evidential proof of sense perception. Philosophy, or metaphysics, is about being and its attributes and could not, he said, describe the attributes of God except in so far as God was being. Thus he could not accept Aquinas' five proofs which argued from facts of ordinary human sense experience to the existence of God. Neither could he accept Augustine's doctrine of illumination which maintained that the correct use of reason would lead to illumined knowledge, for his own separation of reason and revelation meant that he did not accept that natural reason could transcend itself in that way. His view was that knowledge of God could be arrived at through a concept of being that was applicable to both God and God's created universe. In the *Opus Oxoniense* he said of this concept of being that 'It extends to all that is not nothing.'[2] It is a highly abstract concept: it sees being simply as the source of all natures and as something preceding rather than deriving from them. Accordingly, only general modes of being can be deduced from it and particular beings cannot be deduced from it. Its merits are that it embraces both God and his creation and that it allows human understanding to go beyond sensory knowledge. From this univocal, or all-embracing, concept of being Duns Scotus argues for the existence of both infinite and finite being, the latter being created through the will of the former. He maintains that finite causes on their own lead to an infinite regression of such causes but that the idea of a first cause invokes the ideas of **necessity**, omniscience, perfection and infinity.

Scotus differed radically from many of his predecessors in that he rejected doctrines that held that God necessarily created his creatures. He argued instead that although God's intellect knows all possible beings it does not follow that all possible beings necessarily exist; for it is God's *will* that chooses which beings shall exist and his will is the expression of his **essence**. In this way he abolishes a necessary connection between God and his creatures, emphasises God's freedom and disallows any ultimate and total comprehension of God by the beings he had created. The separateness and the importance of faith are thereby reinforced, for one cannot reason one's way to a God who is not necessarily, but only **contingently**, connected with his creatures. Faith therefore may furnish the descriptions inaccessible to reason.

The 'subtlety' of Duns Scotus' thought is clearly revealed in the way in which he dealt with a problem arising out of Aristotelian teaching about forms. The Aristotelian view was that the form of something, that which makes something what it is — a horse a horse, a tree a tree, and so on — can be elucidated in a general definition and so be known by the intellect or reason. But the problem produced by this account is that of how one can know the **particular** individuals that are instances of a **universal** form. Aristotle, and Aquinas following him, had maintained that such particulars were individuated by being different parcels of matter; but this does not render an individual intelligible or knowable, for intelligibility depends on knowledge of the form through definition and not of the matter of a particular individual. Scotus resolved this difficulty by recourse to the notion of *haecceity* or 'thisness'. If the haecceity or ultimate particularity of an individual is understood as belonging with form rather than with matter then it can be seen as intellectually knowable, in principle if not in fact. Thus, for Scotus, the universal form and the individual haecceity belong with the essences created by God and the specific individual is the ultimate actuality of the form.

Duns Scotus strengthened not only the idea of the individual but also the idea of the individual free will. Like Augustine he believed that 'the will commanding the intellect is the superior cause of its action. The intellect, however, if it is the cause of volition, is a subservient cause to the will.'[3] He had to confront complex difficulties about the will, since it was generally characterised as a striving towards the fulfilment or completion of the propensities of one's nature and thus was seen as an essentially egocentric pursuit that was incapable of altruism. Aquinas had tried to deal with this difficulty by making the intellect superior to the will but this was contrary to the Christian tradition. Scotus therefore posited two inclinations of the will, the first towards one's own good and advantage, the second towards the achievement of a justice appropriate to the objective value of all things. In this second tendency of the will things are loved for their own sakes rather than for any good or advantage they might bring to oneself. Scotus called it the *affectio justitiae*, the affection for justice, and described it as 'the first tempering influence on the affection for what is to our advantage'.[4] It was, he said, innate in the will and constituted the will's freedom in that it was able to free one from the natural seeking of one's own advantage. His account points out that this disinterested regard that values each thing for its own sake accords dignity to each human being and wishes others to recognise the values thereby perceived and to share in the appreciation of them.

Duns Scotus' critical acumen and his scepticism concerning the scope of reason paved the way for a more generally critical attitude in the fourteenth century. The dominant theme that his successors took from his work was that philosophical reasoning could never arrive at the concept of a Christian God; only faith can provide such a description. In the twentieth century his abstruse and difficult writing has been studied with deep interest by such diverse persons as the poet Gerard Manley Hopkins, the American philosopher Charles Sanders Peirce, and the German philosopher Martin Heidegger.

Notes

1. G. Leff, *Mediaeval thought* (Penguin, Harmondsworth 1958), p. 263.
2. Duns Scotus, *Opus Oxoniense*, i, 3, 2.
3. Ibid., IV, 49, 2.
4. Ibid., III, 37.

See also in this book

Aristotle, Augustine, Aquinas, Ockham, Peirce, Heidegger.

Duns Scotus' major writings

Tractatus de primo principio (*c.* 1300), ed. M. Mueller (Freiburg in Bresgau, 1941), trans. A. Walter as *Duns Scotus: a treatise on God as first principle* (Franciscan Herald Press, Chicago, 1965)
Opus Oxoniense

Reportata Parisiensia
Scotus' works in Latin are in *Opera omnia*, ed. L. Wadding (12 vols, Lyons, 1639, repr. in 26 vols, ed. L. Vivès, Paris, 1891-5). An English selection is *Duns Scotus: philosophical writings*, ed. A.B. Walter (Bobbs-Merrill, Indianapolis, 1964)

Further reading

Bettoni, E. *Duns Scotus: the basic principles of his philosophy*, ed. B.M. Bonansea (Bobbs-Merrill, Indianapolis, 1964)
Bonansea, B.M. *Man and his approach to God in Duns Scotus* (University Press of America, Maryland, USA 1983)
Copleston, F. *A history of philosophy*, vol. II, Part II (Newman Press, Westminster, Maryland, 1962)
Leff, G. *Medieval thought* (Penguin, Harmondsworth, 1958)

William of Ockham
c. 1285-1349

William of Ockham is famous for a principle of economy known as 'Ockham's razor'. The principle states that 'What can be explained by the assumption of fewer things is vainly explained by the assumption of more things.' Ockham was a radical empiricist who maintained that individual objects of sense were the only reality. He was also a logician and the author of an influential doctrine of **nominalism**. He argued that theological truth could not be arrived at by means of reason.

He was born in the village of Ockham near Guildford, Surrey. He joined the Franciscan order soon after he became a student at Oxford and in due course wrote the customary commentary on the *Sentences* of Peter Lombard.[1] He gave a highly controversial series of lectures on Lombard's *Sentences* and in consequence was summoned in 1324 to the papal court at Avignon to be charged with heresy. Judgement on this matter was delayed for two years during which time Ockham was confined to the Franciscan house at Avignon. In 1326 51 of his written propositions were pronounced heretical. Ockham refused to retract them and later consolidated his rebelliousness by aligning himself with the Spiritual Franciscans who were in controversy with Pope

John XXII. In 1328 he fled from Avignon with Michael of Cesena, General of the Franciscan order and leader of the Spirituals. He was excommunicated by the Pope and thereafter lived in Munich under the protection of the Emperor, Louis of Bavaria, devoting much of his time to writing pamphlets against the Pope. The Black Death was rampant in Europe at the end of the 1340s and Ockham is thought to have contracted it in 1349 or 1350. He was buried in Munich in the Franciscan church but his remains were subsequently taken to an unknown place.

Many of Ockham's ideas were contrary to those of Duns Scotus and he is sometimes seen as working in direct opposition to Scotus. However, the ground of Ockham's empiricism is the belief, shared with Scotus, that everything in the world is **contingent** on the free will of God. Thus they are alike in that they both rejected the views of Thomas Aquinas and other earlier philosopher-theologians about Ideas in the mind of God. These earlier thinkers had incorporated Plato's view that the perfect Forms of all things existed eternally and incorporeally into Christian theology by converting the Forms into Ideas in God's mind. The Ideas were construed as part of God's essence and thus as comprising the pattern according to which God created his world. Since the structure and content of the created world necessarily followed from the Ideas in God's mind, Aquinas and others working in the Augustinian tradition had argued that it was possible to reason from statements about the created world to knowledge of the mind of God. Both Duns Scotus and Ockham thought this account imposed severe limitations on God's freedom to create the world according to his will. They maintained instead that the created world is contingently and not **necessarily** what it is. Ockham argues therefore that there can be no necessary connections from nature to the mind of God and that in order to acquire knowledge we must look at each particular thing: only individual things are real and so only individual things can be known.

The claim that only individual things are real is part of, and is fortified by, Ockham's doctrine of nominalism and the employment of his 'razor' principle. He sees no need to justify our use of general or universal terms such as 'woman', 'fire', 'dog', by reference to Forms or 'essences' which have a special mode of existence distinct from the existence of particular women, fires and dogs. His 'razor' excises the positing of the real existence of Forms or essences because, he says, the universality they are invoked to justify does not reside in such real entities but is simply a property of certain *names* or signs. 'Universal' is a name to be applied to certain words, used in certain ways, rather than to things.[2]

In the Prologue to his commentary on Lombard's *Sentences*, Ockham distinguishes two kinds of knowledge, intuitive and abstractive. Intuitive knowledge is an immediate awareness of either objects of sense or of the mind's activity when engaged in that immediate awareness. Truths of revelation and self-evident truths are also known intuitively. Abstractive knowledge derives from intuitive knowledge and is knowledge not of facts but of propositions. It may be knowledge either of universals that have been formulated by using one's knowledge of many things, or of the judgements we make about our knowledge of existing or non-existing things. Ockham's careful analysis assigns reason to operating only with signs and terms and he distinguishes between natural and conventional signs. He maintains that before we name objects with words our minds contain natural significations of them which are the natural effects of the objects. He says, 'The sign by which I understand man is the natural sign of men ... such a sign can stand for men in mental propositions, just as a word can stand for things in spoken propositions.'[3] The words or terms we give to natural signs are conventional signs with which reason operates.

Since all knowledge, for Ockham, either consists of or derives from the immediate intuitive awareness of particular things, it looks as though he must disavow any possibility of knowing God. This he certainly does but at the same time argues that it is possible to have a certain kind of conception of God by means of the concept of being. Once again the starting point for his discussion is close to that of Duns Scotus on the same topic. Ockham claims that we form the concept of being from the immediate or direct apprehension of particular existing things. This concept may then be used univocally to apply both to creatures and to God; without it we could not conceive of God at all for we could not think of anything without thinking of it as if it existed. But such a procedure, he says, in no way guarantees the existence of God nor does it tell us that his being is in any way like the being of his creatures. All it does is to allow us to form a concept of his existence. In a similar way we can form a concept of 'first' or 'prime' from our immediate knowledge of particular things or creatures and so formulate the concept of a First Being. Again, the ability to develop the concept is something quite distinct from knowing whether that to which the concept is applicable does in fact exist. Ockham reaffirms that whatever further concepts we can draw from the concept of a First Being, any knowledge thereby attained is knowledge of the concepts and not knowledge of God. Of course, what he does allow is that knowledge of God is possible through revelation; but that knowledge is of an entirely different kind, based on entirely different concepts.

Ockham's clear separation of revelation and faith from sensuous and abstractive knowledge had far-reaching effects. It established the theoretical scope and limits for the study of the natural world and so for the development of a well-defined science. Yet it did this within a conception of the universe that was ultimately dependent on the contingency of a divine will that was beyond human apprehension and therefore unchallengeable. God could not be subjected to analysis: he was not conceptually coextensive with the natural world and his power over it was absolute. Gordon Leff has aptly remarked of that concept of omnipotence that 'it served the double end of freeing God from reason and experience from faith'.[4]

Notes

1. Peter Lombard compiled the *Sentences* in the twelfth century. See *Duns Scotus* in this book, pp. 37-9.
2. For more on nominalism see *Hobbes* in this book, pp. 51-7.
3. Ockham, *Sentences*, 1, 2, 7.
4. G. Leff, *Mediaeval thought* (Penguin, Harmondsworth, 1958) p. 290.

See also in this book

Plato, Aristotle, Augustine, Aquinas, Duns Scotus.

Ockham's writings

Ockham's philosophy is intermingled with his theological, scientific and political writings. His logic is contained in his *Summa totius logicae*. His complete works, *Opera omnia philosophica et theologica*, in 25 volumes, are in preparation under the general editorship of E.M. Buytaert (St. Bonaventure, New York and Paderborn). A selection of Ockham's writings is in P. Boehner (ed. and trans.), *Ockham, philosophical writings* (Nelson, Edinburgh, 1957).

Further reading

Copleston, F.C. *Ockham to Suarez*, vol. III, part I of *A history of philosophy* (Newman Press, Westminster, Md., 1950, and Image Books, New York, 1962)
Leff, G. *Medieval thought* (Penguin, Harmondsworth, 1958)
—— *William of Ockham* (Manchester University Press, Manchester, 1975)

Niccolo di Bernardo dei Machiavelli 1469-1527

Machiavelli is popularly taken to be a devious and unscrupulous schemer who wrote his treatise, *The Prince*, in order to ingratiate himself with the Medici family, the powerful Florentine rulers from whose favour he had fallen. *The Prince* is not an overtly or rigorously philosophical work. For one thing, it lacks system; for another, Machiavelli tends to assume a good deal that most philosophers would be concerned to argue for. But his work and personality together represent the great complex of important changes that characterised the late fifteenth century and formed the modern world. Moreover, he sheds as searching a light on modern social and political relations as he does on those of the Renaissance. A philosophy is implicit rather than explicit in his work. It is one that is absorbed rather than observed.

Machiavelli was born in the year in which Lorenzo de Medici assumed power in Florence. Little is known of his youth and early manhood but, after Lorenzo's death and the overthrow of the Medicis in favour of a republic, he was appointed secretary to its Council of Ten. He was then 29 and he held his post at the centre of Florentine politics for 14 years. The republic ended in 1512 and the Medici were restored to power. Machiavelli was arrested, imprisoned and tortured and then released and allowed to live in retirement in the country. There he began to write, hoping that through his work he might re-enter political life, this time in the service of the Medici. He died in 1527, the year of the sack of Rome, without having fully realised that hope. In the latter half of his life he witnessed numerous political upheavals, religious corruption, intrigues and complicated shifts of power. Small wonder, then, that in his enforced retirement and pursuit of reinstatement he turned to pondering on the means by which some kind of enduring political order might be established. He wrote two major political works: *The Prince*, which he was certainly working on in 1513 and which was dedicated in 1516 to the younger Lorenzo de Medici; and *Discourses upon the first decade of Titus Livius*, compiled between 1513 and 1516.

What Machiavelli produces in *The Prince* is a set of prescriptions for the successful management of a state through the procurement of power. Being thoroughly imbued with the values and attitudes of his time, he unashamedly believed that power was good and that it should be sought and enjoyed, along with fame, reputation and honour. As his title, *The Prince*, implies, he favours a monarchy rather than a republic, saying that 'the Condition of Italy makes a Republic Impracticable' and that the somewhat better state of affairs obtaining in France and Spain 'is not so much owing to the goodness of their people, in which they are greatly deficient, as to the fact that they each have a king who keeps them united'.[1] Yet Machiavelli had at one time believed that a constitutional republic of the sort that had been successful in the German lands and in the Swiss Confederation provided the best government. Moreover, in parts of the *Discourses* he reinforces that view by looking, as any Renaissance humanist would, to the past and especially to the classical past and finding there a model of political stability in the Roman republic. But it is arguable that there is no real inconsistency in the shift from a republic to a monarchical position. The idea of a lawgiver, an autocratic and authoritarian figure that enforced the law and restored order, was also well established in antiquity. It was a solution to be adopted when a community had become demoralised and weak.

Machiavelli is extremely blunt concerning the strategies it is permissible for the prince to employ. Ruthlessness may be exercised in order to achieve the desired end. The prince 'should not keep faith when by so doing it would be against his interest' and he must 'learn not to be good'; he 'should not worry if he incurs reproach for his cruelty so long as he keeps his subjects united and loyal ... it is far better to be feared than loved if you cannot be both'.[2] Machiavelli speaks of the *virtu* of a prince or ruler. This is not a virtue compounded of Christian gentleness, justice and compassion but something more like a virtuosity: a competence embracing boldness, drive, decisiveness and political opportunism. The prince needs to observe some prudence, even cunning, in pursuing power. And he needs to develop a perspicacity derived from a profound and unsentimental grasp of what human nature is like. Machiavelli's view of human nature is as follows:

> One can make this generalisation about men: they are ungrateful, fickle, liars, and deceivers, they shun danger and are greedy for profit; while you treat them well they are yours. They would shed their blood for you, risk their property, their lives, their children, so long ... as danger is remote but when you are in danger they turn against you ... Men worry less about doing an injury to one who makes himself loved than to one who makes himself feared.[3]

Machiavelli insists that the generality of people are simple and are easily deceived. The prince should make sure he is seen as a man of compassion, good faith, integrity, kindness and religion: 'everyone sees what you appear to be, few experience what you really are ... the common people are always impressed by appearances and results'.[4]

There is no difficulty in seeing from these extracts what is meant when a person's actions or negotiations are described as 'Machiavellian'. Manipulation, dissembling and deviousness are the popularly known characteristics of the attitude. However, in the last chapter of *The Prince* Machiavelli's tone changes somewhat and his apparent cynicism becomes tempered by a passionate concern for better conditions in Italy. Even this can be seen as his own strategy for currying favour with the reinstated Medici family in Florence. Nevertheless, it is an eloquent and poetic piece of writing that seems to be the genuine expression of, in the words of A.G. Dickens, 'a mind sick of cant and led to envisage heroic and radical solutions in order to extract his countryman from an appalling predicament'.[5] In it Machiavelli endeavours to resuscitate a national spirit which the earlier part of his book seemed to regard as gone for ever. In so doing he exhibits most

interestingly the tacit assumptions as well as the freshly formed ideas and attitudes of his time and circumstances: the shift that had been made from Christian humility to humanist pride; the apotheosising of antiquity; the sense of doom and the hope of glory that always accompany large-scale political changes; above all, the realisation of the acute tensions between politics and morality, the individual and society, so aptly expressed in his own maxim that 'it is sometimes better to seem good than to be good'.[6]

Notes

1. Machiavelli, *Discourses*, I, 17.
2. Machiavelli, *The Prince*, Ch. 17.
3. Ibid.
4. Ibid., Ch. 18.
5. A.G. Dickens, *The age of humanism and reformation* (Prentice-Hall, London, 1972), p. 122.
6. Machiavelli, *The Prince*, Ch. 18.

See also in this book

Rousseau.

Machiavelli's major writings

The Prince (1513), ed. G. Bull (Penguin, Harmondsworth, 1961)
Discourses upon the first decade of Titus Livius (1513-16), trans. L.J. Walker (Penguin, Harmondsworth, 1970)
The art of war, trans. E. Dacres (Tudor Translations, first series, no. 39) (AMS Press, New York, NY. 1967)
History of Florence, ed. H. Hamilton (Harper and Row, London, 1960)
There is a good selection of Machiavelli's writings in *The portable Machiavelli*, ed. P. Bondanella and M. Musa (Penguin, Harmondsworth, 1979).

Further reading

Burckhardt, J. *The civilization of the Renaissance in Italy* (Phaidon, Oxford, 1981)
Jones, W.T. *Masters of political thought*, vol. II, *Machiavelli to Bentham* (George G. Harrap, London, 1947)
Skinner, Q. *Machiavelli* (Oxford University Press, Oxford, 1981)
Fleisher, M. *Machiavelli and the nature of political thought* (Croom Helm, London, 1973)

Francis Bacon   1561-1626

In a letter he wrote at the age of 32 Francis

Bacon said, 'I have taken all knowledge to be my province.' By this he did not mean that he had embarked on a project simply of amassing information. Rather, he had conceived a huge plan for the total reorganisation and development of human knowledge. Moreover, he was deeply concerned not only with a method for its acquisition but with the question how, once acquired, it could best be deployed to increase human dignity and greatness. His ideas created a profound impression during his lifetime and have been widely influential ever since.

Bacon did not inherit the nobility of character ascribed to his parents. His mother, Anne, learned in both Latin and Greek, was sister to the wife of the Lord Treasurer, Burghley. His father, Sir Nicholas Bacon, was Elizabeth I's Lord Keeper of the Great Seal and was described by a contemporary, Birch, as 'most learned, most pious, and wisest of men of the nation'. Francis grew up in the court circle, conversed with Queen Elizabeth from an early age and developed lofty ambitions. When he was 12 he was sent to Trinity College, Cambridge, and at the age of 16 he went to France as a member of the English Ambassador's retinue, fully expecting to become, in due course, a statesman in high office. But his father died when he was 18, leaving very little money and Francis turned to a study of the law, hoping in that way to fit himself for service to the Queen. His interests and competence, even as a young man, were wide: the law, politics, philosophy, history and literature fell easily within his scope and already, during his time in France, he had conceived the plan to organise and deploy the totality of human knowledge.

He entered the House of Commons in 1584 as member for Melcombe Regis. His maiden speech displeased Elizabeth and in spite of his continuing labours in parliamentary and court politics she never granted him the preferment he sought. But his eagerness for office continued, as did his impecuniosity. He seems to have been a complicated mixture. Lytton Strachey said of him: 'He was no striped frieze; he was shot silk.'[1] Macaulay wrote that 'his desires were set on things below, titles, patronage, the mace, the seals, the coronet, large houses, fair gardens, rich manors, many services of plate, gay hangings, curious cabinets'.[2] In fact, he sought splendour and magnificence in everything, not least in the system of knowledge he so ardently laboured to devise and in his vision of the benefits it might furnish for mankind. At the same time his conduct in personal matters appears to have lacked sensibility. Macaulay describes him as seeming to be 'incapable of feeling strong affection, of facing great dangers, of making great sacrifices'.[3] Although he was the close friend of Elizabeth's favourite, the Earl of Essex, when Essex fell from the Queen's favour and planned an insurrection Bacon took part in the ensuing prosecution of the Earl and so was blamed for betraying his friend. After James I's accession to the throne he was knighted, along with 300 others, by the new king.

It wasn't until 1618 that Bacon achieved high office. He was appointed to the Lord Chancellorship, the highest legal position under the Crown. In the same year he became Lord Verulam and, in 1621, Viscount of St Albans. Disaster struck almost immediately. He was charged with bribery, admitted the charge, and was sentenced to a fine of £40,000, disqualification from Parliament, exclusion from court and imprisonment during the King's pleasure. The fine was eventually remitted and his confinement to the Tower lasted only a few days but the disgrace of this episode ended his public career. He continued to study and write as zealously as before and died in 1626 of a feverish bronchitis brought on by the chill he suffered when he filled a chicken's body with snow to see if the flesh could be preserved by the cold.

Bacon is well known for his lucid, epigrammatic essays. The first ten of these were published in 1597. His *Advancement of learning* was published in 1605. Most of the works relating to his major enterprise, *The great instauration*, were published from 1620 onwards. In 1620 the plan of the *Instauration* was published along with its second part, the *Novum organum*. In 1623 the first part of the *Instauration*, which was a revised and latinised version of the 1605 *Advancement of learning*, was published under the title *De augmentis scientiarum*.

The word 'instauration' means 'restoration'. Bacon's aim was to restore to mankind the 'dominion over the universe' that was lost with the Fall of Man. In advocating the unrestrained but highly organised acquisition of knowledge, which for him was the way to restore such dominion, he had to contend with the general view solidly endorsed by seventeenth-century clerics that it was sinful to enquire into nature. He therefore distinguished sharply in the Preface to the *Great instauration* between what he called 'pure and uncorrupted natural knowledge' and the 'proud desire of moral knowledge to judge of good and evil'. He said, 'We do not presume, by the contemplation of nature to attain to the mysteries of God.'[4] In this strict separation of the study of nature from the study of the divine he directly opposed the Thomist doctrine of seeking knowledge of the supernatural through the natural.

In the *Novum organum* Bacon discusses other impediments to learning. These are 'the idols and false notions which are now in possession of the human understanding'. He names four kinds of idols: Idols of the Tribe, Idols of the Cave, Idols of the Market Place, and Idols of the Theatre. The Idols of the Tribe arise from human nature itself, from the fact that 'the tribe or race of men', in their perceptions, tend to distort what is before them. The Idols of the Cave are 'the idols of the individual man'. They are generated by each person's individual propensities, idiosyncrasies and prejudices. Idols of the Market Place are formed through 'the intercourse and association' of people about their daily activities, when 'ill and unfit choice of words wonderfully obstructs the understanding', leading people into 'numberless empty controversies and idle fancies'. The Idols of the Theatre are the dogmas, systems and theories that lodge in the minds of men and which Bacon likens to 'so many stage-plays, representing worlds of their own creation after an unreal and scenic fashion'.[5]

Bacon's own method of overcoming all obstacles to the acquisition of sure and useful knowledge was that of induction. Like many of his contemporaries, including Hobbes and Galileo, he rejected much of the prevailing Aristotelian orthodoxy; not, as William Rawley, his first biographer, reported, 'for the worthlessness of the author to whom he would ever ascribe all high attributes, but for the unfruitfulness of the way'.[6] Aristotle, Bacon maintained, was 'only strong for disputations and contentions, but barren of the production of works for the benefit of the life of man'. His own inductive method would correct all this and abolish all the distortions produced by the Idols.

Induction is the procedure by which general laws or principles are derived from a number of particular instances. It was not, of course, a new procedure in the seventeenth century but Bacon regarded traditional induction as 'a puerile thing' which merely enumerated affirmative examples of particular instances, avoided or explained away negative ones and was generally lacking in organisation and rigour. His own inductive method as expounded in the *Novum organum* is organised in relation to his view of forms. He believed that the underlying structure of nature is quite simple and consists of a basic set of forms, discovery of which will enable us to understand the multifarious complexity of the surface of the world as apprehended through the senses. Baconian forms are the forms of 'simple natures'. Simple natures may be shared by substances and are such things as hot, wet, cold, heavy and so on. They are like 'an alphabet of nature' from which many things can be composed. He refers to the forms as 'laws'.

They are the determinants and the elements of the fundamental structures of the world. He says, 'The Form of a nature is such, that given the Form the nature infallibly follows. Therefore it is always present when the nature is present ... absent when the nature is absent.'[7] Rigorous inductive procedure will draw up a table of instances of the presence of a nature but must not then jump hastily to an inductive generalisation. Negative instances must be sought for, experiments and comparisons must be made, until a comprehensive array of organised tables of data is assembled. Only then can interpretation of nature begin and this, too, must proceed in a disciplined and cautious way so that 'after the rejection and exclusion has been duly made there will remain at the bottom, all light opinions vanishing into smoke, a Form affirmative, solid and true and well-defined. This is quickly said; but the way to come at it is winding and intricate.'[8]

No short account can do justice to the scope and intricacy of Bacon's six-part plan of the *Great instauration*. The closer his work is studied the more it shows itself as a vital and influential part of the great seventeenth-century confluence of intellectual and cultural developments. Yet it runs apart from one major channel in that progressive surge, namely, the mathematically based discoveries and methods of Kepler and Galileo and the related studies of Thomas Hobbes in political philosophy and William Harvey in the circulation of the blood. In a broader cultural perspective Bacon has been seen, in spite of his unequivocally royalist stance, as the eloquent voice of Puritanism and the Revolution. In his book *The great instauration: science, medicine and reform 1626-1660*, Charles Webster wrote:

Bacon's philosophy seemed to be providentially designed for the needs of the Puritan Revolution. Indeed, this suitability was not accidental, considering that the philosopher had an intellectual ancestry largely in common with the English Puritans. Bacon gave precise and systematic philosophical expression to the anti-authoritarianism, inductivism and utilitarianism which were such important factors in the Puritan scale of values.[9]

Certainly, the Royal Society, which received its charter in 1662, owed much to Bacon's ideas and principles. But his influence and inspiration have been far wider than that. In the eighteenth century he was recognised by the French Enlightenment as the originator of scientific advance and in the late eighteenth and early nineteenth centuries the Scottish philosophers of common sense praised him without reservation. The twentieth century has not received him so well. His conviction that the inductive method yielded certain knowledge has not appealed to philosophers who regard induction only as a species of probability; nor do his aphoristic style and tendency to assertion endear him to philosophers demanding hard argument. Yet this is to overlook what much of his greatness actually consisted in: the grandeur of his prophetic vision of science in the service of mankind and the transmission, through his writings, of his infinite zest for and delight in the whole realm of learning.

Notes

1. Lytton Strachey, *Elizabeth and Essex* (Chatto, London, 1928), p. 43.
2. T.B. Macaulay, 'Lord Bacon' in *The works of Lord Macaulay*, vol. VIII, p. 538.
3. Ibid.
4. Francis Bacon, *Works*, I, i, 3, 44-6.
5. Ibid., IV, 53-5.
6. W. Rawley, *Life of Bacon* in J.M. Robertson (ed.) *Philosophical works* (Routledge and Kegan Paul, London, 1905).
7. Bacon, *Works*, I, 230, iv, 121.
8. Ibid., I, 257, iv, 146.
9. Charles Webster, *The great instauration: science, medicine and reform 1626-1660* (Duckworth, London, 1975), p. 514.

See also in this book

Aristotle, Aquinas, Machiavelli, Galileo, Hobbes.

Bacon's major writings

Essays (1597), 10 of a set that eventually numbered 58 (Everyman Library, no. 1010, Dent, London, 1968)

The Advancement of learning (1605), ed. A. Johnson (Oxford University Press, Oxford, 1974)

The great instauration (1620), ed. J. Weinberger (Harlan Davidson, London, 1980)

Novum organum (1620), part II of *The great instauration* (Oxford University Press, Oxford, 1889)

De dignitate et augmentis scientiarum (1623), a revised version of *The advancement of learning*

New Atlantis (1624) (Oxford University Press, Oxford, 1915)

The standard edition of Bacon's writings is *The works of Francis Bacon* in 7 volumes, edited by James Spedding, R.L. Ellis and D.D. Heath (Longman, London, 1857-74). A one-volume selection of Bacon's writings is *Selected writings of Francis Bacon*, ed. Hugh C. Dick (Modern Library, New York, 1955). Bacon's collected *Essays* are in an Everyman edition (Dent, London, 1968).

Further reading

Anderson, F.H. *The philosophy of Francis Bacon* (University of Chicago Press, Chicago, 1948)

Broad, C.D. *The philosophy of Francis Bacon* (Cambridge University Press, Cambridge, 1926)

Farrington, B. *The philosophy of Francis Bacon* (University of Liverpool Press, Liverpool, 1964)

Hesse, M. 'Francis Bacon' in D.J. O'Connor (ed.), *A critical history of Western philosophy* (The Free Press, New York, 1964; Macmillan, London, 1985)

Quinton, A. *Francis Bacon* (Past Masters, Oxford University Press, Oxford, 1980)

Rossi, P. *From magic to science* (University of Chicago Press, Chicago, 1968)

Webster, C. *The great instauration: science, medicine and reform 1626-1660* (Duckworth, London, 1975)

Galileo Galilei 1564-1642

Galileo was a scientist and mathematician whose work has had a profound effect on philosophy as well as on science in general. He was born at Pisa in Italy on 15 February 1564 and was the oldest of seven children. After some schooling in Florence where the family moved when he was six years old he went to the Camaldolese Monastery at Vallambrosa and then matriculated at the University of Pisa in 1582. His father wanted him to study medicine but Galileo rejected the idea. He had come across Euclid's *Elements* and was already fascinated by mathematics, the ideas of Archimedes and the whole range of questions in physics and

cosmology that dominated the natural philosophy of his time. At Pisa he had acquired a reputation for asking pertinent and searching questions and although he left the university in 1585 without a degree he was plainly bent on a life of intellectual enquiry. He taught at the universities of Pisa and Padua, became mathematician and philosopher to the Florentine court and travelled widely throughout Italy to engage in teaching, discussion and enquiry of all kinds in physics, astronomy, engineering, mechanics and mathematics.

Galileo is best known through accounts of two events. One is the account of an experiment in which he is said to have dropped spheres of differing weights from the top of the Leaning Tower of Pisa to demonstrate that, contrary to what Aristotle had maintained, the falling speed of a body is not determined by its weight. The second and far longer story is of the Roman Inquisition's prosecution of him on a charge of 'vehement suspicion of heresy' allegedly perpetrated by him in his *Dialogue* in which he argued for the Copernican **hypothesis** that the earth was not the stationary centre of the universe but a moving planet. The authenticity of the Leaning Tower of Pisa story is doubted, but Galileo's trial is voluminously documented and its issues have been debated by many. The Inquisition first condemned him to indefinite imprisonment but eventually allowed him to spend the remainder of his life in his own villa at Arcetri under the constant supervision of its officers. He died in 1642.

Galileo's importance to philosophy and to science can be understood only through an appreciation of the changes he either instigated or helped to bring about. At the beginning of the sixteenth century the belief was that the earth was an immobile sphere at the centre of the universe, that the sun, the moon and the five planets moved around it in complex circular motions and that beyond this was a sphere in which all was perfection, which contained no fixed stars and which rotated once a day. By the end of the seventeenth century an entirely different view prevailed in the mind of the educated European. By then the belief was that the earth, in common with the other planets, rotated on its axis and that all the planets revolved around the sun in elliptical paths determined by gravity. The idea of a finite universe bounded by an outer sphere of unchanging perfection had been rejected. These profound transformations of the understanding of the universe owe much to the work of Galileo.

At the beginning of the seventeenth century, enquiry into the natural world was still dominated by principles and procedures directly developed from Aristotle's philosophy. This entrenched, comprehensive and powerful Aristotelianism regarded change and, in particular, purposeful motion as fundamental in nature. It was responsible for the belief that the earth was central and stationary and for the separation of the universe into two distinct realms, one elementally composed of earth, air, fire and water, the other composed of the quintessence which was perfect in every respect and subject to no change other than locomotion in perfect circles. The basis of the Aristotelian position was the view that philosophical knowledge, as distinct from practical competence derived from experience, was arrived at only by reasoning. It sought to explain everything by reference to four different types of causes: Formal, Material, Causal and Efficient.[1] At the same time it appealed to a common-sense perception of the world and was, or had been made, comfortably consistent with religious convictions about the separate and superior nature of the heavens and the ordered hierarchy of God's creation. Its detailed comprehensiveness made it difficult to undermine or attack in any way and its espousal and dissemination by theologians rendered it near-sacrosanct in the eyes of those who were taught its tenets. Nevertheless, the gradual accumulation of mathematical, astronomical and physical data during the sixteenth century began, in the early years of the seventeenth, to shape

into a formidable challenge to the Aristotelian world view. In particular, the Polish astronomer, Copernicus, had argued in his *On the revolutions of the heavenly spheres* published in 1543 that the sun was the centre of the universe and the earth a planet that moved. Moreover, the political upheavals that affected much of Europe in the early years of the seventeenth century were creating a climate apt for change and innovation. This meant that Galileo's enquiries were conducted against a background of considerable turmoil and intellectual excitement and with a mounting awareness of possibilities hitherto undreamed of.

Galileo's guiding principle was to measure and quantify. He rejected the Aristotelian presupposition that every material body has a 'place' in the order of things and that motion was to be explained by the natural tendency of each body to seek its own place. Instead, he observed, weighed, measured and calculated in order to test his mathematical hypotheses. He was convinced that mathematics would reveal the structure and laws of the universe. In *The assayer* (1623) he wrote:

Philosophy is written in this grand book, the universe, which stands continually open to our gaze. But the book cannot be understood unless one first learns to comprehend the language and read the letters in which it is composed. It is written in the language of mathematics, and its characters are triangles, circles, and other geometric figures without which it is humanly impossible to understand a single word of it: without those one wanders about in the dark labyrinth.[2]

Thus the philosophical underpinning of Galileo's investigations was the presupposition that mathematics was the key to understanding the universe. But the main thrust of his enquiries was to discern and use the 'language of mathematics' to describe and explain how the universe worked. He is therefore regarded as a scientist rather than a philosopher, and the changing of the philosophical underpinning of scientific enquiry from the Aristotelian reasoning about causes to the Galilean principle of quantification was the basis of the scientific revolution in seventeenth-century Europe. Of course, Galileo was by no means the sole activator of the profound changes that were brought about. Philosophically speaking, he was part of a widespread movement that was seeking to establish a new standard for knowledge, a standard founded on the logical incontrovertibility that characterises the **deductive** reasoning of mathematics. Scientifically speaking, he was inheritor of the ideas of Tycho Brahe, Copernicus and Gilbert and was contemporary with Kepler, Bacon and Descartes. Historians of science sometimes debate whether Galileo was a Platonist, a Pythagorean or even, in some ways, an Aristotelian. There are no clear-cut answers to such questions. Galileo inhabited a cultural climate in which these influences and numerous others were extremely powerful. He can be seen as a Platonist and a Pythagorean in that he conceived the ultimate reality of the cosmos as mathematical and abstract. He can be seen as Aristotelian in his allegiance to the detail and fact of physical reality. It has been suggested, too, that his quarrel with religious authority, culminating in his trial by the Inquisition, was a misinterpreted manifestation of his zeal for Roman Catholicism, in that his attempt to separate scientific fact from biblical and theological pronouncements was actually an attempt to save religious views from being discredited by the advance of science.

The famous story of Galileo's dropping of weights from the top of the Leaning Tower of Pisa marks his discovery of the law of free fall. He did not claim that bodies of differing weights fall at the same speed since that would be true only in a vacuum. His point against Aristotle, who had denied the possibility of a vacuum, was that the difference in time of arrival of differing weights at the ground would not be in proportion to their densities but depended on the resistance of the medium. An experiment he conducted to exemplify this law was that of rolling a metal ball down a slope, testing the measured result against his calculation worked out in accordance with the law. He then related the law of free fall to the idea of inertia, which is the theory that a body will remain in a state of rest or of motion with uniform velocity unless acted on by a force. This directly opposed Aristotle's dictum that motion was not a state but a process and that a moving body would cease to move unless continually acted on by a force. Using a rudimentary concept of inertia, Galileo was able to explain the movements of projectiles and so begin the accurate charting of the movements of astral bodies. His work was later to be refined by Newton but even in its crudest form it constituted a breakthrough from the old conception of a closed universe, part elemental, part heavenly, towards the idea of an infinite one in which the celestial regions were composed of the same kind of matter and were subject to the same laws as the terrestrial.

Galileo first incurred the displeasure of theologians through his discoveries concerning the true nature of the so-called quintessence, the sphere of perfection. In 1609 he built a telescope, working from a description he had been given of a Dutch instrument. He then turned his telescope to the sky, noted what he saw and published his findings in a short book called *The starry messenger*. He declared that the moon was not a perfect sphere but had mountains, valleys and craters, much like the earth. He perceived four moons around Jupiter and used this fact to suggest that those who could not tolerate the thought of the earth attended by its revolving moon annually orbiting the sun, but would consider that the planets did so, might find the movement of the earth more acceptable once they realised that Jupiter, too, had moons. Four years later he discovered that the planet Venus exhibited phases like the moon's. This was important evidence for Venus orbiting the sun rather than the earth. Once again, all this was directly contrary to Aristotle's account of the universe and to his claim that the moon and all the quintessential bodies were perfectly spherical and smooth. Moreover, it contradicted certain biblical texts such as the command of Joshua: 'Sun, stand thou still upon Gibeon; and thou, Moon, in the valley of Ajalon. And the sun stood still, and the moon stayed'[3] which could be interpreted as implying that the sun, except when commanded otherwise, was on the move around a stationary earth.

Tension mounted over the next few years. A minor crisis occurred as the result of a sermon preached in 1614 by a Dominican called Thomas Caccini in which mathematics was denounced and 'the miracle of Joshua' invoked. On this occasion the Inquisition dismissed the case brought to them against Galileo. Shortly after, Cardinal Bellarmine recommended that to treat the motion of the earth as a hypothesis should be acceptable but that it should not be regarded as a truth. A further crisis, the details of which are equivocal, occurred in 1616. It was resolved and Galileo resumed work. By 1632 he was ready to produce his *Dialogue concerning the two chief systems of the world: Ptolemaic and Copernican.* The *Dialogue,* a series of conversations examining the merits of the old and new astronomical systems, quickly ran into trouble. The Inquisition banned all sales of it even though it was a licensed book and the equivocations of the 1616 crisis came again to light, issues were fudged and negotiations face-saving to the Inquisition seem to have taken place behind the scenes. Galileo admitted in a written statement that he had 'gone too far' in the *Dialogue* and that he should make alterations to it. He expected in return that he would be treated leniently, only to be shocked and broken by a sentence of indefinite imprisonment, later commuted to one of confinement in his own home. He died, blind, on 9 January 1642, the year in which Newton was born. During the time of his confinement he wrote *Two new sciences,* which, again in dialogue form, examined the

structure of matter and the laws of motion. Rome had ruled that no book written or edited by Galileo was to be printed, but it was eventually produced at Leyden.

During the 1616 crisis Galileo had written his *Letter to the Grand Duchess Christina.* The *Letter* was an amplification of an earlier *Letter to Castelli* in which he set out his ideas on the relation of science to theology. In the amplified *Letter* he argued, as Kepler had once argued, that there is no need to take certain biblical statements literally because 'if one were always to confine oneself to the unadorned grammatical meaning, one might fall into error'. He further maintained that 'nothing physical which sense-experience sets before our eyes, or which necessary demonstration proves to us, ought to be called in question (much less condemned) upon the testimony of biblical passages which may have some different meaning beneath their words'.[4] It was after this *Letter* had caused a considerable stir in ecclesiastical circles that Galileo was advised by Cardinal Bellarmine that he should treat the Copernican system only as a hypothesis since it appeared not only to violate the scriptures but to be incapable of proof. Historians of science have argued that if Galileo had acted prudently on this advice he would have been able to continue uncensored in his work. But he did not act with the required prudence: perhaps he felt that even more important than his actual discoveries was the need to free, on the one hand, science from any possible fetter, even the fetter of expressing itself in hypothetical terms and, on the other hand, theology from any possibility of ridicule invited by its own short-sighted dogmatism. Whatever his motives, he continued to provoke theological disapproval and force issues that with a little circumspection could have been avoided.

In spite of his trial and condemnation Galileo's ideas survived triumphantly as the key components of the New Philosophy of the seventeenth century. A few days after his death a member of the household of

Cardinal Barberini wrote the following to a friend at Florence:

> Today news has come of the loss of Signor Galilei, which touches not just Florence but the whole world, and our whole century which from this divine man has received more splendour than from almost all the other ordinary philosophers. Now, envy ceasing, the sublimity of that intellect will begin to be known which will serve all posterity as guide in the search for truth.[5]

Notes

1. See *Aristotle* in this book, pp. 22-6.
2. Galileo, *The assayer* in Stillman Drake, *Discoveries and opinions of Galileo* (Doubleday, New York, 1957), pp. 237-8.
3. Joshua x, verses 12-13, *The Bible*.
4. Galileo, *Letter to the Grand Duchess Christina*, trans. Drake in *Discoveries and opinions of Galileo*.
5. Quoted in Stillman Drake, *Galileo* (Past Masters, Oxford University Press, Oxford, 1980), p. 93.

See also in this book

Aristotle, Bacon, Hobbes, Descartes.

Galileo's major writings

The Italian titles of Galileo's writings are lengthy and numerous. I have therefore given English titles and cited some selections of his work. His works and correspondence are in *Le opere di Galileo Galilei*, ed. Antonio Favaro (Florence, 1890-1910, repr. 1929-39). There is a good bibliography in E. McMullin (ed.), *Galileo, man of Science* (Basic Books, New York, 1967).
Galileo against the philosophers (1605), trans. S. Drake (Zeitlin and VerBrugge, Los Angeles, 1976)
The starry messenger (1610), trans. in S. Drake, *Discoveries and opinions of Galileo* (Doubleday, New York, 1957)
Letter to the Grand Duchess Christina (1615), trans. in Drake, *Discoveries and opinions of Galileo*
Dialogue concerning the two chief world systems (1632), trans. S. Drake (University of California Press, Berkeley, Calif., 1953, rev. 1967)

Further reading

Briggs, R. *The scientific revolution of the seventeenth century* (Longman, London, 1969)
de Santillana, G. *The crime of Galileo* (Mercury Paperback, London, 1961)
Drake, S. *Galileo at work: his scientific biography*, 2nd edn (University of Chicago Press, Chicago, 1981)

Koyré, A. *From the closed world to the infinite universe* (Harper and Row, New York, 1958)
—— *Metaphysics and measurement: essays in the scientific revolution* (Chapman and Hall, London, 1968), pp. 1-43
—— *Galileo Studies*, trans. J. Mepham (Harvester Press, Hassocks, Sussex, 1978)
Kuhn, T. (ed.) *The essential tension* (University of Chicago Press, Chicago, 1977)
McMullin, E. (ed.) *Galileo, Man of Science* (Basic Books, New York, 1967)
Wallace, W.A. *Prelude to Galileo* (Reidel, Dordrecht, 1981)

Thomas Hobbes 1588-1679

Thomas Hobbes was born on 5 April 1588, prematurely, John Aubrey tells us, because his mother was alarmed by the news that the Spanish Armada was approaching England. He lived to the magnificent age of 91 retaining his clarity of mind and intellect until a few days before his death. He is one of the great seventeenth-century philosophers. He sought an indubitable foundation for knowledge and was profoundly influenced and inspired by the developing physical sciences and mathematics of his time. Today he is best known, as he was in the seventeenth century, for the political philosophy embodied in his book *Leviathan*.

Hobbes would have liked to spend his life in untroubled security somewhat apart from society in order to reason and reflect about philosophical matters that interested him deeply. But the early and middle years of the seventeenth century were, in many parts of Europe, times of great upheaval. In England the civil war that began in 1642 culminated seven years later in the execution of Charles I and in the uneasy protectorate of Oliver Cromwell. Hobbes's life ran close to this mainstream of momentous events and he knew well a number of the important and powerful men of the day. At one time he was tutor to the Prince of Wales in exile in France. At another he was in fear of being condemned by bishops to burn for his opinions. Twice in his life he deemed it prudent to leave England and live in France for a time. And because of this closeness to great events and because he fervently desired peace and security for his countrymen he decided he must use all his abilities to reason out a solution to the problems of government. *Leviathan*, published in 1651, was the major product of this endeavour. In it Hobbes set forth what he called 'a science of politics': a body of knowledge concerning humankind living in society that would enable a government to establish and maintain a peaceful state for its people. His actual prescription for procuring peace was unexceptional but the method he used to arrive at it was new. His greatness as a philosopher rests chiefly on that innovatory method, derived largely from the physics of his Italian contemporary, Galileo. Hobbes saw that any enquiry that was to command respect must be conducted in such a way that its conclusions could be unequivocally recognised as knowledge: speculation, opinion and pronouncement would not do. And since the deductive reasoning of the kind used in geometry and Galilean physics produced conclusions that were logically incontrovertible, he resolved to reason deductively to arrive at a like knowledge concerning the organisation and conduct of political society.

Geometrical reasoning proceeds from a 'given', a basic premiss or set of premisses, and moves step by step to conclusions which cannot be otherwise. Galileo used this method to analyse events in the physical universe.[1] For example, given data about weights, distances and angles, he was able to deduce and so predict the movements of material bodies. Hobbes's innovation was to transpose this method on to the study of human activities. He decided that if he could establish certain basic facts — a 'given' — about human nature, then he could deduce from them the way in which human beings would behave in certain circumstances. Thus he could discover what causes lead to peaceful coexistence as well as what causes produce strife and could then offer a prescription for a form of government that would infallibly establish and maintain peace

and security. This was the bold and original enterprise of *Leviathan*. Human beings were to be studied as just one aspect of the physical universe. Human passions and proclivities were to be analysed in terms of physical movements and their causes and a prescription formulated for regulating conduct by imposing causes that would produce peace and security.

The foundation of Hobbes's method was the Galilean principle that everything is fundamentally matter in motion. In his *Autobiography* he wrote:

> One thing only is real, but it forms the basis of the things we falsely claim to be something, though they are only like the fugitive shapes of dreams or like the images I can multiply at will by mirrors; fantasies, creatures of our brains and nothing more, the only inner reality of which is motion.[2]

In the first five chapters of *Leviathan* Hobbes develops this claim to show how it encompasses human beings. Human beings, he maintains, are sensory creatures. Sensory experience is caused by 'so many severall motions of matter' and our thoughts, which are also motions of matter and which he calls 'conceptions of the mind', are 'begotten upon the organs of sense'. Having established the conditions for regarding human beings as part of matter in motion, he offers in Chapter 6 his description of human nature: an account of 'voluntary motions, commonly called the Passions'. Here Hobbes is setting out a 'given' from which he will deduce the circumstances required for peaceful coexistence in the state. It is important to realise that his statements about human nature are not deduced from his earlier statements about matter in motion. Such a deduction is not possible, for information about passions and feelings cannot be deduced from information about movements of matter. However, his analysis of the Passions regards them as voluntary *motions* and is entirely consistent with, even though not derivable from, the principle that everything is matter in motion.

Hobbes distinguishes between 'vital' and 'voluntary' motions. The 'vital' motions are those of organs such as the heart and lungs; they are motions which, once generated, maintain life as it were of their own accord. 'Voluntary' motions are instigated by 'Endeavours' which are small movements of the brain. An Endeavour may be either towards or away from whatever causes it. Hobbes's analysis now moves rapidly from the idea of bodily motions to the idea of those motions being desires or aversions which are experienced as either pleasure or pain and which are judged as either good or evil. Movement towards something is experienced, he says, as pleasure; movement away as pain. Moreover, we are said to love and see as good those things we desire and to hate and see as bad those from which we avert. He telescopes ethical values into movements of matter.

In Chapter 13 of *Leviathan* Hobbes describes 'the Naturall Condition'. He maintains that in a natural condition people vary little between each other in their powers and abilities. Moreover, Nature itself and the natural human being are neither good nor evil. In a natural state each individual exercises the natural right to preserve his own life and avoid death. The 'felicity of this life' consists in continual success in obtaining one's desires. But this felicity is never a tranquil contentment because, Hobbes says, 'Life it selfe is but Motion, and can never be without Desire, nor without Feare, no more than without Sense.'[3] Our natural state is one in which, as we move towards what we want, we collide with others similarly engaged. It is a state in which 'there be no Propriety, no Dominion, no *Mine* and *Thine* distinct; but onely that to be every mans that he can get; and for so long, as he can keep it'.[4] Yet the desire to preserve one's life is also a desire for peace since natural human reason recognises that peace is the best condition for the preservation of life. Thus the natural human

being is someone who desires security and peace even though he is perpetually engaged in conflict.

Hobbes sees a way out of this unhappy predicament, a way which employs the passions and the reason of the natural condition as the basis of an artificial structure, the Commonwealth. Just as God made the natural world so must we, in imitation, make the artificial Commonwealth, the Leviathan: a proud, powerful but mortal creature, supreme on earth but subject to divine law. The artificial Commonwealth, basing itself on the natural laws discerned by reason, must preserve the lives of all its citizens and maintain perpetual peace.

Hobbes maintains that the only way to secure perpetual peace is for people to covenant together to place themselves under so powerful a sovereign authority that rebellion against its commands is virtually impossible. This sovereign authority must be authorised to act always for the preservation of the lives of those who submit to it and it must have power great enough to restrain, through its threat of greater harm, the natural warlike passions of its subjects. The sovereign authority is not party to any contract or covenant but is bound by natural law to seek peace and maintain justice and may make whatever artificial laws are necessary to enact those natural laws. For Hobbes, the right to rule depends simply on the power to protect and to preserve perpetual peace.

Leviathan displeased many of Hobbes's contemporaries, and in several ways: because it regarded human beings as bits of matter in motion; because it offered a grim picture of human nature and of life in the natural condition; because it advocated near-absolute power for the sovereign authority; because it eradicated the idea of a sovereign having the divine right to rule and replaced it with the idea of the sovereign's rights being vested simply in the power to enforce laws; and because it divested the Church of its independence, not only by placing it under the authority of the sovereign body but by confronting every aspect of its workings with the penetrating gaze of unsuperstitious reason. Hobbes saw religious dissent as a major source of the breakdown of authority in seventeenth-century England. He argues that there can be no real division between civil and ecclesiastical laws because they are in fact one, and are shown to be so in the Commonwealth he advocates. The sovereign's task is to enact natural law by imposing the civil law, and 'all Subjects are bound to obey that for divine Law, which is declared to be so by the Lawes of the Commonwealth'.[5]

Although it displeased so many in so many ways, *Leviathan* could not be disregarded. Its rigorous method commanded both attention and respect. Moreover, Hobbes's conclusion that the Commonwealth's sovereign authority could be one individual or a body of people so long as it maintained peace and its own indivisibility was a two-edged sword, apt for wielding by both factions in the struggle between Parliament and Crown. The new science of politics was irresistible debating matter for all those eager to lay down new foundations for a society ruined by civil strife.

Hobbes's belief that everything is matter in motion is called metaphysical materialism. It is a materialist doctrine because it holds that everything is matter. It is metaphysical because it is an attempt to supply a unifying principle, a characterisation of reality as a whole that is unaffected by experience or investigation.

Hobbes's metaphysical materialism raised certain philosophical problems which it dealt with in its own way. One such problem concerns language and universal or general terms. In considering the use of language and speech Hobbes distinguishes singular from common names. Singular names such as 'Ann', 'this man', 'this building' indicate particular individuals or things. But common names such as 'woman', 'man,' 'dog' do not indicate particular things and therefore were often called 'universals', which were thought of

as existing immaterially. Hobbes is emphatic that it is simply the common *names* that are universals, for there can be no place for immaterial **essences** in a system consisting entirely of matter in motion. This is his doctrine of nominalism, the view that there are no universal essences that correspond to the common or universal names. For example, the nominalist holds that there is no actual entity which is 'redness'. There are particular red things and there are the words 'red' and 'redness', but not anything which actually is 'redness' itself and which is a kind of universal essence. Hobbes firmly maintains that there is 'nothing in the world Universall but names'.[6]

Hobbes's nominalism is also a criticism of the Aristotelianism that still had, in the mid-seventeenth century, a firm and widespread grip on European thought. Aristotle had taught that the world could be understood through knowledge of the essences of things. He denied that essences existed independently of the things which exhibited them but, nevertheless, his theory became elaborated by others into one in which common nouns such as 'man' and 'tree' were taken to refer to essences which existed non-corporeally and separately from particular material objects.[7] Hobbes described all such references as 'insignificant speech' since the words, in his opinion, signified nothing. For him, a universal or common name is simply a name 'imposed on many things, for their similitude in some quality'.[8]

Nominalism had important implications for Hobbes's account of Commonwealth in *Leviathan*. If there are no independently existing essences such as 'goodness', 'justice', 'evil' and so on, then this means there is nothing that sets absolute standards of right and wrong. Words such as 'goodness' are simply *names* which perform the task of pluralising individual instances and what is good and bad is laid down by the decree of the Sovereign as part of the artificial construction of the great Leviathan, the state.

Hobbes's metaphysical materialism also

raises problems about the freedom of the will. If everything is matter and matter moves in ways which are predictable and inevitable once we know the causal laws that determine their motions, then can the human will be said to be free? Hobbes's answer to this question is forthright, clear and entirely consistent with his materialist tenets. Certainly, he says, everything that takes place does so because it is causally necessitated and human beings are as much a part of the causal system as everything else. But human freedom is not to be understood as freedom from causal **necessity**. On Hobbes's account, to will or want something is to tend to move towards whatever it is that one wants. Thus, if my movement towards what I want is unimpeded then I am acting freely. If my movement is hindered or prevented in some way then I am not able to act freely. These external impediments to my movements are checks on my freedom. If, however, I cannot get or do what I want because of something that is a part of me — if, for instance, I cannot leap over to the other side of that fence because I haven't the physique to jump so high — then that is not a restriction on my freedom but just a natural lack of ability in me. Hobbes uses the example of flowing water. Water descends freely along a channel when there is no blockage to impede what it naturally tends to do. But water cannot of its own accord ascend, because it is not in its nature for water to do so. However, we do not therefore say that the water is not *free* to ascend, because the inability to ascend is part of the nature of water rather than an impediment external to it. We have by nature a range of powers and abilities and freedom is their unimpeded exercise. By a careful statement about what is meant by 'freedom' Hobbes is able to draw a distinction between occasions when we are free and occasions when we are not, yet still maintain that everything we do is necessitated. The general view that human freedom is compatible with universal causal necessity is often called 'soft determinism' or simply 'compatibilism'.

Hobbes attempted a very ambitious synthesis. Like other seventeenth-century philosophers he sought a firm foundation for knowledge and found it, like them, in the type of reasoning used in mathematics. At the same time he held that everything is analysable as matter in motion and that sense experience is the ultimate source of thought and knowledge. Sensory knowledge, he says, is of *whole* things, of what a particular whole thing is: 'the whole object is known more than any part thereof'. It is knowledge of fact. But sense experience by itself is not sufficient for philosophy. The work of philosophy is to search for the causes of things, to analyse the general nature of something rather than its particular existence. Hobbes calls it 'the science of causes'. He says:

the cause of the whole is compounded of the causes of the parts; but it is necessary that we know the things that are to be compounded, before we can know the whole compound. Now, by parts, I do not here mean parts of the thing itself, but parts of its nature; as, by the parts of man, I do not understand his head, his shoulders, his arms, etc. but his figure, quantity, motion, sense, reason, and the like; which accidents being compounded or put together, constitute the whole *nature* of man, but not the (*particular*) man himself.[9]

The clarity of this kind of knowledge of 'parts' depends on giving precise definitions of general terms: 'motion', 'reason', 'sense' and so on must be defined as rigorously as mathematical terms such as 'circle', 'equal', 'divide'. From exact definitions **deductive** reasoning will produce incontrovertible conclusions. But here we encounter something puzzling in Hobbes. For he seems to be speaking at one moment of understanding the causes of things, at the next of reasoning from definitions. What we have to understand is that, for him, there is no difference between understanding something by its constitutive causes and understanding something by reasoning out the logical implications of its definition. For instance, the definition of a triangle was regarded by Hobbes as the cause of a triangle and the implications of the definition were regarded as the effects of the cause. Similarly, he speaks of analysing the strife of civil war, a mass of effects, into its constituent causes. These causes turn out to be certain basic elements of human nature which are also definitions of that nature. By identifying causes with definitions Hobbes thought he could arrive at undeniable knowledge concerning the physical world of causes and effects. It was an ambitious attempt at the synthesis of disparities which, under one aspect or another, are central in numerous philosophical problems.

It isn't easy for us to appreciate the strength of the feelings of outrage that Hobbes's ideas provoked. For many it was unthinkable that they should reject the traditional Aristotelian conception of the universe which derived from, and appealed to, common sense. Common sense inclines us to say of a blue-covered book that the blue is *in* the cover; that the cheese's smell is the smell *of* the cheese. The Aristotelian world-picture is built from just such common-sense accounts. It construed motion as a change *in* the moving body and it regarded the cosmos as a closed, finite system which could not be described mathematically since mathematical concepts could not deal with the perceived qualities, as distinct from the quantities, of things. Anyone prepared to consider the strange 'new philosophy' had to set aside traditional convictions and take seriously the thought that a theory formed without reference to common-sense ideas might enable them to understand the physical universe more fully; that, in Galileo's phrase, 'the book of nature is written in geometrical characters'. A major intellectual effort was required in order to accept the idea that motion, as much as rest, is a state of existence and not a process that has a purpose. But all this was required if certain and incon-trovertible knowledge was to be acquired.[10] Hobbes possessed an intellectual adventurousness that readily took to the new ideas and saw their application to social and political as well as natural states. The force and originality of his thinking meant that he was regarded as an atheist and an enemy of religion, terrifyingly wicked and blasphemous. He was, in the seventeenth century, a very modern man. He would, I believe, be quite at home with a lot of the ideas of the twentieth century, largely because he was already advocating them in the seventeenth. Theorists of linguistic meaning are, in the late twentieth century, showing a renewed interest in his nominalism.

Notes

1. See *Galileo* in this book, pp. 47-51.
2. Thomas Hobbes, *Autobiography* (The Rota, Exeter, Devon, 1979).
3. Thomas Hobbes, *Leviathan*, Ch. 6.
4. Ibid., Ch. 13.
5. Ibid., Ch. 26.
6. Ibid., Ch. 4.
7. See *Aristotle* in this book, pp. 22-6.
8. Hobbes, *Leviathan*, Ch. 4.
9. Hobbes, *De corpore, English works*, vol. I, p. 67.
10. See *Galileo* in this book, pp. 47-51.

See also in this book

Galileo, Descartes, Spinoza.

Hobbes's major writings

De cive (1642), *Latin works*, vol. II, trans. as *Philosophical rudiments of government and society* (1651) in *English works*, vol. II
Leviathan (1651), *English works*, vol. III and in C.B. Macpherson (ed.), *Hobbes: Leviathan* (Penguin, Harmondsworth, 1951)
Of liberty and necessity (1654), *English works*, vol. III, 4
Behemoth (1668), *English works*, vol. VI
Hobbes's writings are collected in *English works*, 11 vols, and *Opera Latina (Latin works)*, 5 vols, ed. W. Molesworth (J. Bohn, London, 1839, and Oxford, 1961). A wide selection of Hobbes's writings is in R.S. Peters, *Body, man and citizen* (Collier-Macmillan, London, 1962).

Further reading

Briggs, R. *The scientific revolution of the seventeenth century* (Longman, London, 1969)

Kuhn, T. (ed.) *The essential tension* (University of Chicago Press, Chicago, 1977)

Peters, R.S. *Hobbes* (Penguin, Harmondsworth, 1956)

Raphael, D.D. *Hobbes: morals and politics* (Allen and Unwin, London, 1977)

Sorell, T. *Hobbes* (Routledge and Kegan Paul, London, 1986)

Stephen, L. *Hobbes* (Macmillan, London, 1904)

René Descartes 1591-1650

Descartes is regarded as the founder of modern philosophy. He was a mathematician as well as a philosopher. His ambition was to begin philosophy anew, establishing it on grounds certain enough to support an edifice of indubitable knowledge. As one of the foremost participants in the burgeoning intellectual and scientific activity of his time he fully appreciated the importance of the new methods and discoveries that were then emerging and he recognised the challenge they presented to the ideas and assumptions of entrenched Aristotelianism. His famous declaration, 'I think therefore I am,' known as his 'cogito', is his purported proof of his own existence as a thinking being and the starting point of his search for certainty. He uses a similarly celebrated 'method of doubt'. This method is brilliantly exemplified in a set of six *Meditations* in which, starting from a conjectured position of near-total scepticism, he arrives at a set of claims he holds to be incontrovertibly true. From the 'cogito' he developed an argument for the existence of two distinct created **substances**, one corporeal the other non-corporeal, and thereby presented philosophy with Cartesian **dualism** and, concomitantly, with the problem of saying how the human mind and the human body are able to affect each other.

Descartes was born at La Haye, in France. He was educated at the Jesuit college of La Flèche and at Poitiers, graduating in law in 1616. From then until 1628 he travelled extensively and frequently in Germany, Italy, Holland and France, for some of that time serving as a soldier, first with a Protestant, then with the Catholic Bavarian army. It was probably at Ulm that he had the opportunity in a bitter winter to spend several days in a stove-heated room reflecting on and developing the approach he wanted to make in his philosophy. He completed his first major work, *Rules for the direction of the understanding*, in the 1620s though it remained unpublished until 1701. His *Le monde*, completed in 1634, offered a scientific theory of the origins and workings of the universe but he withheld it from publication because it espoused the Copernican system of astronomy for the teaching of which Galileo had recently been condemned. His *Discourse on method* was completed, along with some scientific and mathematical works, in 1637 and these were followed by the six *Meditations on first philosophy* in 1641 and the *Principles of philosophy* in 1644. Five years later he was persuaded to go to Sweden to join a group of scholars assembled there by Queen Christina. The Queen is said to have required him to teach her philosophy at five o'clock each morning. In consequence Descartes fell prey to the cold northern winter and died of pneumonia less than a year after moving to Sweden. In a brief memoir John Aubrey gives us an endearing glimpse of Descartes the mathematician. He writes:

> He was so eminently learned that all learned men made visits to him, and many of them would desire him to show them his Instruments (in those days mathematical learning lay much in the knowledge of Instruments, and, as Sir Henry Savile sayd, in doeing of tricks) he would draw out a little Drawer under his Table, and shew them a paire of Compasses with one of the legges broken; and then, for his Ruler, he used a sheet of paper folded double.[1]

The first step of Descartes' method for attaining certainty was to see whether it was possible to doubt everything: his memory, the evidence of his senses, the existence of the world around him and the existence of his own body. In the *Meditations* he conjectures that there might be 'some deceiver, supremely powerful, supremely intelligent who purposely always deceives me'.[2] But he finds it impossible to doubt one thing, namely, that he is thinking: even if the thoughts he thinks are false, he says, he is nevertheless thinking when he has them. He uses the term 'thinking' (cogitans) to cover all conscious mental activity; thus his doubting is a form of thinking. What he now understands is that simply in considering the proposition 'I think' he establishes its truth and cannot therefore doubt that he exists as a thinking thing. He says: '*I* am, *I* exist; that is certain ... For the present I am admitting only what is necessarily true; so "I am", precisely taken, refers only to a conscious being ...'[3]

The certainty that he is 'a thinking thing' gives Descartes the basis he requires for constructing his edifice of knowledge. He has established it by the method of doubt and by the exercise of what he calls 'the light of reason'. He goes on to offer two **arguments** for the existence of God. The first argument starts from his recognition of himself as a being who, in virtue of his doubts, is imperfect, yet who is able to entertain the idea of God as a perfect being. This perfect idea, he maintains, can come only from a perfect being; therefore God must exist as its source. The argument, which is a version of the **cosmological** argument, relies almost entirely on the **scholastic** principle that there is at least as much reality in the cause as in the effect; that is, if the idea is perfect, then its cause is likewise perfect. The second of Descartes' arguments for the existence of God, the **ontological** argument, is related to the same scholastic dictum. It points out that the idea of a most perfect being is of a being containing every perfection and thus containing reality in every degree. The idea of a most perfect being therefore contains the idea of existence and this means that God's **essence** contains his existence. Descartes is now able to argue that since God is perfect he will not

deceive or lead anyone into error and that correct use of one's human faculties will therefore result in knowledge. In the last meditation he argues again that God, being good, does not deceive us about the ideas we believe are produced in us by physical objects; hence there are physical objects.

Descartes' 'cogito' and all his arguments in the *Meditations* have been the subjects of extensive and detailed criticism ever since they were written. The legitimacy of his claim to the certainty of his existence as a thinking being has been challenged and many flaws have been found in his arguments for the existence of God. These criticisms do not affect Descartes' stature as a highly original innovator and independent thinker whose work marks and was an important part of the great shift from scholasticism and Aristotelian physics towards **rationalism** and scientific method.

Descartes is well known for the dualist problem of mind and matter that was generated from his conclusion that mind is a noncorporeal substance that is distinct from material or bodily substance. By 'substance' he means, as did Aristotle before him, 'anything which has *independent* existence; which does not depend on anything else for its existence'. He further maintains that 'every substance has a principal property that constitutes its *essential* nature';[4] that is, every substance has a property it *must* have in order to be what it is. Consciousness is the essential property of mind substance; extension in length, breadth and depth is the essential property of bodily or material substance. Descartes' realisation that he cannot doubt that he exists as a thinking substance, even though he can still doubt that he has a body, convinces him that mind can exist independently of matter. When he then proves to his own satisfaction that matter and hence his body do exist, he is faced with the problem of saying how the two distinct substances of body and mind interact to form the union that we call a person. He is unable to provide a satisfactory solution to the problem. He rejects the Aristotelian idea of the soul or mind as that which animates the body and he maintains that 'my soul is not in my body as a pilot in a ship; I am most tightly bound to it ...';[5] that is, the mind does not influence the body by, as it were, operating levers and switches which set the body into the required motions but there is, he insists, a much closer union in which the mind *directly* moves the body and directly experiences, rather than observes, the pains and pleasures generated by means of the body. Yet in the *Passions of the soul*, a work written towards the end of his life, he gives a wholly causal account of this union, declaring that the interaction between mind and body takes place by means of 'a certain very small gland',[6] namely the pineal gland which is situated at the base of the brain. His suggestion is that the double impressions he supposes we receive in virtue of having two ears, two eyes, two hands, and so on, are united 'in this gland by the intermission of the spirits which fill the cavities of the brain' before arriving at the soul. But of course this account goes no way towards showing how a material substance actually can affect a non-material substance. As a consequence, the Cartesian version of the mind–body problem has probably been the most popular and most worked-over philosophical problem of the last three centuries. In the twentieth century J.B. Watson and B.F. Skinner have tried to solve it in one way by advancing the theory that psychological activity is entirely explicable in terms of the data of observed behaviour. Another quite different type of resolution of the problem was propounded by Gilbert Ryle, who argued that mental concepts may be analysed in terms of overt behaviour, and yet another by Ludwig Wittgenstein, who maintained that mental activity is made intelligible only by reference to criteria that are publicly accessible. Descartes was certainly aware of the inadequacy of his account for many objections were made to it in his own lifetime. Princess Elizabeth of Bohemia, with whom he exchanged a series of letters on the topic, wrote this to him:

> I beg of you to tell me how the human soul can determine the movement of the animal spirits in the body so as to perform voluntary acts — being as it is merely a conscious substance. For the determination of movement seems always to come about from the moving body's being propelled ... but you utterly exclude extension from your notion of soul, and contact seems to me incompatible with a thing's being immaterial.[7]

Quite so.

Descartes' concern to establish secure foundations for knowledge was not confined to philosophy. Mathematics was, for him, the model for all knowledge because its truths are undeniable. Anyone seeking truth, he said, should not trouble themselves about any object concerning which they cannot have a certainty equal to arithmetical or geometrical demonstration. He regarded metaphysics, physics and the natural sciences as related to each other within one organic-like structure and he was fired by a vision of securing knowledge of God and the human soul, as well as of all scientific and natural phenomena, that was as certain as the conclusions of a geometrical proof. In all this he relies on reason, the human capacity to perceive something 'clearly and distinctly' without reference to sense experience. He says:

> I term that 'clear' which is present and apparent to an attentive mind, in the same way that we see objects clearly when, being present in the regarding eye, they operate upon it with sufficient strength. But the 'distinct' is that which is so precise and different from all other objects that it contains nothing within itself but what is clear ...[8]

An idea, Descartes says, may be clear without also being distinct; but if an idea is distinct then it is also clear. His **analogy** between the clarity of our ideas in the mind and physical objects seen by the eye should not distract us from realising that here Descartes is working entirely within the realm of reason and with 'ideas' that have the clarity and distinctness of geometrical definitions. This approach was of profound importance to the philosophies of **rationalism** and **empiricism** that developed in Descartes' wake, for it was the basis of a distinction made between primary and secondary qualities; between, on the one hand, solidity, extension, shape, motion and number, which were regarded as primary qualities of matter; and on the other, colour, scent, smell and taste, regarded as its secondary qualities. Descartes maintains that ideas of primary qualities are not derived from sense experience but are innate. In the second of the *Meditations* he considers the changes that take place in a lump of wax if it is put near a fire: 'the fragrance evaporates, the colour changes, the shape is lost, the size increases; it becomes fluid and hot, it can hardly be handled, and it will no longer give out a sound if you rap it'.[9] In spite of all these changes perceived by the senses Descartes still knows that what is before him is the lump of wax. He concludes that he has a purely intellectual conception of matter as something extended and capable of an infinity of changes and that it is this 'idea of reason' that enables him to apprehend the continuing identity of the wax. It is, he says, the mind that knows rather than the senses.

Descartes is often described as a timid man, fearful that his innovative ideas might offend the Jesuits who educated him and provoke punishment from higher quarters of the sort meted out to Galileo. Nevertheless, independence and originality are apparent in all his thought. He wrote the *Discourse on method* in French instead of Latin in order to reach a wider audience. His style is elegant, personal and individualistic in a fresh and stimulating way. His arguments inspired debate, criticism and admiration from the most eminent and influential people

of his time: from Thomas Hobbes, Benedict de Spinoza, Marin Mersenne, Antoine Arnaud, Fermat, the Princess Elizabeth, William Cavendish and many theologians. Above all, he propagated a confidence in the power of the human intellect to reach an understanding of the world and in the power of each individual to make reasoned judgements. In *Rules for the direction of the mind* he remarks that 'we shall never be philosophers if we have read all the arguments of Plato and Aristotle but cannot form a solid judgement on matters set before us'.[10]

Notes

1. John Aubrey, *Aubrey's brief lives* (Penguin, Harmondsworth, 1978) p. 254.
2. Descartes, *Meditations on first philosophy*. Meditation 2.
3. Ibid.
4. Descartes, *Principles of philosophy*, Part I, 53.
5. Descartes, *Meditations on first philosophy*, Meditation 6.
6. Descartes, *Passions of the soul*, Part I.
7. Descartes, *Correspondence*, no. 30; Letter from the Princess Elizabeth.
8. Descartes, *Principles of philosophy*, Part I, 45-46.
9. Descartes, *Meditations on first philosophy*, Meditation 2.
10. *Rules for the direction of the mind*, Rule III.

See also in this book

Bacon, Galileo, Hobbes, Spinoza.

Descartes' major writings

Rules for the direction of the mind (1628)
Discourse on method (1637)
Meditations on first philosophy (1641)
Principles of philosophy (1644)
The passions of the soul (1649)
The standard edition of Descartes' works in French is *Oeuvres de Descartes*, ed. C. Adam and P. Tannery (12 vols and supplement, Paris, 1897-1910; Index général, Paris, 1913). The standard English translation of Descartes' writings is *The philosophical works of Descartes*, trans. E.S. Haldane and G.T.R. Ross, 4th edn, 2 vols (Cambridge University Press, Cambridge, 1967). There is a good selection of Descartes' writings in *Descartes: philosophical writings*, trans. E. Anscombe and P. Geach (Nelson, London, 1971). Another selection is *The essential Descartes*, ed. Margaret D. Wilson (Mentor Books, New York, 1969).

Further reading

Balz, A.G.A. *Descartes and the modern mind* (Oxford University Press, Oxford, 1952)

Gaukroger, S. (ed.) *Descartes: philosophy, mathematics and physics* (Harvester, Brighton, 1980)

Haldane, E.S. *Descartes: his life and times* (Murray, London, 1905)

Kenny, A. *Descartes: a study of his philosophy* (Random House, New York, 1968)

Popkin, R. *History of scepticism* (Harper and Row, London, 1968)

Williams, B.A.O. *The project of pure enquiry* (Penguin, Harmondsworth, 1978)

Wilson, M.D. *Descartes* (Routledge and Kegan Paul, London, 1978)

Benedict de Spinoza
1632-1677

Spinoza belongs with the illustrious group of seventeenth-century philosophers most of whose members were mathematicians and scientists as well as philosophers and whose number includes Descartes, Leibniz and Hobbes. He maintains that there is only one substance and that it is God. His philosophical arguments are presented in the form of geometrical theorems: he supplies Definitions and Axioms from which he derives Propositions, Proofs and Corollaries. Because he maintained that the one substance was God he was said by some to be 'obsessed with God'. But for the same reason others regarded him as a **materialist** and an atheist; for, they said, if everything is God, then God is the material universe. Spinoza's intention in all he wrote was to use reason to discover the true good and thereby to possess a joy continuous and supreme to all eternity'.

Spinoza was born in Amsterdam of Jewish parents who were refugees from the Spanish Inquisition. He was brought up as an orthodox Jew and studied the work of many Jewish philosophers, including Maimonides,[1] but was formally expelled from the Jewish community in 1656 for what were said to be his heresies. Thereafter he earned his living by polishing lenses and made his friends among a group of Protestants known as the

'Collegiants', a sect without priests. In 1661 he started writing his *Treatise on the correction of the understanding*, a work which shows the influence of and also criticises Descartes. He began to write his major philosophical work, the *Ethics*, in 1663 but it was not completed until 1675 because he laid it aside in order to write a treatise in defence of liberty of thought and speech. This treatise was published anonymously in 1670. It shocked the orthodox, who soon discovered who the author was, and Spinoza was attacked and vilified in numerous publications and articles. In the tolerant atmosphere of seventeenth-century Holland he came under no restraint but he nevertheless judged it best not to publish more books. During the remainder of his short life he completed the *Ethics* and worked on a *Treatise on Politics* which was published in an unfinished form after his death. His deep interest in science and mathematics is evident from the range of titles of his modest library which was sold in 1667. The sale document shows that his collection of books included volumes on geometry and algebra, astronomy, physics, anatomy, alchemy and, of course, on optics. In company with Galileo, Descartes, Hobbes and many others, he believed that mathematics was the means to discovering the truth about the universe.

Spinoza thought that if he could know the truth of how things are he would be able to learn how to act well and attain blessedness. The basis of his search for truth was the concept of substance. He defines substance as that which exists in itself and is conceived through itself; it is that which does not depend on anything else for its existence. In Part 1 of the *Ethics* he argues that there can be only one substance that is conceived through itself, namely, 'God or Nature'. It was this identification of God with the physical universe that Spinoza's contemporaries found so deeply shocking. However, if substance is, by definition, that which is independent of anything else, then to posit the created universe as a substance distinct from its creator is to produce a contradiction. Thus, Spinoza insists, the creator and all his creation must be one substance. God and Nature are one; God is immanent and not transcendent and God or Nature, regarded as a whole, is self-creating and therefore entirely free. For Spinoza, all the relations within the one great system are logical relations and to know the truth about the whole system would be to know the logical connections that hold between all its parts. Since logical connections are **necessary** connections, if one could come to know all the truths of the system and their inter-connections, one would then see that the universe contains nothing that is **contingent** or that could be other than it is. Spinoza says: 'In the nature of things nothing contingent is admitted, but all things are determined by the necessity of divine nature to exist and act in a certain way'.[2] This means that although God or Nature as a whole is free, within nature everything is determined and everything is logically deducible from the concept of God. God is free simply in virtue of being self-determining and he determines to produce things in a logically necessary manner.

The claim that within nature everything is determined has implications for Spinoza's account of human freedom, but to understand these implications something more about Spinoza's system must be made clear. He held that the one substance, God, has an infinity of attributes but that the limited human intellect can conceive of things under two of these attributes, Thought and Extension; that is, we can think of the universe either as a system of minds or thoughts, or as a system of physical entities. An attribute constitutes an essence of a substance, a fundamental nature without which the substance would not be what it is. Thus, extension is essential to corporeal things and so is essential to that aspect of the one substance we call God. But we are never to think of Thought and Extension as the separate bases of parallel systems of existents. They are simply different aspects of the one substance. Spinoza also speaks of 'Modes'. A Mode, he says, is a modification of substance. A human body, and any body, is a Mode of the attribute of Extension. It is an arrangement or structure of particles of matter differentiated from the rest of matter by its particular structure. A human mind is likewise a Mode of the attribute of Thought. It is the mental aspect of the substance of which the body is the material aspect. Spinoza says: 'The human mind is the idea of the human body',[3] not meaning thereby that one's mind has a complete conception or 'idea' of every part and function of one's body, but that every Mode or modification of Extension necessarily has a correlate that is conceived as a Mode or modification of Thought. By positing one substance of which Thought and Extension are attributes, Spinoza has avoided the Cartesian difficulty of having to say how two distinct substances can interact.[4]

Although individual human beings are not distinct substances, each person or individual entity, Spinoza maintains, 'endeavours to persist in its own being'. He calls this endeavour '*conatus*'. The clearest example of it is in organic life: in the way in which organisms react to ward off injury or harm and repair any damage inflicted on them. Considered as thought, *conatus* is one's conscious striving or desire to maintain one's existence and as such it is that which constitutes an individual identity. Spinoza says, 'The endeavour (conatus) wherewith each thing endeavours to persist in its own being is nothing more than the actual essence of the thing itself.'[5] But, as already mentioned, Spinoza's universe is one in which everything that occurs does so in accordance with the strictest necessity. Thus every striving and endeavour and, indeed, all a person's movements and actions, are elements in a causal chain which is also a sequence of logical deductions the source of which is God. Everything is what it is of necessity and cannot possibly be other than it is. This account of the way things are for human beings, as well as for every other part of the universe, follows from Spinoza's definition of God as the one substance, self-causing and immanent. He says:

There is no mind absolute or free will, but the mind is determined for willing this or that by a cause which is determined in its turn by another cause, and this one again by another, and so on to infinity.[6]

Even God's freedom seems to be circumscribed by what reason conceives as possible for a Perfect Being. Spinoza argues in the following way:

All things depend on the power of God. That things should be different from what they are would involve a change in the will of God, and the will of God cannot change (as we have most clearly shown from the perfection of God): therefore things could not be otherwise than as they are.[7]

Spinoza's uncompromising doctrine of determinism was described as his 'hideous hypothesis'. Yet Part V of the *Ethics* has the title *Concerning the power of the intellect or human freedom*, and it opens with the words: 'I pass on at last to that part of the Ethics which concerns the manner or way which leads to liberty.' The way to liberty is by means of the best use of one's intellectual powers. Earlier in the *Ethics* Spinoza distinguishes between three levels of knowledge. The lowest level is that of knowledge acquired through the senses. Spinoza describes it as 'vague experience', since it is a mixture of a person's own ideas of his body and ideas acquired by sensing objects external to him. Strictly speaking, this kind of experience is not knowledge at all; for knowledge, according to Spinoza as to other rationalist thinkers, is always the conclusion of deductive reasoning and not merely a collection of unrelated ideas or propositions. Knowledge at the second level is provided by 'adequate ideas'. These are general ideas, widespread in human thought, which

Spinoza calls 'common notions', and they form the basis required for erecting the third level of knowledge. Motion, solidity and the propositions of mathematics are examples of common notions which, once they are conceived clearly and distinctly, provide the materials with which reason operates at the third level. In his treatise *On the correction of the understanding* Spinoza remarks that 'The mind, by acquiring an ever-increasing stock of clear ideas or knowledge, eo ipso acquires more "instruments" to facilitate its progress.'[8] He holds that the person who has a true idea 'knows at the same time that he has a true idea': one cannot doubt a true idea because it is necessarily or logically true and its denial produces a contradiction. This is the standard we have to accept for truth. An adequate idea is one that is logically coherent within itself and the test of its truth is that logical coherence.

Spinoza calls his highest level of knowledge 'intuitive knowledge'. Using the 'adequate ideas' of the second level it proceeds to knowledge of 'the essence of things'. This knowledge is 'the intellectual love of God' because it discerns and understands everything in relation to God, recognising God as the source of all things and perceiving the necessary connections between all things. Complete knowledge of this kind can belong only to God. Human beings, who are finite Modes, have only partial and fragmentary understanding. Spinoza argues that 'the more we understand particular objects, the more we understand God', for, within his system, the more physical experiences we have, the more material we have for producing adequate ideas from which to derive knowledge of essences. If our ideas are confused and 'inadequate' then, he maintains, our minds are passive. We must actively seek knowledge because 'the more objects the mind understands by the second and third kinds of knowledge, the less it suffers from those emotions that are evil and the less it fears death'.[9] Human freedom is freedom from passivity and suffering; it is the rational understanding of why everything is as it is. Human misery is always the consequence of privation of knowledge and happiness and peace of mind are always proportionate to genuine knowledge. Thus 'He who clearly and distinctly understands himself and his affects loves God, and loves him better the better he understands himself and his affects ... From the third kind of knowledge arises the greatest possible peace of mind.'[10]

Spinoza is the supreme **rationalist** and the character of his philosophy follows from that fact. Many of the theorems of the *Ethics* are difficult to follow, requiring that we trace their deductions back through many stages but, even if we are defeated by Spinoza's geometry of the cosmos, there remains the enjoyment of numerous perspicuous declarations contained in his propositions, notes and corollaries. The rigorous austerity of his method was not the vehicle for a solemn and punishing ethic; rather, it yielded dicta of a just and refined common sense. It is pleasing to know that an edifice of deductive reasoning supports the following attractive conclusion: 'There cannot be too much merriment, but it is always good; but, on the other hand, melancholy is always bad.'[11]

Notes

1. See *Maimonides* in this book, pp. 31-3.
2. Spinoza, *Ethics*, Part I, Prop. XXIX.
3. Ibid., Part II, Prop. XIII.
4. See *Descartes* in this book, pp. 57-61.
5. Spinoza, *Ethics*, Part III, Prop. VII.
6. Ibid., Part II, Prop. XLVIII.
7. Ibid., Part I, Prop. XXXIII, note 2.
8. Spinoza, *Treatise on the correction of the understanding*, Part VII, 39.
9. Spinoza, *Ethics*, Part V, Prop. XXXVIII.
10. Ibid., Prop. XXVII.
11. Ibid., Part IV, Prop. XLII.

See also in this book

Maimonides, Hobbes, Descartes, Leibniz.

Spinoza's major writings

Treatise on the correction of the understanding (started 1661, published in 1677), trans. Andrew Boyle in

Everyman Library no. 481 (Dent, London, 1910, 1959, 1963)
Treatise on theology and politics (1670)
Ethics (started in 1663, completed in 1675, published in 1677), trans. Andrew Boyle in Everyman Library no. 481 (Dent, London, 1910, 1959, 1963)
The standard Latin edition of Spinoza's writings is *Spinoza opera*. ed. C. Gebhardt (4 vols, Heidelberg, 1924). Spinoza's writings in an English translation are collected in *The chief works of Benedict de Spinoza*, trans. R.H.M. Elwes (2 vols, Dover Publications, New York, 1956).

Further reading

Bennett, J.A. *A study of Spinoza's ethics* (Cambridge University Press, Cambridge, 1984)
Hampshire, S. *Spinoza* (Penguin, Harmondsworth, 1951)
Parkinson, G.H.R. *Spinoza's theory of knowledge* (Clarendon Press, Oxford, 1954)
Wolfson, H.A. *The philosophy of Spinoza* (Harvard University Press, Cambridge, Mass. 1983)

John Locke   1632-1704

John Locke is described by Bertrand Russell as 'the most fortunate of philosophers' because his philosophical and political views were widely understood and warmly welcomed by many of his contemporaries. For much of his life England was engaged in radical political reform that sought to limit the power of kings, establish the regular assembly of parliament, overthrow authoritarianism and secure religious freedom. Locke was an embodiment of these aspirations and was active in politics as well as philosophy. His theory of knowledge, set out in his *Essay concerning the human understanding* (1690), is of major importance in the **empirical** philosophy that succeeded the continental **rationalism** founded by Descartes. The *Essay* is a critical inquiry 'into the original, certainty, and extent of *human knowledge*, together with the grounds and degrees of *belief*, opinion and *assent*'. Equally important are his *Two treatises of government*, also published in 1690, in which he argues against the divine right of kings and maintains that all men are free and equal in the state of nature and possess certain natural rights. Locke's political doctrines were incorporated into the American Constitution and into the constitution established in France in 1871. During his lifetime he published most of his political writings anonymously, preferring to keep them separate from the *Essay* which he regarded as his most important work.

Locke was born at Wrington in Somerset. His father was an attorney and a parliamentarian who fought against Charles I. Locke attended Westminster School and then Christ Church, Oxford, receiving his BA in 1656. He stayed on to take his master's degree and in 1664 was appointed censor of moral philosophy. He embarked on the study of medicine and became well qualified, although he never practised. In 1665 he went with Sir Walter Vane on a diplomatic mission to the Elector of Brandenburg but refused subsequent offers of diplomatic work, went back to Oxford and began to concentrate his attention on philosophy. He soon found a kindred soul in the Earl of Shaftesbury, who invited Locke to live in his London house as his personal physician. In that household politics and philosophy flourished side by side and Locke was at the centre of influential and volatile public affairs. In 1683 Shaftesbury was in danger of being impeached for treason. He fled to Holland and died there. Locke, too, exiled himself to Holland, spending much of the time until the end of the Stuart despotism on study and the writing of the *Essay concerning the human understanding* but also involving himself closely in the plans to set William of Orange on the English throne. After the revolution of 1688 Locke returned to England, escorting the Princess of Orange who was to become Queen Mary. His two major works, the *Essay concerning human understanding* and the *Two treatises of government*, provoked lively debate when they were published in 1690. Locke's health by now was poor but he continued to engage in work and public service as much as he could. For the last thirteen years of his life he lived at Oates, the home of Sir Francis and Lady Masham, still writing, corresponding and debating, and enjoying the affection and respect of many. He died at Oates on 28 October 1704 while Lady Masham was reading the Psalms to him.

Locke's main philosophical concern, like that of so many other philosophers of the seventeenth and eighteenth centuries, was with questions about the capabilities of the human mind and the nature of knowledge. In a famous passage in the 'Epistle to the Reader' that introduces the *Essay* he describes the task of the philosopher as that of an 'underlabourer' who must clear the ground a little, 'removing some of the rubbish that lies in the way of our knowledge'. He felt that rationalism had allowed that the power of reason could do far more than was actually the case and had thereby provoked a sceptical reaction that was equally excessive. For his part he thought that if he could discover the extent of the mind's powers then this knowledge might make people more cautious in 'meddling with things' that exceed the mind's comprehension; it would enable them 'to stop when it is at the utmost extent of its tether; and to sit down in a quiet ignorance of those things which, upon examination, are found to be beyond the reach of our capacities'.[1]

Like his fellow empiricists Locke held that human knowledge is ultimately derived from sense experience. In the first book of the *Essay* he therefore considers and rejects the view that there are certain ideas that are innate; that is, that we have some ideas not acquired by experience but present as part of the constitution of the human mind. In the second book he maintains instead that the mind is as 'white paper, void of all characters, without any ideas' and asks 'How comes it to be furnished?' His answer is that experience, in the form of sensations and reflections, provides raw materials which the mind then works with, analysing and organising them in complex ways. Sensations are received when the sense organs are stimulated and then produce effects in consciousness; reflection is 'that notice which the mind takes of its own operations and the manner of them' and is dependent for its material on other mental activities engendered by sensation. Anything of which the mind is thus aware Locke calls an 'idea' and he distinguishes between simple ideas such as bitter, sour, cold, hot, which contain no other ideas and which cannot be created by us, and complex ideas which are produced by the mind when it compounds and combines simple ideas. Complex ideas may be of strange things such as unicorns or satyrs that have no actual existence but will always be analysable into a medley of simple ideas acquired through experience. In the course of three revisions of the *Essay* Locke elaborated his account of ideas, sometimes producing inconsistencies between the details of the four accounts of them. But they are vital to his view of the human mind since he sees them as signs that represent the world to us: they are the means by which we perceive the world external to us, our own thoughts and the thoughts of others. His resulting theory of perception is a causal theory: we have to think of physical stimuli operating on the senses and thereby causing ideas in the mind. But the consequences of the theory seem to be that we never perceive the world directly because we perceive only the *ideas* caused by stimulation of the senses.

The objections to such a theory are numerous. For example, if it is only ideas that we are actually acquainted with, can we know anything at all about external objects? And in the same vein: can we really place credence on a theory which on the one hand employs notions of external physiological processes affecting our senses and, on the other, asserts that we can have no direct knowledge of such processes?

Locke's account of what can be known of physical objects is consonant with the science of his contemporaries, those 'masterbuilders' such as Boyle and Newton whose work he commends in the 'Epistle to the Reader' and for whom he describes himself as an 'underlabourer'. These scientists worked to explain the world in terms of its structures rather than its qualities and believed that our experience of qualities such as colour, scent and so on can be explained in terms of the structures rather than as entities distinct from the structures. Adopting a similar standpoint, Locke distinguishes between what are generally named as primary and secondary qualities. Primary qualities are those which are 'utterly inseparable from the body, in what estate soever it be; and such as in all the alterations and changes it suffers, all the force can be used upon it, it constantly keeps'. As an example he cites a grain of wheat, pointing out that however much we break it into parts, each part 'has still solidity, extension, figure and mobility' which are its primary qualities. Secondary qualities, he says, are 'nothing in the objects themselves but powers to produce various sensations in us by their primary qualities, i.e. by the bulk, figure, texture and motion of their insensible parts, as colours, sounds, tastes, etc.'[2] Thus, bulk, number, figure and so on are actually in objects, but such things as colour, scent, and warmth and cold are not. Locke calls the primary qualities *real* qualities because they are present in objects 'whether anyone's senses perceive them or no'. As for secondary qualities, he says:

> Take away the sensation of them; let not the eyes see light or colours, nor the ears hear sounds; let the palate not taste, nor the nose smell, and all colours, tastes, odours and sounds, as they are such particular ideas, vanish and cease, and are reduced to their causes, i.e. bulk, figure and motion of parts.[3]

In his espousal of this theory Locke is challenging the Aristotelian view that colours, tastes and smells are things in themselves. He also specifies a third type of quality possessed by objects. This third quality is the power bodies have to make 'such a change in the bulk, figure, texture and motion of *another body* as to make it operate on our senses differently from what it did before'.[4]

Locke's example is of the power of fire to make lead soft and fluid. Once again, this quality is possessed by an object in virtue of its primary qualities; it is not something distinct from them.

The notion of substance is a problem for Locke. In Chapter XXIII of Book II of the *Essay* he points out that groups of simple ideas 'go constantly together'; that is, they form objects that we call trees, apples, dogs and so on. And he says, 'not imagining how these simple ideas can subsist by themselves, we accustom ourselves to suppose some *substratum* wherein they do subsist, and from which they do result, which therefore we call *substance*'.[5] Someone pressed for precise details about what exactly this substratum is could only reply, he says, that it is 'something, he knew not what'. Since Locke has claimed that all our concepts are derived from experience he might be expected to reject the notion of substance as meaningless. But in fact he does not. In letters to Dr Stillingfleet, Bishop of Worcester, he explains that he does not dispense with the concept of substance because it would be contradictory to hold that qualities *exist* but that they can do so with the support of substance. In saying this he is supposing that the concept of existence necessarily includes the concept of substance; but this is not by any means self-evident. Locke is often criticised for not fully accepting the consequences of his own empiricism. It seems that he could not completely discard the well-established traditions that had their source in Aristotle.

Language is the topic of Book III of the *Essay*. Locke's account is dependent on his causal theory of perception which leads to the conclusion that we are directly aware only of our ideas. Since ideas are private to the persons who have them Locke decides that language is a system of signs consisting of 'sensible marks of our ideas' that enable us, when we wish, to communicate with one another. He holds that ideas can have intelligibility on their own, without words, and that words are simply for the public expression of thought and are meaningful only if backed by ideas.

Locke explains how we come by general words, which signify general ideas, by appeal to the notion of abstraction. All things that exist, he says, are particular but, as we develop from infancy to adulthood, we observe common qualities in people and things. From seeing many particular men, for example, and by 'separating from them the circumstances of time and place, and any other ideas that may determine them to this or that particular existence' we can arrive at the general idea of 'man'.[6] This is the process of abstraction. But, he insists, '*general* and *universal* belong not to the real existence of things, but are the inventions and creatures of the understanding, made by it for its own use, and concern only signs, whether words or ideas'.[7] It would not have been consistent with an empiricist standpoint to allow that the general or the universal had some kind of real existence. What Locke does allow is that each distinct abstract idea is a distinct essence; that is:

a circle is as essentially different from an oval as a sheep from a goat; and rain is as essentially different from snow as water from earth, that abstract idea which is the essence of one being impossible to be communicated to the other.[8]

Book IV of the *Essay* is called 'Of Knowledge and Opinion' and is widely regarded as its least successful part. It has been described as a rationalist conclusion to a work of empiricism. Locke says that knowledge is a perception of 'the connection and agreement, or disagreement and repugnancy of any of our ideas'.[9] He lists four sorts of agreement or disagreement and distinguishes between what he calls 'actual' and 'habitual' knowledge. One's knowledge is deemed 'actual' when one has proved something to be the case and has the proofs in mind, or 'in actual view'. If the proofs are not 'in actual view' then one's knowledge is to be described as 'habitual' knowledge. He also makes an important though not original distinction between 'demonstrative' and 'intuitive' knowledge and identifies three degrees of certainty. Intuitive knowledge is acquired when the mind 'perceives the agreement or disagreement of two ideas *immediately by themselves* ... Thus the mind perceives that white is not black, that a circle is not a triangle, that three are more than two and equal to one and two'.[10] This intuitive knowledge carries the highest certainty that 'human frailty is capable of'. Demonstrative knowledge relies on a sequence of intuitions but is less certain than intuitive knowledge because it involves memory. The third level of certainty is that pertaining to 'sensitive knowledge'. This is knowledge of 'particular external objects, by that perception and consciousness we have of the actual entrance of ideas from them'.[11] By this Locke means that sensitive knowledge is only of what I am perceiving; I should not claim to *know*, for example, that there is a corridor outside this room in which I write and a kitchen downstairs, since I am not at present perceiving them. This is to uphold a very restricted sense of the word 'knowledge', one that would radically alter our everyday use of the word, were we to observe it. When Leibniz criticised Locke's three degrees of certainty he wrote: 'Perhaps *opinion*, based on likelihood, also deserves the name of knowledge; otherwise nearly all historical knowledge will collapse, and a great deal more.'

Locke's political philosophy is known largely through the second of his *Two treatises of government*. Its second chapter begins with the declaration that we are all naturally in a state of perfect freedom. People are free 'to order their actions, and dispose of their possessions, and persons as they think fit, within the bounds of the Law of Nature, without asking leave, or depending on the will of any other man'. Locke sees the law of nature as stemming from God's will and as discoverable by the use of reason. It is the responsibility of each individual to enact the law of nature which binds them to preserve peace and to refrain from harming one another; but when some individuals fail in this, civil government is formed: men contract between each other to form a body politic that will uphold natural law and the natural rights to life, liberty and certain property. If the ruler of this society violates the rights of individuals or seeks to obtain absolute power then the people are entitled to remove him.

Although Locke writes of individuals as entering into contracts or, as he calls them, 'compacts', to establish civil societies, he does not mean that everyone deliberately, at some particular time, makes a contract. His point is that people do undertake the obligation of obedience to government by, in one way or another, consenting to existing political arrangements. Consent, Locke maintains, may be *tacit*, in that 'every man that hath any possession or enjoyment of any part of the dominions of any government doth thereby give his tacit consent, and is as far forth obliged to obedience to the laws of that government'.[12] Because consent, even when tacit, is freely given, then, Locke holds, obedience is obligatory as long as the terms of the contract are observed. This account is not entirely immune from criticism. It has been argued, for example, that while it is possible to give tacit consent to some arrangement by merely agreeing to it, it is not possible to make a tacit undertaking to do something: thus the notion of tacit consent is not sufficient to justify the individual's obligation to obey the government.

Locke described himself as merely an 'underlabourer' and some of his critics have described his empiricism as timid or halfbaked. Nevertheless his influence both in his distinguished lifetime and in the centuries since his death has been profound and farreaching. D.J. O'Connor has remarked that 'without Locke's work, that of Berkeley, Hume, Mill, Russell and Moore would have looked very different'.[13] So might the constitutions of many political societies and the ideas of political thinkers such as Paine and Jefferson who found inspiration in his work.

Notes

1. John Locke, *Essay concerning human understanding*, Book I, Ch. 1, 4.
2. Ibid., Book II, Ch. 8, 9.
3. Ibid., Book II, Ch. 8, 17.
4. Ibid., Book II, Ch. 8, 23.
5. Ibid., Book II, Ch. 13, 2.
6. Ibid., Book III, Ch. 3, 6 and 7.
7. Ibid., Book III, Ch. 3, 11.
8. Ibid., Book III, Ch. 3, 14.
9. Ibid., Book IV, Ch. 1, 2.
10. Ibid., Book IV, Ch. 2, 1.
11. Ibid., Book IV, ch. 2, 14.
12. John Locke, *An essay concerning the true origin, extent and end of civil government*, Chapter 8, 19.
13. D.J. O'Connor, 'Locke' in D.J. O'Connor (ed.), *A critical history of Western philosophy* (The Free Press, New York, 1964; Macmillan, London, 1985), pp. 204-19.

See also in this book

Descartes, Leibniz, Berkeley, Hume, Rousseau.

Locke's major writings

A letter concerning toleration (1689), ed. J. Tully (Hackett, Indiana, USA, 1983)
An essay concerning human understanding (1690), ed. P.H. Nidditch (Oxford University Press, Oxford, 1979)
Two treatises of government (1690), ed. P. Laslett (Cambridge University Press, Cambridge, 1960)
Correspondence, ed. E.S. de Beer (8 vols, Clarendon Press, Oxford, 1975-)
Locke's collected writings are in preparation at the Clarendon Press: *The works of John Locke*, ed. P. Nidditch (Clarendon Press, Oxford, 1975-)

Further reading

Aaron, Richard I. *John Locke*, 3rd edn (Clarendon Press, Oxford, 1971)
Bennett, J. *Locke, Berkeley, Hume: central themes* (Clarendon Press, Oxford, 1971)
Colman, J. *John Locke's moral philosophy* (Edinburgh University Press, Edinburgh, 1983)
Cranston, M. *John Locke, a biography* (Oxford University Press, Oxford, 1985)
Dunn, J. *Locke* (Past Masters, Oxford University Press, Oxford, 1984)
Hunter, M. *Science and society in restoration England* (Cambridge University Press, Cambridge, 1981)
Mackie, J. *Problems from Locke* (Clarendon Press, Oxford, 1976)

O'Connor, D.J. *John Locke* (Penguin, Harmondsworth, 1952; New York, 1968)
Parry, G. *Locke* (George Allen and Unwin, London 1978)
Tipton, I.C. (ed.) *Locke on human understanding* (Clarendon Press, Oxford, 1977)
Woolhouse, R.S. *Locke* (Harvester Press, Brighton, 1983)

Gottfried Wilhelm Leibniz 1646-1716

Leibniz ranks as an outstanding polymath even among the intellectual giants of the seventeenth century. He was a mathematician, scientist and philosopher; a lawyer, diplomat, engineer, inventor and historian. He saw his work in all these fields as underpinned by his **metaphysical** system. He maintains that reality ultimately consists of an infinite number of non-material substances that he calls monads: 'simple substances without parts and without windows through which anything could come in or go out'.[1] God, he argues, is an infinitely perfect being who, from an infinite number of possible worlds, creates the best possible world within which everything unfolds in accordance with a pattern he has pre-established and which follows from his first decrees. Leibniz believed that philosophy was of great practical importance and that it could resolve theological and political issues as well as provide a coherent basis for scientific and mathematical developments. His vision was of a great synthesis of knowledge, a universal encyclopaedia that would be accessible through catalogues, abstracts and indices to the international community of scholars who, when confronted with large political and social problems, would be able to sit down together and calculate correct solutions. He saw himself as a citizen of the world rather than of the small state of Hanover which he served for much of his life and this breadth of outlook is apparent in the numerous brilliant and wide-ranging projects that constitute his prodigious output.

Leibniz was born in Leipzig a few years

before the Thirty Years War ended. His father, who was a professor of philosophy at Leipzig University, taught him to read at an early age and thereafter his intellectual abilities developed rapidly. He was enrolled in the university at the age of fourteen, graduated two years later and proceeded to work for and obtain a doctorate in law which was awarded him in 1666 at the University of Altdorf. He refused a professorship there but worked for a short while as secretary to a Nuremberg society interested in alchemy, a topic in which he retained an interest for the whole of his life. He then entered the service of the Archbishop of Mainz who sent him on a mission to Paris. There he met, among others, the philosopher Malebranche; Arnauld, the theologian and philosopher, and Huygens, the Dutch physicist. He extended his knowledge of mathematics and invented a calculating machine superior to one made by Pascal. He visited London in 1673 and was elected a member of the Royal Society. In that year the Archbishop of Mainz died and Leibniz found himself without a job. Somewhat reluctantly, because it did not appeal to him, he eventually accepted the post of Librarian to the Duke of Brunswick at Hanover. On the way to taking up the work he went to Amsterdam where he visited Spinoza with whom he enjoyed four days of lively discussion. Sadly, this was his last opportunity for engaging in stimulating philosophical exchanges. Thereafter he lived and worked in Hanover save for the few journeys required by his work and had contact with other scholars only through letters and the exchange of papers. His main task as Librarian was to write a history of the House of Brunswick but whilst compiling this he worked in many other fields as well. He was involved in a most unhappy controversy about the discovery of the infinitesimal **calculus**. It seems that both he and Newton, as well as other European mathematicians, were working on the calculus at the same time and a dispute arose over who in fact was to be deemed its author

or discoverer. Newton was able to stand aside from the dispute for many of his friends vigorously made a case for him. But Leibniz had fewer defenders to rally to his aid and had to resort to pleading his own case. He did this by writing anonymously in his own defence: a wretched procedure to have to engage in, and particularly so since his authorship of his defence was soon apparent. Whatever the precise truth of the controversy may be time has shown that Leibniz's notation, which is still used, is regarded as more satisfactory than Newton's. Leibniz's biographers have pointed out that he was disappointed, too, in that his highly original work in logic was not acknowledged by his contemporaries. His achievements in logic are now recognised but his copious writings on the subject lay disregarded in the Royal Library in Hanover until early in the twentieth century. His death in 1716 was more or less ignored by the Hanoverian court, the Royal Society in London and the Academy of Berlin. A number of factors contributed to this unpopularity, among them his tendency to be snobbish and arrogant; but most of the hostility seems to have been provoked by Leibniz's opposition to nationalism and his vision of a single universal society. In this, as in so many of his ideas, he was much in advance of his time.

Leibniz's best-known works are the *Discourse on metaphysics* (1686), the *New essays concerning the human understanding* (1704), the *Theodicy* (1710) and the *Monadology* (1714). Only the *Theodicy* was published in his lifetime. Equally famous are the series of letters he exchanged with Antoine Arnaud concerning freedom and the concept of an individual, and with Clarke concerning the Newtonian universe. But no mere listing of his writings, even if it were comprehensive, can indicate the scope of his interests, abilities, inventiveness, sheer intellectual power and prodigality. The task of compiling a complete edition of his works did not begin until 1923 and is not yet finished.

Whereas Descartes maintained that reality consists fundamentally of two **substances** and Spinoza maintained that there is only one, Leibniz argued a case for infinitely many substances: the monads. Leibnizian monads are the simplest units of existence and each monad is a different simple substance which is unextended and without parts. Thus, ultimate reality, for Leibniz, does not consist of anything physical. We have to think of the monads as energy rather than matter and as differing from each other in virtue of possessing differing degrees of consciousness. A human being is a colony of monads in which the dominant monad is a spirit monad that unifies the colony in being conscious, to a certain extent, of its members. The individual monads can only be created or annihilated 'all at once' by God and each monad carries within itself, from its creation, the potentiality of all it will ever be. Each monad unfolds its being in a way which is harmonious with the unfolding of every other monad but without ever affecting or being affected by any other monad. In creating the universe God is able to conceive of an infinite number of possible worlds and he creates the best of all possible worlds. He does not create a perfect world, for that is logically impossible. To create a perfect world God would have to reproduce himself exactly. But since God is non-extensive spirit, a reproduction of his qualities would be indiscernible and so non-existent. Thus the best of all *possible* worlds is the one containing as much existence as possible compatible with the greatest degree of perfection. God knows and foresees every detail of the unfolding of every monad and every relationship and complex of relationships through which every monad will pass as it unfolds itself. In para. 59 of the *Monadology* Leibniz says, 'Now this *connection* or adaptation of all created things with each, and of each with all the rest, means that each simple substance has relations which express all the others, and that consequently it is a perpetual living mirror of the universe.' Because each monad mirrors the universe from a different point of view 'it is,' he says, 'as if there were as many different universes, which are however but different perspectives of a single universe in accordance with the different points of view of each monad'.[2] Each monad is in a sense representative of the whole, although it does not reflect the whole, for only a divinity could do that. Leibniz says: 'It is not in the object, but in the modification of the knowledge of the object, that monads are limited.'[3] The apparent interaction of things in everyday experience is in fact the consequence of God's ordination. It is the working out of a pre-established harmony known in its entirety only to God.

Leibniz bases his philosophy on some very general principles. The first is that reality consists of substances and their attributes. Logically, or grammatically, this is to say that he thought in terms of subjects to which predicates are ascribed. He also accepted certain fundamental principles of thought: the principle of contradiction, which holds that any statement containing a contradiction is false and its opposite is true; and the principle of sufficient reason, which holds that there is a sufficient reason for everything being as it is. A particular type of truth derives from each of these two principles. Truths of reason, which are **necessary** truths the opposites of which are impossible, derive from the principle of contradiction. Truths of fact, which are **contingent** truths the opposites of which are possible, derive from the principle of sufficient reason.

Necessary truths are shown to be so by analysis. The necessary truth 'A bachelor is an unmarried male' is shown to be necessary once one considers the definitions of the terms 'bachelor' and 'unmarried male'. For truths of fact there are sufficient reasons; but if one enquires into the reasons for a particular state of affairs, say for the fact that a particular table is occupying a particular position, then it is possible to go on and on adducing more and more 'reasons'. In Leibniz's system only God can know all the reasons for a contingent truth's being what it is. God is the ultimate and sufficient reason for every contingent truth and his intellect can grasp everything pertaining to a truth so that, for him, every contingent truth is as analytically true as a truth of reason. This is simply another aspect of the doctrine that a monad, when created, contains within it all that it will ever be. The logical expression of the doctrine is that in any true proposition the concept of the predicate is contained in the concept of the subject; the complete concept of a monad and, by extension, of any aggregate of monads, contains everything that can truly be said of it.

An important consequence of Leibniz's doctrines is that many of our ordinary beliefs about our ability to make choices and our capacity to influence or be influenced by others seem to be untenable. Just this objection was made by the theologian, Antoine Arnauld, and was met by Leibniz in letters exchanged between the two. In 1686 Leibniz sent a summary of his *Discourse on metaphysics* to Arnauld, who, upon reading it, declared that it contained many startling things, and wrote to his patron, Landgraf Ernst Von Hessen-Rheinfels, in the following terms:

> I find in these meditations so many things which frighten me, and which, unless I am much mistaken, all mankind will find so shocking, that I do not see that any purpose would be served by a piece of writing which will manifestly be rejected by the whole world.[4]

Leibniz's doctrine, Arnauld said, seemed to impose restrictions not only on the liberty of individuals but on that of God as well; for if the concept of an individual involves everything that will ever happen to him, the liberty of God is restricted in that having once decreed the existence of an individual that existence will follow a relentless course which God would be unable to alter; and the liberty of the individual is quite non-existent since the events of his life are pre-chosen. Thus if God, in allowing Adam to exist, knows all that Adam will do, we can only conclude that Adam is determined and has no choices. Likewise God, having brought about the existence of Adam as a colony of monads containing the potentiality of all that Adam will ever be, can only allow Adam to be just that and nothing else.

To this Leibniz replies by invoking the distinction between truths of reason and truths of fact and by emphasising some points he has already made in paragraphs 8 to 13 of the *Discourse*. Adam, he says, does not do all he does out of logical necessity: upon waking in the morning it is logically possible for Adam that he may rise and walk or may lie longer in the Garden, enjoying its delights. There will be sufficient reasons for what he in fact does and these reasons will be known to God. But although God has decreed and knows what Adam will do, so that it is certain that Adam will do what he does, it is never logically necessary that Adam does what he does and it is always logically possible that he might do otherwise. To the objection that his theory restricts God's freedom Leibniz answers that God's freedom is not exemplified in arbitrary acts. The greatest freedom is to act in accordance with what is good and this is what God freely chooses to do. He has freely chosen to create the best of all possible worlds and the whole orderly system of the world as we know it stems from God's first decree.

Arnauld is not satisfied with Leibniz's replies. His own view is that the concept of an individual such as himself includes 'only what is of such a nature that I would no longer be myself if it were not in me', rather than 'everything that will ever happen to me'.[5] He believes that he is defined by a range of features essential to his being himself but that 'everything which is of such a nature that it might either happen to me or not happen to me without my ceasing to be myself, should not be considered as involved in my individual concept'.[6] Thus, according to Arnauld, if an individual is defined as a *type* of human being, for example as male, celibate, a theologian, then his human freedom would consist in his living out the details of these roles in his own particular way. But such a view is inadmissible to Leibniz's metaphysics, the basis of which is the concept of the monad as self-contained, complete, and chosen by God to be everything that it will be.

To some, Leibniz's account of the way things really are may sound strange, even fantastic. For Leibniz himself the postulation of an infinite number of extensionless and self-contained substances, created by a God possessing infinite perfection and cognisant of all possibilities and actualities, was simply the conception of reality that resulted from rational reflection concerning the way things ultimately must be. Moreover, he believed that rationally conceived principles must provide the grounds of the **empirical** sciences; in short, that the logico-metaphysical structure arrived at by the process of reason is a fully adequate foundation for the world of appearances: for the phenomena of matter, bodies, space, time, motion and the interactions of human beings.

Notes

1. Leibniz, *Monadology*, para. 7.
2. Ibid., para. 57.
3. Ibid., para. 60.
4. See G.H.R. Parkinson (ed.), *Leibniz: philosophical writings* (Dent, London, 1973), p. 48, note 2.
5. *The Leibniz–Arnauld Correspondence*, letter from Arnauld to Leibniz, 13 May 1686.
6. Ibid.

See also in this book

Descartes, Spinoza, Locke, Berkeley, Hume.

Leibniz's major writings

Discourse on metaphysics (1686), trans. P. Lucas and L. Grint (Manchester University Press, Manchester, 1961)
The Leilbiz–Arnauld correspondence (1686-90), trans. H.T. Mason (Manchester University Press, Manchester, 1967)
New essays concerning the human understanding (1704), trans. P. Remnant and J. Bennett (Cambridge University Press, Cambridge, 1981, 1982)
Theodicy (1710), trans. E.M. Huggard (Routledge and Kegan Paul, London, 1952)
Monadology (1714) in *Leibniz: selections*, ed. P. Wiener (Scribner's, New York, 1951, and Bobbs-Merrill, New York, 1965)
The Leibniz–Clarke correspondence (1715-16), ed. H.G. Alexander (Manchester University Press, Manchester, 1956)
There is a good selection of Leibniz's writings in P.P. Wiener, (ed.), *Leibniz selections* (Charles Scribner's Sons, New York, 1951)

Further reading

Broad, C.D. *Leibniz: an introduction*, ed. C. Lewy (Cambridge University Press, Cambridge, 1975)
Brown, S. *Leibniz* (Harvester Press, Brighton, 1984; paperback, 1986)
Ishiguro, H. *Leibniz: philosophy of logic and language* (Duckworth, London, 1972)
Rescher, N. *Leibniz: an introduction to his philosophy* (University Press of America, Lanham, 1979)
Saw, R.L. *Leibniz* (Penguin, Harmondsworth, 1954)

George Berkeley   1685-1753

The main thrust of Berkeley's philosophy is the claim that there is no such thing as matter. He held that all the objects we perceive and ordinarily take to exist in the world outside ourselves are simply collections of ideas existing only in minds. This somewhat startling proposal embodies what Berkeley regarded as a plainly apparent fact. He wrote:

Some truths there are so near and obvious to the mind, that a man need only open his eyes to see them. Such I take this important one to be, to wit, that all the choir of heaven and furniture of the earth, in a word all those bodies which compose the mighty frame of the world, have not any subsistence without a mind, that their being is to be perceived or known; that consequently so long as they are not actually perceived by me, or do not exist in my mind or that of any other created spirit, they must either have no existence at all, or else subsist in the mind of some eternal spirit.[1]

This philosophy, and other philosophies that similarly take the view that the external world is somehow produced by the mind, is known as 'idealism'. Berkeley maintains that God implants ideas in us in an orderly manner and that in God's mind all things exist at all times. Reality consists of the eternal mind of God and our finite minds, between which rational communication takes place by means of ideas. By rejecting matter Berkeley disposes of the knotty problems with which his predecessors wrestled of giving an account of material substance and of the interaction of minds and matter, and restores God to the role of the sustaining and **necessary** source of all things. However, the rejection generates the difficulty of how to think of the physical sciences; for these sciences purported to establish truths about a physical universe which Berkeley declares to be non-existent. He eventually resolves this difficulty by arguing that the pronouncements of science are useful theories rather than factual accounts. This view was largely unacceptable to Berkeley's contemporaries but in the twentieth century has found favour with scientists and philosophers who recognise that theoretical structures are employed for the useful and predictive purchase they exert rather than for their factual truth.

Berkeley was Irish by birth though of English descent, his grandfather having moved to Ireland at the time of the Restoration. He was born at Kilkenny and attended Kilkenny College. When he was 15 he went to Trinity College, Dublin, where he received a very up-to-date education which included a study of Locke's philosophy. He graduated in 1704 but stayed in Dublin to study and was elected to a fellowship in 1707. His first work, *An essay towards a new theory of vision*, was published when he was only 24. A year later he published *A treatise concerning the principles of human knowledge*, his most important and influential work, known generally as *The principles*. In 1713 he went to London, published *Three dialogues between Hylas and Philonous*, and met Addison, Pope, Swift and Steele. Subsequently he travelled on the continent and then moved for a short while to Newport, Rhode Island, intending to establish a college in Bermuda that would train Indians, Negroes and white American colonists for the ministry. But government funding was not forthcoming and the venture had to be abandoned. He returned to London in 1732 and in 1734 was made Bishop of Cloyne, Ireland. He apparently took a close interest in the well-being of the poor people of his diocese and, having become convinced that tar water contained valuable medicinal properties, he published in 1744 *A chain of philosophical reflexions and inquiries concerning the virtues of tar-water*, a book now known as *Siris* and containing philosophical reflection as well as practical advice. This was Berkeley's last piece of philosophical writing but over a century later two notebooks were discovered, started by him in 1705 and containing remarks on the development of his philosophical views. These fascinating notes were published in 1871 by their discoverer, A.C. Fraser, and are now known as *The philosophical commentaries*. A piece of advice Berkeley wrote in the notebooks for himself runs as follows: 'Mem. Upon all occasions to use the utmost modesty — to confute the mathematicians with the utmost civility and respect, not to style then Nihilarians, etc. N.B. To reign in ye satirical nature.'[2]

Berkeley retired to Oxford in 1752, occupying a house in Holywell Street. He died suddenly on a Sunday evening in January 1753 while listening to his wife reading aloud from the Bible.

In the early years of the eighteenth century the dominant view of the nature of things was firmly and confidently grounded in the new science that had burgeoned so magnificently in the seventeenth century. That science, often known as 'the new philosophy' or 'the corpuscularian philosophy', maintained that the material universe was atomic or 'corpuscular' in its structure and mechanical in its operation. The explanation of the way in which the world worked was entirely in terms of mass, shape, size and motion, these properties generally being thought to be the primary qualities of matter. So-called secondary qualities, such as the tastes, colours and temperatures we ordinarily ascribe to things, were held not to be in the things themselves but in us, although produced in us by 'powers' in the external bodies. Perception was generally analysed as a causal process in which a stimulus is transmitted from the sense organs to the brain which then causes 'ideas' to be produced 'in the mind'. And, it was argued, it is these ideas rather than the external objects themselves that are actually perceived. The major exponent of this theory was John Locke and it is largely as a critical response to the implications of Locke's views, founded as they were on the new science, that Berkeley's philosophy is to be understood.[3]

Berkeley agrees with Locke that it is ideas in the mind that are the objects of perception. Thereafter his reasoning reaches conclusions very different from Locke's. He attacks Locke's distinction between primary and secondary qualities by arguing that it is not in fact the case that primary qualities are in objects, secondary qualities in us. Locke had said that secondary qualities are in us because they vary in accordance with the state or the surrounding conditions of the person observing them but Berkeley points out that this applies equally to our perceptions of so-called primary qualities: perceived shapes, for instance, alter as we move around and our judgements of rates of motion vary with our distance from the moving objects. We have, Berkeley insists, no way of knowing when or if our ideas of things are correct representations of what they are supposed to represent: we have no reason to suppose that they are caused by external objects and the whole theory of perception as a causal process does not stand up to critical examination. Common sense suggests therefore that we should relinquish belief in a material substance. He says:

'When we do our utmost to conceive the existence of external bodies, we are all the while only contemplating our own ideas.'[4]

A central tenet of Berkeley's exposition in the *Principles* is that to exist is to perceive or be perceived; that is what it means to exist. He regards it as a major error that some people had assumed that there are existing things which neither perceive nor are perceived. In the *Philosophical commentaries* he remarks that the confusion produced by former philosophers 'sprang from their not knowing what existence was and wherein it consisted. This was the source of all their Folly. 'Tis on the discovering of the nature and meaning and import of Existence that I chiefly insist.'[5] His own view is that only two kinds of things exist: spirits and ideas. Spirits perceive and ideas are perceived. Ideas are passive but spirits are active and able to cause ideas. Human beings are finite spirits, but God is an infinite spirit who causes many of our ideas. God causes the ideas of what we ordinarily think of as our immediate perceptions of the external world. Subsequent reflections on what we have perceived, as when, for example, I think about the wood pigeons I saw and heard this morning, are caused by ourselves. Berkeley believes not only that this thesis of immaterialism disposes of or, rather, prevents the generation of the tricky problems concerning substance, perception and knowledge that had afflicted earlier philosophies, but that it is a natural consequence of plain, common-sense thinking. For those made anxious by the apparent insubstantiality of what he proposes he writes the following:

The only thing whose existence we deny, is that which philosophers call matter or corporeal substance ... If any man thinks this detracts from the existence or reality of things, he is very far from understanding what hath been premised in the plainest terms I could think of. Take here an abstract of what hath been said. There are spiritual substances, minds, or human souls, which will or excite ideas in themselves at pleasure: but these are faint, weak, and unsteady in respect of others they perceive by sense, which being impressed upon them according to certain rules or laws of Nature, speak themselves the effects of a mind more powerful and wise than human spirits. Those latter are said to have more *reality* in them than the former; by which is meant that they are not fictions of the mind perceiving them. And in this sense, the sun that I see by day is the real sun, and that which I imagine by night is the idea of the former. In the sense here given of *reality*, it is evident that every vegetable, star, mineral, and in general each part of the mundane system, is as much a *real being* by our principles as by any other. Whether others mean anything by the term *reality* different from what I do, I entreat them to look into their own thoughts and see.[6]

Thus it is not that Berkeley is requiring that we attempt to make a bizarre transformation of human existence in which we refuse to treat the world and our own bodies as if they were in some sense not really there. 'We are not', he declares, 'by the principles premised ... deprived of any one thing in Nature.'[7] What he does wish to transform is the conceptual apparatus which, in the attempt to explain the nature of things, had produced logical incongruities, profound doubt about the capacity of human beings for knowledge and a relegation of God to the role of inventor of a mechanical universe that was no longer dependent on him. Another part of that conceptual apparatus that came under his critical scrutiny was Locke's account of abstract ideas, an account Berkeley deemed to be the source of 'innumerable errors and difficulties in all parts of philosophy and in all the sciences'. Briefly, Locke had maintained that an abstract idea is formed by abstracting from a number of things a common property, such as redness, which they share. Having formulated this idea of redness, it is then used to identify redness in other objects. Berkeley regarded this account as unnecessary and also impossible. It was unnecessary because recognition of redness in some things, he says, does not depend on invoking an 'abstract idea' of redness with which to make a comparison; all that is required is that an object is seen to resemble other red objects in the relevant way. But it is also impossible, Berkeley argues, that there can be abstract ideas; for words must be able to refer to some perception or idea of sense and Locke's account does not allow for this. There cannot be, for example, an abstract idea of man, because 'the idea of a man that I frame to myself, must be either of a white, or a black, or a tawny, a straight, or a crooked, a tall, or a low, or a middle-sized man' and it is impossible to *abstract* from these properties and so formulate the kind of general idea of man that Locke was positing. Berkeley admits that he can separate particular elements of an idea — 'I can consider the hand, the eye, the nose, each by itself abstracted or separated from the rest of the body' — but denies that he 'can frame a general notion by abstracting from particulars'.[8] What is at issue here is something that is of radical importance in Berkeley's philosophy, namely, the principle that meaningful discourse is possible only in respect of what can be perceived. His own account of a general word as being used to refer to a number of particulars that are relevantly alike, rather than as referring to an idea 'abstracted' from particulars, is consistent with that important principle, since the resembling particulars are perceivable ideas whereas the abstract idea seems, upon analysis, to be an impossibility.

When Berkeley comes to speak of spirits he finds it difficult to maintain consistency. Since ideas are only ideas of sense there cannot be an idea of a spirit; moreover, ideas, he says, are 'passive and inert' but spirits are active beings and cannot therefore be ideas. He continues: 'Though it must be owned at the same time that we have some *notion* of soul, spirit, and the operations of the mind such as willing, loving, hating, in as much as we know or understand the meaning of these words.'[9] Later in the *Principles* he argues that we have an indirect knowledge of spirits: 'I perceive several motions, changes, and combinations of ideas, that inform me there are certain particular agents, like myself, which accompany them and concur in their production.'[10] And just as we do not directly perceive our fellow spirits, he says, so do we not directly perceive God:

> all the difference is that, whereas some one finite and narrow assemblage of ideas denotes a particular human mind, whithersoever we direct our view, we do at all times and in all places perceive manifest tokens of the Divinity — everything we see, hear, feel, or anywise perceive by sense, being a *sign* or *effect* of the power of God.[11]

In Berkeley's system everything is dependent at all times on the will of God. It is God who 'maintains that intercourse between spirits whereby they are able to perceive the existence of each other'.[12] Nature is not distinct from God, but is simply 'the *visible series of effects or sensations* imprinted on our minds, according to certain fixed and general laws'.[13] Anticipating objections that the 'monsters, untimely births, fruits blasted in the blossom, rains falling in desert places, miseries incident to human life, and the like' generated in nature can scarcely be seen as the immediate products of God's will, Berkeley points out that the ordered and law-governed sequences of nature are necessary 'for our guidance in the affairs of Life'; that 'the very blemishes and defects of Nature are not without their use'; and that 'the mixture of pain or uneasiness which is in the world ... is indispensably necessary to our well-being'. In short, it is our failure to take the large view and to recognise the connections between all things that leads us to see some things as evil. Comprehensive-

ness of mind would enable us to recognise 'the divine traces of Wisdom and goodness that shine throughout the Economy of Nature'.[14] Berkeley closes the *Principles* with an exhortation to give God and Duty a first place in our studies.

There is a wonderful economy in Berkeley's view of reality and an appealing drawing together, in his philosophy, of the great themes of God, man and nature. He is an **empiricist** in his adherence to sense experience as the measure of meaning and reality, but when we set that empiricism in the context of his rejection of matter it is as if we have given a shake to a kaleidoscope: everything has changed, and yet it is all still there. Berkeley whisks away the ground from under our feet, and our feet as well; yet he does not, in consequence, allow us to continue merely *as if* it were all still there, but assures us that it *is* still there. This, I think, is to perform a very skilful piece of conceptual conjuring. It attempts a conflation of the concepts of 'matter' and 'idea' but the attempt is not, in the end, successful; the illusion dazzles but does not ultimately convince. This failure does not detract from the value of the details and perceptions of many of Berkeley's arguments against particular aspects of Lockean philosophy.

Even the briefest account of Berkeley's thought cannot exclude the two famous pieces of verse that enshrine his doctrine that 'to be is to be perceived'. The first is a limerick by Ronald Knox:

> There was a young man who said, 'God
> Must think it exceedingly odd
> If he finds that this tree
> Continues to be
> When there's no one about in the Quad.'

To which the second is the reply:

> Dear Sir:
> Your astonishment's odd:
> I am always about in the Quad,
> And that's why the tree

Will continue to be,
Since observed by
Yours faithfully,
God.[15]

Notes

1. Berkeley, *A treatise concerning the principles of human knowledge*, Part I, para. 6.
2. Berkeley, *The philosophical commentaries*, Notebook A, 633.
3. See *Locke* in this book, pp. 64-9.
4. Berkeley, *Principles*, Part I, para. 23.
5. Berkeley, *Commentaries*, Notebook A, 491.
6. Berkeley, *Principles*, Part I, para. 36.
7. Ibid., para. 34.
8. Ibid., Introduction, para. 10.
9. Ibid., Part I, para. 27.
10. Ibid., para. 145.
11. Ibid., para. 148.
12. Ibid., para. 147.
13. Ibid., para. 150.
14. Ibid., paras. 152-4.
15. See B. Russell, *History of Western philosophy* (Allen and Unwin, London, 1967), Ch. 16, p. 623.

See also in this book

Locke, Leibniz, Hume.

Berkeley's major writings

An essay towards a new theory of vision (1709) (Everyman Library, no. 483, Dent, London)
A treatise concerning the principles of human knowledge (1710) (Everyman Library, no. 483, Dent, London)
Three dialogues between Hylas and Philonous (1713) (Everyman Library, no. 483, Dent, London)
Berkeley's writings are collected in *The works of George Berkeley, Bishop of Cloyne*, ed. A.A. Luce and T.E. Jessop (9 vols, Thomas Nelson and Sons, London, 1948-57). A good selection of his writings is in M.R. Ayers (ed.), *Berkeley: Philosophical works* (Dent, London, 1975).

Further reading

Armstrong, D.M. *Berkeley's theory of vision* (Melbourne University Press, Melbourne, 1960
Bennett, J. *Locke , Berkeley, Hume: central themes* (Oxford University Press, Oxford, 1971)
Flage, D.E. *Meaning and notions in Berkeley's philosophy* (Croom Helm, 1986)
Ritchie, A.D. *George Berkeley: a reappraisal* (Manchester University Press, Manchester, 1967)
Thomson, J.F. 'Berkeley' in D.J. O'Connor (ed.), *A critical history of Western philosophy* (The Free Press, New York, 1964; Macmillan, London, 1985)

Tipton, I.C. *Berkeley* (Methuen, London, 1974)
Urmson, J.O. *Berkeley* (Oxford University Press, Oxford, 1982)
Warnock, G.J. *Berkeley* (Blackwell, Oxford, 1982)

Joseph Butler   1692-1752

Joseph Butler, Bishop of Durham, linked his moral philosophy to a natural theology rather than to a theology of revelation. He advocated the practice of enlightened self-love, arguing that self-love includes benevolence to others. He regarded human nature not as a mere aggregate of appetites and propensities but as a hierarchical system of related parts with conscience as its governor. This view of humankind is consistent with his theology, for he maintained that what religion teaches us is consonant with the natural government bestowed on us by 'the acknowledged dispensations of Providence'.

Butler was born at Wantage in Berkshire, the eighth child of a retired draper. Because the family was Presbyterian, Joseph attended one of the special academies that provided excellent education for the children of families who dissented from the established church. In spite of this he gravitated towards the Church of England, a move to which his family made no objection. In 1715 he was entered as a commoner at Oriel College, Oxford. After ordination he occupied several livings and in 1726 published his *Fifteen sermons*, a book embodying his moral philosophy. Subsequently he lived for several years in seclusion and was described by Archbishop Blackburne as 'buried, but not dead'. But in 1736 he was appointed Clerk of the Closet by Queen Caroline. Each evening he joined the group of scholars whose company the Queen enjoyed and she, on her deathbed, asked that he should be given preferment. He became a bishop at Bristol and then at Durham. He died in 1752 at Bath, having gone there to try to restore his failing health.

When Butler looks at human nature he finds it to consist of several elements, or 'principles', such as appetites, passions, affections and the ability to make judgements. The natural arrangement of these elements in a person is such that the superior principles are in command. When a lesser principle becomes dominant then one's essential nature is violated. Butler classified passions and appetites in general as constituting the lowest level of the hierarchy; benevolence the next level; self-love the next; and conscience the highest level. A person is called 'benevolent' if he possesses 'a habitual temper of benevolence'. Self-love proper is to be contrasted with 'supposed self-love' which gives a false idea of what will produce happiness. Self-love proper is 'reasonable self-love' that manifests a 'cool and reasonable concern' for one's own happiness rather than 'immoderate self-love' or 'overfondness for ourselves'. It operates in relation to one's particular passions and inclinations, working to obtain what will increase happiness. Butler maintains that only very rarely will doing what is right conflict with a person's *real* happiness. He says: 'Self-love, then ... does in general perfectly coincide with virtue, and leads us to one and the same course of life.' Thus, virtuous behaviour by no means requires neglect of one's own interests and pleasure. Butler writes:

> ... the temper of compassion and benevolence is itself delightful; and the indulgence of it by doing good affords new positive delight and enjoyment ... benevolence and self-love ... are so perfectly coincident that the greatest satisfactions to ourselves depend upon our having benevolence in a due degree.[1]

Self-love, when it is cool and reasoned, discovers what is in one's best interest. Conscience, which is superior to though not necessarily stronger than self-love, discerns what is right and wrong, good and bad. Butler's account of conscience is given in his Sermons 2 and 3. He remarks of it: 'Had it strength as it has right, had it power as it has

manifest authority, it would absolutely govern the world.'[2] He seems to have believed that there always is a consensus of opinions about the judgements human beings make through the exercise of conscience. And conscience, he says, 'without being consulted, without being advised with, magisterially exerts itself, and approves or condemns'.[3] It seems that conscience is a natural and God-given faculty bestowed on humanity for the purpose of affirming the everlasting principles of natural morality and for distinguishing between them and 'the false teachings of custom'. Butler writes of the authority of conscience as follows:

> Nor is it at all doubtful in the general what course of action this faculty ... approves ... It is that which all ages and all countries have made profession of in public ... it is that which the primary and fundamental laws of all civil constitutions over the face of the earth ... enforce the practice of upon mankind; namely justice, veracity, and regard to common good.[4]

Questions concerning culturally determined differences in values do not seem to have troubled Butler. We have to think of conscience simply as pronouncing to each individual, in the course of daily life, what is right or wrong, remembering that when the hierarchy of principles is functioning in its natural order then there is no conflict between conscience, benevolence and self-love. There is more than a hint of circularity in Butler's argument for acting in accordance with our nature and he provides very little justification for his analysis of human nature.

Butler's account of human nature strongly opposes that of Thomas Hobbes.[5] Hobbes had maintained that our nature is so constituted that everything we do is motivated to secure our own preservation and power: all our apparently benevolent or compassionate actions are performed in order to acquire friends, appease enemies or make ourselves secure or superior; and we cannot, Hobbes maintains, do other than act for our own preservation. Against this view Butler invokes common sense to put some searching questions. If Benevolence is to be understood as a means of furthering one's power, how, he asks, does Hobbes explain the fact that we are sometimes pleased when a person's misfortunes are alleviated by someone other than ourselves? How, too, can Hobbes explain that we sometimes prefer to be good to one person rather than another? Butler's views also differ from those of his contemporary, Anthony Ashley Cooper, Earl of Shaftesbury, who, although he maintained that humankind possesses an instinct for benevolence, did not recognise a ruling conscience in human nature. Butler felt this was an inadequate account of human nature since it allowed for no means of restraining the person who saw that happiness might be obtained through a vicious rather than a virtuous action.

Butler's best-known writing on natural theology is contained in *The analogy of religion, natural and revealed, to the constitution and course of nature* (1736). He sees nature as the result of providential design and believes that study of it can inform us not merely of what we are like but also of what we should be like. Using the observation that we undergo natural changes without being destroyed, he points out that it is perfectly possible, on an **analogy** with these natural processes, to undergo the great changes wrought by death but yet survive in an afterlife. He also argues that our experience of nature shows that some actions produce satisfaction and pleasure, some pain and displeasure. What we learn from these interactions with nature is analogous to what religion teaches concerning the punishment of the wicked and the rewarding of the virtuous. There is also an analogy between our natural capacity to form habits by disciplining ourselves and living in conformity with natural principles and the possibility of preparing in a similar manner for a life hereafter.

Butler draws further analogies between nature and revealed religion. All living creatures, he suggests, are brought into the world and nurtured by others. In the same way God governs the world by mediation and Jesus Christ is our mediator. Scripture does not explain the efficacy of this mediation but the fact that it is mysterious is not to be used as an argument against it since it is but one of many matters that lie beyond the natural reach of our faculties. There is, Butler maintains, a great deal of historical evidence to support Christianity; the whole 'is perfectly credible' and the body of positive evidence for it cannot be destroyed even though parts of it may be questioned. In the last part of the *Analogy* he offers a rather laboured defence of his analogical method. It may be objected, he says, that it is a poor thing to solve difficulties in revelation by saying that they are the same in natural religion; for what is required is that we deal with the difficulties in both. But then the epithet 'poor' could be applied to many attempts to solve life's difficulties. What he does in the analogy, he declares, is to give a direct answer to those who say that religious doctrines are incredible. For his analogy is between what is certain in ordinary experience and the doctrines of religion. It seems that if we accept the certainty of ordinary experience then there is no reason to find the tenets of religion incredible.

Butler occupies an important place in the development of moral philosophy. He is part of the move away from reliance on revealed religion towards the study of human nature and the idea of the individual conscience as a guide to moral conduct. He revised the views of his predecessors and contemporaries in order to amend what he saw as their deficiencies. His shrewd arguments against Hobbe's theory that human beings always act to secure their own preservation and pleasure have become justly famous as a refutation of that kind of view of human nature.

Notes

1. Butler, *Fifteen sermons*, Sermon 3, §8, and Sermon 1, §6.
2. Ibid., Sermon 2, §14.
3. Ibid., §8.
4. Butler, *Dissertation 2, On the nature of virtue*, §1.
5. See *Hobbes* in this book, pp. 51-7.

See also in this book

Hobbes, Kant, Mill.

Butler's major writings

Fifteen sermons preached at the Rolls chapel (1726), ed. W.R. Matthews (G. Bell and Sons, London, 1949)
The analogy of religion, natural and revealed, to the constitution and course of nature (1736)
Dissertation 2, Of the nature of virtue (1736), an appendix to the *Analogy*. (SPCK, London, 1970)
Butler's collected writings are published in 2 volumes, ed. J.H. Bernard (Macmillan, London, 1900).

Further reading

Broad, C.D. 'Butler' in *Five types of ethical theory* (Routledge and Kegan Paul, London, 1930)
Duncan-Jones, A.E. *Butler's moral philosophy* (Penguin, Harmondsworth, 1952)
Mossner, E.C. *Bishop Butler and the age of reason* (Blom, New York, 1936, and Ayer, Salem, New Hampshire, USA, 1969)

David Hume   1711-1777

Hume's philosophy has exerted a major influence on the development of western thought since the mid-eighteenth century. It is a profoundly sceptical philosophy springing from the empiricist principle that 'nothing is in the mind that was not first in the senses' and it argues compellingly against many of the claims and conclusions of the rationalist philosophers of the seventeenth century. Hume maintained that we are not justified in claiming knowledge of God, of the human soul or of absolute moral values. His aim was to examine human nature and the human understanding; for, he said, 'there is no question of importance, whose decision is not compriz'd in the science of man'.[1] His method was to deploy 'experience and observation'. In the Introduction to his *Treatise of human nature* he writes:

> And 'tho we must endeavour to render all our principles as universal as possible, by tracing up our experiments to the utmost, and explaining all effects from the simplest and fewest causes, 'tis still certain we cannot go beyond experience; and any hypothesis, that pretends to discover the ultimate original qualities of human nature, ought at first to be rejected as presumptuous and chimerical.[2]

Hume was born in Edinburgh. His father owned Ninewells, a small estate near Berwick. His mother came from a family of lawyers and was an independent and highly intelligent woman who, after her husband's death when David was two years old, dedicated herself to the education and upbringing of her family. David was urged towards the law. When he was twelve he was admitted to Edinburgh University but found, he said, that he had 'an unsurmountable aversion to everything but the pursuits of philosophy and general learning'.[3] He left the university without taking a degree but continued a life of study at home. His first, and probably his best philosophical work, the *Treatise of human nature*, was published anonymously, the first two books in 1739 and the third book in 1740. It was virtually ignored and Hume wrote of it that 'It fell deadborn from the press, without reaching such distinction as even to excite a murmur among the zealots.'[4] In 1740 an anonymous abstract of the *Treatise* appeared in print and it is now known that Hume was the author of this abstract. In succeeding years he failed to be elected to professorial chairs at Edinburgh and Glasgow. He tutored the young Marquis of Arrandale, who was found to be insane, served as secretary to General St Clair, whom he accompanied on military exploits abroad, and in 1752 accepted the post of Librarian to the Faculty of Advocates in Edinburgh. In this latter capacity he wrote his six-volume *History of England* concerning which Voltaire pronounced that: 'Mr Hume, in his *History*, is neither parliamentarian, nor royalist, nor Anglican, nor Presbyterian — he is simply judicial.'[5] In 1763 Hume went to Paris, a city where he was well loved, to be secretary to the Earl of Hertford at the embassy there. By this time he was established as a writer, not only because of the much-admired history but because of a series of books and pamphlets on philosophical, political, moral and religious subjects. Boswell described him in 1762 as 'the greatest writer in BRITTAIN'.[6] After three years as the intellectual darling of Paris, Hume returned to England bringing Jean-Jacques Rousseau with him as a political refugee. This kindness had unhappy consequences for Rousseau was suspicious of his benefactor and misunderstanding ensued. Rousseau returned to France and in 1769 Hume returned to his native Edinburgh, had a house built in the New Town and there enjoyed philosophical reflection and the company of friends and fellow citizens. Two years of illness preceded the death in 1777 of this most genial man, whose own description of himself, given in what he called his 'funeral oration', was wholeheartedly endorsed by those who knew him. He wrote:

> I was a man of mild dispositions, of command of temper, of an open, social and cheerful humour, capable of attachment, but little susceptible of enmity, and of great moderation in all my passions. Even my love of literary fame, my ruling passion, never soured my temper, notwithstanding my frequent disappointments.[7]

In the *Treatise* Hume begins by examining the ways in which a human being perceives the world. He says that our perceptions are of two kinds: impressions, which are 'all our sensations, passions and emotions as they make their first appearance in the soul'; and ideas, which are 'the faint images of these [impressions] in thinking and reasoning'.[8] Impressions and ideas may be either simple or complex and, Hume maintains, all simple ideas are derived from simple impressions. Impressions cause ideas but ideas do not cause impressions. We have a faculty of memory which retains ideas in the order in which they occur and a faculty of imagination which is able to rearrange ideas already derived from impressions. Thus imagination might combine the ideas already derived from impressions of 'gold' and 'mountain' to form the complex idea of 'a golden mountain'. New simple ideas are derived only from impressions.

For Hume the major difference between impressions and ideas is a difference of degree of forcefulness, impressions being the more vivid of the two kinds of perceptions. This means that he had disposed of the distinction made by the rationalists between sense experience and reason and with it the rationalists' accordance of superiority to the workings of reason. Hume gives credence only to claims which can be analysed to show that they refer in the first instance to sense impressions. He therefore rejects all claims to knowledge of the existence of God, of the soul, and of substance understood as a kind of colourless something which supports qualities, because he can find no impressions of sense from which these concepts arise. He accounts for **abstract** or general ideas by in the first instance agreeing with Berkeley that ideas are always of particulars and not of abstracted generalities; he then points out that ideas that resemble one another become associated together so that one particular idea can 'stand for' a group of ideas that have become associated.

In the *Treatise* Hume enunciates an important doctrine concerning our ways of speaking about the world. He says:

> All the objects of human reason or enquiry may naturally be divided into two kinds, to wit, Relations of Ideas, and Matters of Fact. Of the first kind are the sciences of Geometry, Algebra, and Arithmetic; and in short, every affirm-

ation which is either intuitively or demonstrably certain ... Propositions of this kind are discoverable by the mere operation of thought, without dependence on what is anywhere existent in the universe ... Matters of fact, which are the second object of human reason, are not ascertained in the same manner; nor is our evidence of their truth, however great, of a like nature with the foregoing. The contrary of every matter of fact is still possible; because it can never imply a contradiction ... *That the sun will not rise tomorrow* is no less intelligible a proposition and implies no more contradiction than the affirmation, that it will rise.[9]

This doctrine is sometimes known as 'Hume's Fork'. Its import is that any meaningful proposition must either express some kind of relationship between ideas and be **necessarily** true or false in virtue of the meanings of their terms, or state a putative fact which is only **contingently** and not necessarily true or false. Propositions concerning God, the soul, and so on, already rejected since they do not derive from sense impressions, cannot be accommodated on either prong of the fork, and at the end of the *Enquiry concerning the human understanding* Hume writes:

> If we take in our hand any volume; of divinity or school metaphysics, for instance; let us ask, *Does it contain any abstract reasoning concerning quantity or number?* No. *Does it contain any experimental reasoning concerning matter of fact and existence?* No. Commit it then to the flames: for it can contain nothing but sophistry and illusion.[10]

Hume's insistence that every meaningful idea must derive from an impression of sense gave him considerable trouble when he tried to account for the maxim 'Every event has a cause.' Since the causal maxim is of supreme importance in all our practical calculations and arrangements it could not be dismissed as an illusion or chimera. Moreover, we do seem to hold that there is some necessary connection between causes and their effects. This connection, Hume argues, is not the necessary connection that obtains in the relations of ideas; nor do we acquire our ideas of causation by actually observing a kind of power, which we call cause, operating between two things which we take to be causally related. I do not, for example, receive a sense impression of some entity, 'a cause', operating between a billiard cue and a billiard ball when the former strikes the latter. All one actually observes is that a movement of the cue is followed by a movement of the ball. 'This', Hume says, 'is the whole that appears to the *outward* senses ...'. Consequently there is not in any single, particular instance of cause and effect, any thing which can suggest the idea of *power* or *necessary* connection.' [11] How, then, do we come to our idea of causality?

Hume's answer is that we are continually observing pairs of events, such as flames producing heat, and because of this the one of a pair puts us in mind of the other: we come to expect heat when we see flames. In the end we come to say that a flame *must* produce heat and we call the flame the cause of the heat. It is therefore, according to Hume, a habit of mind developed through our experience of things that gives us our idea of cause and effect. 'Every event has a cause' is thus safely classified as a proposition concerning a matter of fact: it derives ultimately from experience and observation. The necessity we impute to the effect in succeeding the cause is not part of the way things are in the world but, rather, is in us and is a result of our minds operating in the ways they do operate. All we observe are constant conjunctions of certain events and there is no guarantee that such conjunctions will continue. Having been burned by flames we come to believe that fire will burn us in the future. This belief, like all beliefs, is the result of the operation of natural instincts rather than a process of reasoning. What

Hume has offered, using his method of observation, is a description of the way in which beliefs arise.

Hume is equally ruthless in applying his method to the concept of the self. He considers the view held by 'some philosophers' that 'we are at every moment intimately conscious of what we call our *self* and, opposing it, maintains that we do not have an idea of self; for, he says:

> It must be some one impression, that gives rise to every real idea. But self or person is not any one impression, but that to which our several impressions and ideas are supposed to have a reference. If any impression gives rise to the idea of self, that impression must continue invariably the same, thro' the whole course of our lives; since self is suppos'd to exist after that manner. But there is no impression constant and invariable. Pain and pleasure, grief and joy, passions and sensations succeed each other, and never all exist at the same time. It cannot, therefore, be from any of these impressions, or from any other, that the idea of self is deriv'd; and consequently there is no such idea.[12]

He concludes that what we call the self is simply a 'bundle of perceptions' and says that

> when I enter most intimately into what I call *myself*, I always stumble on some particular perception or other ... I can never catch *myself* at any time without a perception ... If anyone upon serious and unprejudic'd reflection, thinks he has a different notion of *himself*, I must confess I can no longer reason with him. He may perhaps, perceive something simple and continu'd, which he calls *himself*; tho' I am certain there is no such principle in me.[13]

In an appendix to the *Treatise* Hume returns to the question of the self, confessing that he finds his earlier account very defective. What he finds he is unable to explain is how perceptions, each of which is distinct and separate from all others, become connected to each other to constitute a 'bundle'. 'This difficulty', he bluntly declares, 'is too hard for my understanding.'[14]

When Hume turns his attention to morality he uses exactly the same observational method of enquiry as he uses for all other topics, although this involves introducing a refinement to his doctrine of impressions. This refinement is the positing of 'impressions of reflection', that is, of impressions received by reflection on our own inward states, of anger, say, or happiness, from which we then derive ideas of anger and happiness. The difficulty for Hume in giving an account of morality and moral judgements is that of saying what particular perceptions could possibly produce our impressions and thence our ideas of virtue and vice, good and evil, and so on; for we do not perceive virtue and vice as such and even if we then say that we perceive particular acts of virtue or vice there remains the difficulty of indicating the actual vice or virtue in the particular act. In a famous passage in the *Treatise* he writes:

> Take any action allow'd to be vicious; Wilful murder, for instance. Examine it in all lights, and see if you can find that matter of fact, or real existence, which you call *vice*. In whichever way you take it, you find only certain passions, motives, volitions and thoughts. There is no other matter of fact in the case. The vice entirely escapes you, as long as you consider the object.[15]

Hume resolves the difficulty of perceiving virtue and vice by resort once again to natural human propensities. Vice, he argues, cannot be found 'till you turn your reflexion into your own breast, and find a sentiment of disapprobation, which arises in you, towards this action. Here is a matter of fact; but ... it lies in yourself, not in the object.'[16] Vice, virtue and other moral qualities are dependent on our natural reactions. They are 'impressions of reflection', generated by reflecting on our own feelings. Hume has at once accounted for any disagreement between our moral judgements and demolished the rationalists' conception of the existence of eternal moral values accessible through the use of reason. For him, morality is a matter of feeling rather than reason.

Hume's analysis of the causal connection as a regular conjunction of events rather than as a necessary connection between a cause and its effect has implications for his views on free will. In the *Enquiry concerning human understanding* he maintains that although verbally we lay claim to freedom from causal necessity in our actions, in practice we acknowledge that we expect to find causal regularities in the behaviour of our fellow beings as much as we expect them in nature and in all physical events. Just as we expect the production of a flame from the striking of a match so do we expect certain actions to follow from certain motives. His explanation of why we will not acknowledge this in words even though we tacitly recognise it in practice is that we tend to think, when we observe things outside ourselves, that we see a necessary connection between conjoined events; yet when we reflect on our own conduct we have no sense of a similarly binding connection between our motives and our actions. And so we say our actions are exempt from these connections because we do not *feel* a link between them. But in fact, Hume says, it is the same for everything and everyone: the regularity we observe in matters outside ourselves applies to ourselves as well. At the same time, the connection is not one of necessity. It is simply that there is a regular or constant conjunction between certain events and a tendency in our own minds to make an inference from one event to another to which it is regularly conjoined. This is what 'necessary connection' amounts to, and human liberty does not consist in exemption from such 'necessity' but in being free to do what we want to do: we are free when we are not restrained from doing what

we want to and when we are not compelled to do something we do not want. Liberty is not opposed to necessity but to constraint. This view of human freedom, which Hume shared with Thomas Hobbes and which has powerfully influenced many subsequent discussions in the free will debate, is often known as 'soft determinism' or 'compatibilism'. By defining freedom as freedom to do what one wants rather than as exemption from causality it makes a belief in causal determinism compatible with a belief in human freedom.

Hume's philosophy is one of naturalism as well as scepticism: he gives an account of human *nature*, and in doing so argues that the beliefs formed by the propensities of our human nature are not able to be justified by reason. Yet he has used his own reasoning powers to come to this conclusion and towards the end of Book I of the *Treatise* he confronts the dilemma he has produced in using reason to confound reason. If he rejects all 'refin'd or elaborate reasoning' then that is to 'cut off entirely all science and philosophy'. But if, in accordance with 'parity of reason', he gives due consideration to everything, then he is guilty of contradiction, for that is to acknowledge and deploy parity and thereby the very reason that is in question. 'I am', he says, 'confounded with all these questions, and begin to fancy myself in the most deplorable condition imaginable.' Reflecting on this impasse and, indeed, reasoning about it, he concludes that 'since reason is incapable of dispelling these clouds, nature herself suffices to that purpose and cures me of this philosophical melancholy ... I dine, I play a game of backgammon, I converse, and am merry with my friends'.[17] The dilemma he describes and the revelations concerning his despondency are perhaps meant to make vivid something about human beings that Hume has already asserted; namely, that 'Nature, by an absolute and uncontrollable necessity has determined us to judge as well as to breathe and feel.'[18]

Notes

1. David Hume, *Treatise of human nature*, Introduction.
2. Ibid.
3. David Hume, *My own life*.
4. Ibid.
5. Voltaire, *Oeuvres complètes* (52 vols, Paris, 1883-7), vol XXV, pp. 169-73.
6. See David Hume, *Treatise of human nature*, ed. E. Moosner (Penguin, Harmondsworth, 1969), Editor's Introduction, p. 24.
7. Hume, *My own life*.
8. Hume, *Treatise*, Book I, section I.
9. Ibid., Appendix B.
10. Hume, *An enquiry concerning human understanding*, XII, iii.
11. Ibid., VII, i.
12. Hume, *Treatise*, Book I, section VI.
13. Ibid.
14. Hume, *Treatise*, Book III, Appendix.
15. Hume, *Treatise*, Book III, Section I.
16. Ibid.
17. Ibid., Book I, section VII.
18. Ibid.

See also in this book

Hobbes, Locke, Berkeley.

Hume's major writings

A treatise of human nature, Books I and II (1739) and Book III (1740), ed. L.A. Selby-Bigge, revised P.H. Nidditch (Oxford University Press, Oxford, 1902, 1975, 1978)
An abstract of a treatise of human nature (1740), ed. J.M. Keynes and P. Sraffa (Cambridge University Press, Cambridge, 1938)
An enquiry concerning human understanding (1748) and *An enquiry concerning the principles of morals* (1751), ed. L.A. Selby-Bigge, revised P.H. Nidditch (Oxford University Press, Oxford, 1902, 1975, 1978)
Four dissertations (1757): *Natural history of religion, Of the passions, Of tragedy, Of the standard of taste* in *The philosophy works of Hume*, ed T.H. Green and T.H. Grose (Longmans, Green, London, 1895)
Autobiography: My own life (1777), printed as appendix A in E.C. Mossner, *The life of David Hume*, 2nd edn (2 vols, Oxford University Press, Oxford, 1980)

Further reading

MacNabb, D.G.C. *David Hume* (Hutchinson, London, 1951)
Mossner, E.C. *The life of David Hume*, 2nd edn (2 vols, Oxford University Press, Oxford, 1980)
Passmore, J. *Hume's intentions* (Duckworth, England, 1980)
Smith, N. Kemp *The philosophy of David Hume: a critical study of its origins and central doctrines* (Macmillan, London, 1941)
Stroud, B. *Hume* (Routledge and Kegan Paul, London, 1977)

Jean-Jacques Rousseau
1712-1778

One of the most quoted remarks in the whole of political philosophy is the sentence with which Rousseau opens Chapter 1 of *The social contract*: 'Man is born free and everywhere he is in chains.' The chains he refers to are not those of a particular despotic rule but of legitimate government in general and his chief concern is to discover a justification for submitting to this kind of bondage. Rousseau is popularly thought to be the champion of an attitude that saw virtue in natural things and 'the noble savage' as the ideal human being, but his mature thought rejected much of this view, recognised the benefits and advantages of civil society and considered its 'chains' justified so long as it enacted what the general will of the people decreed was for their real good. Freedom was supremely important to him and his whole theory was designed to secure it for everyone; not, however, in the form of a removal of all constraints but as a positive freedom to participate in the activity of legislating for the common good. For Rousseau it is law rather than anarchy that sets people free. In *The social contract* he investigates the principles underlying this freedom, examining 'men as they are' and 'laws as they can be'. He seeks to elucidate a form of political association which, he writes, 'will defend and protect with the whole common force the person and goods of each associate, and in which each, while uniting himself with all, may still obey himself alone, and remain as free as before'.[1]

Rousseau was born at Geneva. His upbringing and education were unconventional. His mother died when he was a few days old and his father's care of him was somewhat erratic. In 1728 he left Geneva and thereafter travelled and studied, tried his hand at tutoring and working on a new method of musicial notation and met a number of interesting and influential people. He was, though only briefly, (because of a quarrel) secretary to the French Ambassador at Venice. The publication of his writings began in 1750 when he was awarded a prize by the Academy of Dijon for an essay on 'Whether the restoration of the Sciences and the Arts has had a purifying effect on morals', a work now known as his first *Discourse*. In 1755 he published a second, much longer work, the *Discourse on the origin of inequality*, again in response to a question set by the Academy of Dijon. His work reached a high peak in 1762 when *Emile*, his treatise on education, and then *The social contract* were published. *Emile* was condemned by the Paris Parlement and Rousseau fled to Neuchatel to live under the protection of the King of Prussia. In 1765 the Scottish philosopher, David Hume, invited Rousseau to England but the two quarrelled, largely because Rousseau became irrationally convinced that Hume wished to humiliate and vilify him. He returned to France in 1767 and for three years moved from place to place, eventually settling in Paris in 1770. He moved in 1778 to the estate of the Marquis de Girardin at Ermenonville but died there within two months of the move. In the last few years of his life he wrote about his personal and emotional life: some dialogues, an unfinished reverie, and the famous *Confessions*, published post-humously, which describe the first 53 years of his life.

In *The social contract* Rousseau suggests that the structure of society in general is that of the family writ large. The ruler of a society is like the father of a family and people yield up their freedom to the ruler as children yield it to a father, in order to preserve their safety. Might, he says, does not create right. We obey only legitimate might. The contract that is made between ruler and people is a just one in that it entails reciprocal rights and obligations. Moreover, in Rousseau's scheme of things, it is citizens in association who constitute the sovereign ruler and who therefore determine legislation. His social contract works only if every individual gives up all rights. He says 'Each of us contributes to the group his person and the powers which he wields as a person, and we receive into the body politic each individual as forming an indivisible part of the whole.'[2] Individuals together become a collective moral body, a kind of dispersed self which, in its wholeness, is the sovereign power. The sovereign is a moral concept, a rational abstraction which is the basis of the equality and freedom of the people it comprises. It transforms natural liberty into civil liberty and is that through which a moral will can be expressed. The social contract, too, is an abstraction: it is a concept that describes the kind of association that obtains in a state or civil society rather than any specific agreement drawn up at some particular time and place.

Rousseau distinguishes between what he calls 'the will of all' which is the totality of individual self-interested wishes and the General Will, which is arrived at only when each citizen reflects on what will produce the good of all. The General Will must be general not only in its origins but also in its application: 'What makes the will general is not the number of citizens concerned but the common interest by which they are united ... the sovereign knows only the nation as a whole.'[3] Rousseau maintains that the General Will is always right. This is not to say that the actual deliberations of the people are always right but that when every citizen is adequately informed and deliberates rationally for the general good then the conclusions arrived at will be right. More-over, the enactment of the General Will is a culmination and fulfilment of freedom, for the initial contract that establishes the collective sovereign person is freely entered into by its members who then put themselves under laws of their own making. As subject to the sovereign the citizen participates in the making of legislation; as an individual he or she is recipient of rights thereby allocated: 'Sovereign and subjects', Rousseau says, 'are simply the same people in different respects.' We compel ourselves to be free.

The problem of how the mass of the

people together, however well intentioned, can actually determine the General Will troubled Rousseau greatly. 'How', he asks, 'can a blind multitude, which often does not know what it wills because it rarely knows what is good for it, carry out for itself so great and difficult an enterprise as a system of legislation?'[4] His solution to the difficulty was the concept of the Legislator, someone who is neither magistrate nor sovereign but who has an intelligence that can articulate the objective good sought by the many for their society. The Legislator is completely outside the structure of the legislation he suggests. Yet he has a god-like quality that evokes the recognition in his utterances of ideals only half-sensed by most people but nevertheless sought by them. This curious concept in Rousseau's system has provoked much discussion. In particular he has been accused, in introducing the idea of Legislator, of producing a political theory that in the last analysis invites despotism. It is as if he suddenly loses faith in the unaided natural goodness of humanity and has to find some force to send it in the right direction. In a similar vein, towards the end of *The social contract*, he introduces the idea of a profession of allegiance to the state to which every citizen would be bound for life. This, too, has shocked liberal-minded readers. Others have regarded him as a champion of revolution, largely because of the tone of his earlier writings in which he rails against the decadence of the culture around him and the way in which, to his mind, it has corrupted human nature. Certainly, by 1791, thirteen years after his death and two years after the beginning of the French Revolution, his name was on many lips in France and his ideas on egalitarianism and the General Will were common parlance.

In *Emile*, the treatise on education, Rousseau considers the development of a child growing up in the country and tries to analyse the principles underlying a natural process of maturing from infancy to adulthood. He affirms his belief in a natural human goodness, albeit one that is vulnerable to vice and error, and advocates a quiet and gentle nurturing that is related to the needs of each stage of a child's development and that is especially sympathetic to the thought that 'Nature wants children to be children before being men.' As the child matures, relationships with others begin to be more important; moral and political awareness follows and eventually the individual becomes a fully social human being who is well able, if his education has spared him unnatural stimulations and tensions, to exercise his natural powers to the full within a community of rational beings.

Rousseau's writing has an intense and personal quality that compellingly transmits his vision of a society in which each person is able to be fulfilled, happy and free. His views have been widely influential, in part because of their vitality and passion but also because they focus on issues of freedom and human relationships that are of perennial interest as well as being difficult — perhaps impossible — to resolve. He traced the inspiration for all his ideas to the thoughts that flooded overwhelmingly into his mind when he contemplated the question set by the Dijon Academy about the influence of the arts and sciences on morals. In a letter to Malesherbes, written in 1762, he described how he sat beneath a tree, weeping over those thoughts. He wrote: 'All that I have been able to retain of those swarms of great truths that enlightened me under that tree have been scattered quite feebly in my main works ...'[5]

Notes

1. Rousseau, *The social contract*, Book I, Ch. 6.
2. Ibid.
3. Ibid., Book II, Ch. 4.
4. Ibid., Ch. 6.
5. Rousseau, *Second letter to Malesherbes*, 1762.

See also in this book

Hobbes, Locke, Hume, Kant.

Rousseau's major writings

A discourse on the arts and sciences (1750)
A discourse on the origin of inequality (1755)
A discourse of political economy (1755)
The social contract (1762)
The above works are translated by G.D.H. Cole in *The social contract and discourses*, revised and augmented by J.H. Brumfitt and John C. Hall (Everyman Library, Dent, London, 1973).
Emile (1762), trans. B. Foxley (Dent, London, 1974)
Confessions (1781), trans. J.M. Cohen (Penguin, Harmondsworth, 1971) Rousseau's collected works in French are in *Oeuvres complètes de Jean-Jacques Rousseau*, eds. B.G. Pléiade and M. Raymond (Paris, 1959-71), English translations of the political writings and in *Political writings*, ed. C.A. Vaughan (2 vols, Cambridge University Press, Cambridge, 1915).

Further reading

Broome, J.H. *Rousseau: a study of his thought* (Edward Arnold, London, 1963)
Masters, R.D. *The political philosophy of Rousseau* (Oxford University Press, Oxford, 1968)

Immanuel Kant   1724-1804

Kant ranks with Plato and Aristotle as one of the most important philosophers in Western culture. His work is highly original and very wide-ranging. It was produced at a crucial time in the development of philosophy when there was tension between the continental allegiance to rational thought and the British espousal of sense experience. Kant attempted a synthesis of these two themes and thereby changed the course of philosophy. He recognised the strength of the **empiricist** claim that sense experience is the source of all our beliefs but could not accept its **sceptical** conclusion that those beliefs cannot be justified. At the same time he rejected the **rationalist** claim that factual truths about what does and does not exist can be conclusively established by the use of reason alone. Accordingly, he saw his task as that of finding out whether it is possible to have **metaphysical** knowledge, that is, knowledge of such matters as the existence of God, the immortality of the soul and whether human beings have free will. The task was undertaken in his *Critique of pure reason*, published in 1781. The *Critique* was immediately recognised as a work of major importance but because of Kant's cumbrous style and his use of numerous technical terms it proved difficult to translate from the German. As a result its influence spread only slowly. In spite of this Kant's greatness has duly received full acknowledgement. His large output deals with the philosophy of religion, morality, art, history and science, as well as with the **epistemology** and metaphysics treated in the *Critique*.

Kant was the son of a saddler of Konigsberg in East Prussia, a town now part of the Soviet Union and renamed Kaliningrad. He attended his local high school and then the University of Konigsberg. After graduating he became a private tutor to Prussian families but continued his own studies and in 1755 took a master's degree at Konigsberg, thereafter lecturing at the university and becoming a professor of logic and metaphysics there in 1770. His writing until this time was largely concerned with the natural sciences. These works sometimes exhibit the germs of his later thought, but it was only with the publication of the *Critique of pure reason* that his originality began to manifest itself in a profoundly critical attitude to rationalist claims to knowledge of metaphysical matters. Further works followed rapidly in the wake of the first *Critique*: in 1783, the *Prolegomena to any future metaphysics*, a simplified presentation of the *Critique*'s main ideas; in 1785, the *Groundwork of the metaphysic of morals*; in 1788, the *Critique of practical reason*, a fuller version of the *Groundwork*; in 1790, the *Critique of judgement*. During these years Kant also produced his *Metaphysical foundations of natural science*. In 1793 the publication of his *Religion within the limits of reason alone* caused something of a stir. It was disapproved of by Fredrick William III who made Kant promise not to punish any further theological writings.

Kant continued writing until the time of his death. He lived a quiet and orderly life in Konigsberg, travelled very little and acquired a legendary reputation for punctu-

89

ality. On one of the rare occasions when he was late in setting out for his afternoon walk it was, we are told, because he had been reading Rousseau's book, *Emile*. He had many friends and was respected and admired by all who knew him but his social life was as regulated as his working hours and seems never to have affected the prodigious flow of his written output. It has been remarked of him that 'he came as near as anyone ever has to combining in himself the speculative originality of Plato with the encyclopaedic thoroughness of Aristotle'.[1]

Something of the power and originality of Kant's philosophy may be glimpsed by looking at his treatment of the concept of causality. It was David Hume, Kant said, who first interrupted his 'dogmatic slumber'. Hume has pointed out that the claim 'Every event has a cause' was not **necessarily** true, that is, x is the cause of y is not deducible from the concept of x; but nor is the claim derived simply and directly from sense experience, since all that sense experience acquaints us with is that y regularly follows x, not that it necessarily does so.[2] This meant that there was no justification for the broad claim that all events have causes and thus no justification for the whole Newtonian system of nature. Hume went on to analyse the necessity we impute to the causal maxim as being a product of our own mental processes working on the sense impressions received when we observe regularly conjoined events; in frequently observing regularly conjoined pairs of events the occurrence of one of a pair puts us in mind of the other, and we come then to say that one is the cause of the other and to believe that the two are necessarily connected. But Hume's psychological explanation of how the mind arrives at a belief is not a justification for the truth of what is thereby believed. Kant recognised that Hume had 'proved irrefutably' the ungroundedness of the causal principle and he saw, too, that some other propositions — for example that God exists and that the human soul is immortal — held by meta-

physicians to be necessarily true, were similarly unjustifiable. In his 'dogmatic slumber' he had not questioned the capability of reason to discover truths that went beyond experience but, wakened from that slumber, he resolved to make a critical study of the scope of human reason and to ask the question 'whether such a thing as metaphysics be even possible at all?' He described his resulting analysis as 'revolutionary' because it rested on a position that was the complete reversal of Hume's. Briefly, whereas Hume had argued that our idea of cause is derived ultimately from the sensory experience of regularly conjoined events, Kant turned the whole matter round and argued that we have to have the concept of cause in order to have any objective experience.

To deal with his question about the possibility of metaphysics Kant examines the structure of human experience. He wants to elucidate the conditions required for knowledge. He argues that knowledge is founded on subjective experiences which are produced by external entities that affect the senses. What is thus passively received becomes knowledge by being apprehended according to certain formal principles of the understanding: passive, sensory receptivity is succeeded by activity of mind. He uses an elaborate battery of terms in this analysis. The term 'objects' is used generally to refer to the external entities that affect the senses. When sensibility is thus affected he speaks of it as 'receiving representations'. These representations are comparable with Locke's 'ideas' and Hume's 'impressions'. Sensibility supplies the mind with 'intuitions' and intuitions, in Kant's terminology, are always sensory. Once supplied they may become thought by means of the activity of the understanding. In this way a subjective, sensory experience may, he says, be transformed into objective conceptual knowledge.

What actually is present to us in sense experience Kant calls 'appearances'. They are appearances because what is thus present to us is what *appears* to us in virtue of our mode of receiving what is given to sense. He distinguishes between matter and form in an appearance. Matter is what is given in sensation, but we have to think of form as being 'in the mind'. Kant maintains that the forms whereby sensations are received are Space and Time and that they are in the mind a priori, that is, independently of any sense experience. He calls them 'pure forms of intuition'. Concerning knowledge acquired through the senses he writes

> all our intuition is nothing but the representation of appearance ... the things we intuit are not in themselves what we intuit them as being, nor are their relations so constituted in themselves as they appear to us ... As appearances they cannot exist in themselves, but only in us. What objects may be in themselves and apart from all this receptivity of our sensibility, remains completely unknown to us.[3]

Here Kant is urging a distinction that is at the core of his theory of knowledge. He is saying that what we intuit in appearances are not the things as they are *in themselves* but only things as they *appear to us* in virtue of our mode of experiencing them. Things-in-themselves cannot be known 'even if we could bring our intuition to the highest degree of clearness'. They are the non-sensible causes of what we intuit. Kant calls the thing-in-itself a 'transcendental object' or 'noumenon'. By 'transcendental' he means 'at the base of all experience' and his philosophy is sometimes called 'transcendental idealism'.

Since the transcendental object is unknowable there are severe limitations on what can be said about it. Since it is that of which appearances *are* the appearances we may say that it is the source of all possible perceptual experience. But we cannot, Kant argues, think of it as something that might be knowable by means of a special kind of knowledge, different from sensory knowledge. We may think of it only negatively, as noumenal rather than phenomenal, and so as non-sensible and non-intuitable.

The account of our passive receiving of sensible intuitions describes the first of three main stages that together produce knowledge. Kant summarises the stages as follows:

> What must first be given — with a view to the *a priori* knowledge of all objects — is the *manifold* of pure intuition; the second factor involved is the *synthesis* of this manifold by means of the imagination. But even this does not yet yield knowledge. The concepts which give *unity* to this pure synthesis ... furnish the third requisite for the knowledge of an object; and they rest on the understanding.[4]

The second stage in acquiring knowledge, 'the synthesis of the manifold', involves activity in contrast with the passive receiving of intuitions of the first stage. The synthesis unites the various elements of a representation so that they can be brought under a concept, as when one recognises something, for instance, as a table. The concepts applied in this synthesis are concepts derived from experience but, Kant says, their application 'does not yet yield knowledge'. For knowledge we need *pure* concepts of understanding; that is, formal principles not derived from experience, but in the mind **a priori**. He calls the understanding 'the faculty of judgements'. Its pure concepts are *forms* of judgements that may be made concerning the concepts derived from experience. To become knowledge our concepts of experience must be judged in accordance with one or other of the forms of judgement produced by the pure concepts of understanding. By this means, subjective experiences may be transformed into objective knowledge.

One such form of judgement, or principle, is: 'Every event has a cause.' Thus any judgement that something is the case must, if it is to count as knowledge, allow that the event judged must have a cause. By applying the causal principle what might have had only the status of a mass of subjective impressions is able to count as a possible experience for others and so as objective experience for the person who has the impressions. The principle confers objectivity by enabling an event to be 'placed' in a succession of events in time, with the cause necessarily preceding the event it produces. The event is a possible experience for others because it is subsumed under a necessary and universal law. Kant insists that the pure concepts of understanding, one of which is the concept of causality, are useless unless exemplified in experience. Thus the causal maxim is to be seen as part of the structure of all human minds, not something acquired by sensory means but as requiring what Kant describes as 'application in experience'. We are justified in using the causal maxim because it is one of the universal conditions that make objective experience of the world of appearances possible, just as space and time are other such conditions, for us, of a single common world.

In propounding a case for humankind's being predisposed to experience the world in a particular way Kant effects an important change in a doctrine that had been relied upon in one way or another by many **rationalists** and **empiricists**. This is the doctrine, already mentioned in connection with Hume's analysis of the causal maxim, that any true proposition is either a truth of reason, **necessarily** true in that its negation produces a contradiction but empty in that it tells us nothing about the world, or a truth of fact, established by observation but only **contingently** true. Hume had managed to accommodate the causal maxim in the class of matters-of-fact propositions and had dismissed metaphysical propositions, which fell into neither class, as 'sophistry and illusion', but Kant regarded Hume's strategy as inadequate since it left the causal principle without any justification. His own account establishes a third class of propositions, one whose propositions, like those stating matters of fact, tell us something about the world and are **synthetic** rather than **analytic** but which are also necessary in that they have an *a*

priori element, that is, an element that is not derived from sense perception. Kant calls these 'synthetic *a priori* propositions'. 'Every event has a cause' is one of them; it is synthetic because its truth is not established by analysis of its terms, and it is *a priori* and necessary because the concept of causality is a pure concept of understanding that is part of our intellectual structure, and is a prior and necessary condition of our experiencing the world as we do experience it. Kant argues that we *can* have knowledge of causality in the world of appearances, for the pure concept of causality is exemplified for us in the observable phenomena of that world and our judgements made in accordance with it are universally valid. What we cannot have knowledge of are things-in-themselves, the noumenal aspects of phenomena. Nor can we know the truth of metaphysical propositions such as 'God exists' or 'Humans have immortal souls' because concepts such as 'God' and 'soul' are not exemplified in sense experience. Kant calls such concepts Ideas of Reason. Such concepts, he says, may be thought; they are useful, inspiring and profoundly important. But they cannot be objects of knowledge for we can only know what can be an object of possible experience. In drawing these conclusions Kant overcomes Hume's **scepticism** concerning knowledge of the world of nature but endorses his scepticism concerning **metaphysical** propositions.

The denial of metaphysical knowledge has the great merit that it 'leaves room for faith' in morals and religion. When Kant deals with moral philosophy, in the *Groundwork of the metaphysic of morals* and the *Critique of practical reason* it is moral conviction rather than any kind of speculative metaphysics that he uses as a foundation. He sees freedom as the condition that makes morality possible, but against this has to set the consideration that the causality in nature that he has already established implies a physical determinism that is universal in the world of phenomena. It is therefore arguable that if our actions are regarded as natural occurrences, as much subject to causality as all other parts of nature, then human beings can scarcely be regarded as free and hence morally responsible for their deeds. Kant resolves this difficulty by recourse to the notion of Reason, 'a faculty by which man distinguishes himself from all other things, even from himself so far as he is affected by objects', and by reference again to the noumenal, or things-in-themselves. He argues that when we exercise reason in directing our wills we may think of ourselves not simply as parts of nature but also as under quite different laws, formulated by reason. Freedom is an Idea of Reason and as such is not knowable in the way that concepts of understanding are knowable; but one may, Kant says, consider the will not only as causality of oneself regarded as a phenomenal self, but also as a kind of causality of one's noumenal self. The noumenal self can be conceived of only negatively: as not intuitable in space and time, as unknowable, and as not subject to causal necessity. This does not mean that, as phenomenal beings, we are ever exempt from causal necessity. The sequences of nature proceed, and must proceed, according to natural causality but the same series of events looked at from a different viewpoint may be thought of as the result of the causality of the noumenal self. However, we cannot ever know when, or if, it is reason rather than natural causality that determines an action.

If we dismantle the structure with which Kant supports his moral theory we can see how close his thought lies to our everyday moral convictions and assumptions. That we acknowledge a natural causality but at the same time think, but do not know, that freedom is somehow possible, is borne out by our everyday practices. For any action that I claim to have chosen freely there is always an explanation in terms of a natural causality of the movements that accomplish it and no account of the action that ignores the possibility of an explanation in terms of natural

causality is objectively acceptable. At the same time the action itself is understood by reference to the intentions relating to it; that is, it is explicable by reference to *reasons*. We think of the action as being performed because of certain reasons although we do not deny that the movements required by it are in accordance with natural causality.

Kant's influence on philosophy has been immeasurable. The penetration of his intellect and the grandeur and comprehensiveness of his thinking are apparent in all his writing, revealing themselves in spite of what has so often been pronounced the most turgid and clumsy prose imaginable. Part of the power and, indeed, the fascination of his philosophy is that within its monumental and labyrinthine edifice are housed the whole range of our common sensibilities, convictions and aspirations; each having within the total structure a position that admirably displays its significance and qualities in relation to everything else. And as in the philosophy, so in the person. For the well-ordered and carefully regulated structure of the life of this man, whose punctuality was so precise that the citizens of Konigsberg could set their clocks by his afternoon walk, seems to have housed a most radiant personality. His pupil Johann Herder wrote:

I have had the good fortune to know a philosopher ... In his prime he had the happy sprightliness of a youth; he continued to have it, I believe, even as a very old man. His broad forehead, built for thinking, was the seat of an imperturbable cheerfulness and joy. Speech, the richest in thought, flowed from his lips. Playfulness, wit, and humour were at his command ... He was indifferent to nothing worth knowing. No cabal, no sect, no prejudice, no desire for fame could ever tempt him in the slightest away from broadening and illuminating the truth. He incited and gently forced others to think for themselves; despotism was foreign to his mind. This man, whom I

93

name with the greatest gratitude and respect, was Immanuel Kant.

Notes

1. A.M. Quinton, 'Kant' in John Van Doren, ed., *The great ideas today 1977* (Encyclopaedia Britannica Inc., Chicago, 1977) p. 228.
2. See *Hume* in this book, pp. 81-6.
3. Kant, *Critique of pure reason*, A 42, B 59.
4. Kant, *Critique*, A 78-9, B 104.

See also in this book

Locke, Hume, Schopenhauer.

Kant's major writings

Critique of pure reason (1781), trans. N. Kemp Smith (Macmillan, London, 1929; corrected, 1933)
Prolegomena to any future metaphysics that will be able to present itself as a science (1783) (Bobbs-Merrill, Indianapolis and New York, 1950)
Groundwork of the metaphysic of morals (1785), trans. H.J. Paton (Harper and Row, New York, 1964)
Critique of practical reason (1788), trans. L. Beck (University of Chicago Press, Chicago, 1949)
Critique of Judgement (1790), trans. J.C. Meredith (Clarendon Press, Oxford, 1952)
The standard edition of Kant's works in German is *Sämtliche Werke*, ed. Preussische Akademie der Wissenschaften (22 vols, Berlin, 1902-55)

Further reading

Bennett, J. *Kant's analytic* (Cambridge University Press, Cambridge, 1966)
Korner, S. *Kant* (Penguin, Harmondsworth, 1955)
Paton, H.J. *The categorical imperative: a study in Kant's moral philosophy* (Hutchinson, London and New York, 1947)
Smith, N. Kemp *A commentary to Kant's Critique of pure reason* (Macmillan, London, 1923)
Strawson, P. *The bounds of sense* (Methuen, London, 1966)
Walsh. W.H. *Kant's criticism of metaphysics* (University of Edinburgh Press, Edinburgh, 1975)

Jeremy Bentham   1748-1832

Jeremy Bentham propounded a moral doctrine based on the Principle of Utility. The doctrine derives from the phrase 'the greatest happiness of the greatest number' which Bentham found in a pamphlet written by Joseph Priestley, concerning whom he wrote: 'Priestley was the first (unless it was Beccaria) who taught my lips to pronounce this sacred truth ... that the greatest happiness of the greatest number is the foundation of morals and legislation.' He devoted much of his life to the work of reforming jurisprudence and legislation in accordance with this principle of producing the greatest happiness for the greatest number. His best-known philosophical work is the *Introduction to the principles of morals and legislation* published in 1789. His written output was enormous, but much of it was produced by him in manuscript or draft form to be worked over and completed by others and writers on Bentham have had difficulty in distinguishing the fully authentic matter from that which has undergone significant editorial change. Bentham worked closely with James Mill, father of John Stuart Mill, on political and social issues and exerted a powerful influence on John Stuart Mill's education and development. As a part of his utilitarian doctrine he propounded a 'felicific calculus' intended to calculate the quantity of happiness likely to result from actions.

Bentham was born in London and was educated at Westminster School and Queen's College, Oxford. In 1763, when he was 15, he entered Lincoln's Inn and was called to the bar in 1768. Three years later he published anonymously his *Fragment on government*, a critical examination of Blackstone's *Commentaries on the laws of England.* He visited his brother in Russia from 1785 to 1788 and published the *Introduction to the principles of morals and legislation* on his return, having spent long periods of time working on it in a remote part of Russia. Thereafter the range of his interests and activities expanded rapidly. Revolutionary events in France absorbed much of his attention and he became involved in a great many social and political activities. He planned a model prison, known as the Panopticon, and worked for many years to gain its acceptance and realisation, but without success. Meanwhile his legal reputation was becoming established on the continent through the work of a Frenchman, Dumont, who had compiled and edited many of his papers to produce the *Traités de législation civile et pénale*.

The friendship with the Mill family began in 1808 and thereafter the two households were regularly amalgamated for several months each year. During these later years Bentham was preparing an enormous work, his *Constitutional code*, and writing many pamphlets advocating law reform and criticising bad legislation. He died on 6 June 1832. After his death his close friends and followers, a number of whom attended the ceremonial dissection of his body in Webb Street, formed themselves into a Benthamite party within the House of Commons. Edwin Chadwick, who was living in Bentham's house at the time of his death where the two, it is reported, were 'surrounded by 70,000 sheets of manuscript on the theory of law and all conceivably related subjects', dedicated himself to working across the whole gamut of Bentham's reforming ideas. Thus a host of friends and followers made this great and indefatigable innovator's work important, among them John Stuart Mill, who developed Bentham's rather crude exposition of utiliarianism into an influential and widely subscribed-to ethical doctrine.

On first acquaintance it is perhaps surprising to find that the Principle of Utility is in fact to do with happiness, and with happiness regarded as the supreme moral value. Bentham had adopted the term from Hume but he eventually came to feel that it was unfortunately chosen and said, 'the word "utility" does not so clearly point to the ideas of *pleasure* and *pain* as the words *happiness* and *felicity* do'.[1] In the *Fragment on government*, his first published work, he maintained that all actions tend to aim at producing happiness 'and this *tendency* in any act we style its *utility*'; but later, in the 1820s, he made it clear that he preferred the utilitarian principle to be called 'the Greatest Happiness Principle' and added footnotes to this effect in new editions of his earlier works.

The two terms link together informatively once it is realised that Bentham's 'utility', or usefulness, is a usefulness for producing happiness.

The principle became the foundation of all Bentham's work of legislative reform and the tool he used to criticise all social institutions and practices. For him it was to be the shaping force for resolving large issues in society. Later, in the hands of John Stuart Mill, it was explored and developed as a principle of personal and individual morality.

The fullest account of Bentham's utilitarianism is in *An introduction to the principles of morals and legislation*. Central to it is, first, a psychological theory asserting that human behaviour is governed by pain and pleasure and that each person acts to secure his or her own good; second, a moral theory that asserts that happiness, or pleasure, is the supreme good for humanity and that the greatest happiness of the greatest number is the end of right action. Since, according to Bentham, each person is psychologically disposed to seek his or her own happiness, but morality requires that one acts to bring about the greatest good for everyone, his task is to show how legislation can effect a coincidence of individual and societal interests; he has to present a system 'the object of which is to rear the fabric of felicity by the hands of reason and law'.[2] The legislator must therefore be able to gauge the relative values of pleasures and pains in order to impose sanctions in accordance with what Bentham calls the Duty-and-Interest-Juncture-Producing-Principle. Punishment, he maintains, is 'primarily mischievous'; it has utility only if it serves to minimise pain and increase pleasure. To calculate amounts of pain and pleasure Bentham identifies seven properties that he believed were quantifiable: intensity, duration, certainty, propinquity, fecundity, purity and extent. He also distinguishes different kinds of pleasures and pains and points out that in estimating their quantities in particular cases it is necessary to take into account the fact that people vary enormously in their individual capacities and predilections. This is the basis of the 'felicific calculus', probably the most stringently criticised element of Bentham's utilitarianism. The doctrine was strongly disapproved of for other reasons as well, chief among them its uncompromising secularity. It made no appeal to religious authority or revelation in the formulation of its happiness principle, nor did it invoke religious motives for actions. Bentham believed that his principle accorded with reason and that moral mistakes arose simply from mistakes in calculation. Moreover, he held that from the legislative point of view 'quantity of pleasure being equal, push-pin is as good as poetry', a remark that engendered heated debate when John Stuart Mill produced his own version of utilitarianism and tried to transpose the doctrine from the public to the personal domain.[3]

Bentham was thoroughly detested by opponents such as Thomas Arnold, Carlyle and Macaulay. Yet the heart of his doctrine was the urgent desire to benefit all humankind; and his followers, the Benthamites, were upright and earnest men of the same persuasion. Bentham bequeathed his body for the purposes of dissection to the Webb Street School of Anatomy at a time when only the bodies of executed murderers were legally procurable for teaching purposes. The campaign for change succeeded soon after his death when the Anatomy Act made it legal for bodies to be given for dissection, thereby realising Bentham's hope that humanity 'may reap some small benefit by my disease'.

Notes

1. Bentham, *An Introduction to the principles of morals and legislation*, Ch. 1, 1.
2. Ibid. Ch. 1.
3. See J.S. Mill's essay, 'Bentham', in *Dissertations and discussions*, vol. I, and his *Utilitarianism*, Ch. 2. Both are in M. Warnock (ed.), *Utilitarianism* (Fontana, London, 1962).

See also in this book

Hume, Mill.

Bentham's major writings

Fragment on government (1776), ed. F.C. Montague (Greenwood Press, London, 1980)
Introduction to the principles of morals and legislation (1789), ed. J.H. Burns and H.L.A. Hart (Methuen, London, 1982)
Traités de législation civile et pénale (1802)
The book of fallacies (1824), ed. H.A. Larrabee (Oxford University Press, Oxford, 1952)
Bentham's writings are in *The collected works of Jeremy Bentham* (Clarendon Press, Oxford, 1983).

Further reading

Halévy, E. *The growth of philosophic radicalism* (Faber and Faber, London, 1928)
Harrison, R. *Bentham* (Routledge and Kegan Paul, London, 1985)
Plamenatz, J. *The English utilitarians* (Blackwell, Oxford, 1949)
Steintrager, J. *Bentham* (Allen and Unwin, London, 1977)
Stephen, L. *The English utilitarians*, vol. I (Duckworth, London, 1900)

Georg Wilhelm Friedrich Hegel 1770-1831

Hegel was a philosophical idealist: he believed that Mind or Spirit was the ultimate reality. He was also a philosophical monist in that he held that everything is interrelated within one vast, complex system or whole which he called the Absolute. His particular form of idealism did not entail a disbelief in the existence of material objects. At the same time he held that only the Absolute is entirely real and its seemingly distinct parts have reality only in virtue of being parts of the whole. Much of his philosophy is difficult and extremely complicated. He tries to incorporate in it and make coherent a large number of philosophical intuitions with the result that his attempts to reconcile conflicting views sometimes produce obscurities and contradictions. These difficulties reappear in the varying interpretations of his thought made by those who write about him.

Hegel was born at Stuttgart in 1770. He

was educated at the Gymnasium in Stuttgart and then at the University of Tübingen. Almost his whole life thereafter was spent in teaching and writing philosophy. He tutored at the universities of Bern and Frankfurt and in 1801 went to Jena where he finished his *Phenomenology of mind* the day before the battle of Jena. His last two professorial posts were at Nuremberg and Berlin. His philosophy reveals several important influences: the early Greeks, Spinoza, Kant, the New Testament, Fichte and Schelling. He lived through the French Revolution and was deeply sensible of the religious, social and political troubles of his times and the fragmentation of society that they were producing. It is not surprising that he saw a practical and philosophical redemption in a doctrine of mystical unity, wholeness and freedom of spirit.

The monistic idealism of Hegel's *Phenomenology of mind* commits him to the belief that there is just one thinking or mental **substance**. His theory of truth connects with this, for he held that the real is what is rational and that 'the true is the whole'. Reality and truth are the entire system in which all propositions are coherently and rationally related and in which the contradictions apparent in propositions concerning only parts of the whole are resolved. The whole is continually changing and its development takes place through a process of dialectic. The term 'dialectic' derives from a Greek word meaning 'to argue'. In Hegelian dialectic development proceeds by means of three definite stages. First, a thesis, embodying a particular view or position; second, an antithesis providing an opposing or contrary position; third, a synthesis which reconciles the two previous positions and then becomes the basis of a new thesis. The dialectic always works by rejecting what is not rational and retaining what is rational. It is an activity that increases the self-consciousness of Mind by giving all its objects of thought their proper and rationally conceived place in the whole. Hegel

maintained that the seemingly independent objects dwelt upon in thought are not really independent but are simply estranged aspects of the one Mind which must eventually be restored to wholeness. The rational dialectic *is* the process of restoration and development of self-consciousness that will eventually achieve the unity and the freedom that result from complete self-knowledge. The idea that Mind, in dwelling on apparently independent objects, is estranged from itself was later used by Karl Marx, but Marx transposed the idea into material terms using a word that is translated as 'alienation' to expound his theory that, under certain conditions, human beings become cut off and estranged from important elements in their own lives.[1]

In his *Philosophy of history* Hegel developed a theory based on the view that the State is the reality of Mind's progress towards unity with Reason. He sees the State as the embodied unity of objective freedom and subjective passion; it is the rational organisation of a liberty which is merely capricious and arbitrary if left to individual whims. He has four classifications for the members of a State: the citizen, who is passive under the laws of the state and has no awareness of personal or civil liberty; the person, who is aware of and active in personal liberty; the hero, whose will to personal liberty is consonant with the larger historical movements of the time and who has a sense of how to act in the political arena; and the victim, whose desires and interests are so inward and personal that they relate scarcely at all to the larger movements of life and who therefore falls victim to anything in the great tide of events that happens to run counter to his personal concerns. Hegel maintains that Mind, as it moves inexorably towards ultimate wholeness and freedom, employs all these types of individuals towards the achievement of its end. There is a sense in which all individuals are victims in that all individual passions are deployed by Reason to achieve an ultimate and total self-consciousness. History is the embodiment of Mind's dialectic with the great epochs of world history serving as the theses, antitheses and syntheses in the movement towards a wholly rational condition. Hegel writes:

Reason is the Sovereign of the World ... the history of the world, therefore, presents us with a rational process. This conviction and intuition is a **hypothesis** in the domain of history as such. In that of philosophy it is no hypothesis. It is there proved by speculative cognition, that Reason — and this term may here suffice us, without investigating the relation sustained by the Universe to the Divine Being — is *Substance*, as well as *Infinite Power*; its own *infinite material* underlying all the natural and spiritual life which it originates, as also the *Infinite Form*, that which sets the Material in motion. Reason is the *substance* of the universe.[2]

Hegel maintained that philosophy, religion and art are ways of comprehending the Absolute. His theory of art, largely contained in his *Lectures on aesthetics*, is developed from ideas in Schiller's *Letters on the aesthetic education of mankind*. In the *Lectures* Hegel argued that beauty is rationality embodied in sensible form and that this embodiment occurs in symbolic, classical and romantic art. In symbolic art the deployed form symbolises by referring to or indicating a rational element that is beyond itself, as when a dove symbolises the rational conception of peace. In classical art the deployed form does not refer to what is beyond itself but instead is an adequate realisation that completely exemplifies the rational notion it embodies. Thus, a classical statue completely exemplifies the ideal human form. In romantic art, regarded by Hegel as supreme, subjective freedom becomes manifest in the work of art and the finite perfection of classicism is transcended. Romantic art is superior because it is an extension of self-consciousness and so consti-tutes a significant movement towards the restoration of the self-consciousness of Mind as a whole.

Commentators disagree in their descriptions of Hegel's religious stance. He is variously described as atheistic, **pantheistic**, theistic and panentheistic, the last being the view that all things in the universe are parts of God but that God, in virtue of being the whole that is greater than the sum of all parts of the universe, is something more than just the totality of the universe. In the *Phenomenology of mind* Hegel described what he called 'the unhappy consciousness', a state of mind in which the individual is inwardly divided, wanting partly to be independent of the physical and material aspects of life and to realise a profound spirituality, and partly to acknowledge and come to terms with what is physical and material. Hegel opposed any religious doctrine that produced this sort of division in the human soul. He believed that the superior and spiritual qualities with which people invest a remote and unattainable God are in fact as much human qualities as those generally regarded as baser, and that when human beings take the finer qualities to be separate from themselves they are manifesting just another aspect of their estrangement not only from parts of their own nature but from the Absolute or whole. This certainly seems to suggest that Hegel was some kind of pantheist since the implication of his thought is that the attributes of God are actually our own. However, as many have pointed out, Hegel was a member of the Lutheran church, regarded the doctrines of the Incarnation and the Trinity as religious manifestations of the ultimate wholeness of all things, and considered himself a staunch defender of the Christian religion. Peter Singer has suggested that Hegel saw God as an **essence** needing to manifest itself in the world and then perfect itself by perfecting the world, and although this does not resolve the difficulties about whether or not God is to be regarded as identical with the world, it is consonant, on the whole, with many themes of Hegel's thought.[3]

Hegel regarded philosophy as a higher form of comprehension than art and religion. It is higher because its comprehension of the absolute is a conceptual one and this means that it is conscious of its own method and of the methods of art and religion. Thus philosophy, he maintains, contributes very positively to the development of the self-awareness of the whole and thereby to the freedom from the conflicts and apparent contradictions of partial knowledge.

After Hegel's death in 1831 his pupils and followers split into two distinct factions. Those who became known as the Old Hegelians regarded Hegel's ideas on religion as compatible with orthodox Protestant Christianity. They concentrated on his later philosophy and propagated the political and social ideas worked out in his *Philosophy of right*, interpreting the development and condition of the Prussian state as the exemplification and culmination of the Hegelian dialectic. The influence of the Old Hegelians was powerful for a time, especially in Berlin, but had declined by the middle of the nineteenth century.

The story of the Young Hegelians is a very different one. They saw Hegel's system as a blueprint for the practical and inevitable realisation of a better human world. But they could not accept that Mind was the ultimate reality. Two Young Hegelians, David Friedrich Strauss and Ludwig Feuerbach, effected a revolutionary change at the very heart of Hegel's philosophy by arguing that it is the physical and material life of human beings that determines consciousness and thought and not, as Hegel had maintained, that mind is the source and reality of all things. It was this reversal of Hegel's main thesis that was adopted later by Karl Marx and from which Marx developed his theory of alienation.

No brief account of Hegel's philosophy can convey the scope, detail and grandeur of his ideas. Everything he wrote exemplifies as well as argues for his thesis concerning mind's ever-developing consciousness of itself. The pattern of his thinking is always triadic and dialectical, not only in the static arrangements of his categories, classifications and their subdivisions but dynamically as well, in that he sees the large movement of history as dialectical in its progress towards total self-awareness. The inflexibility of his complicated and interlocking formal structures frequently forces the heterogeneous constituents of history into inappropriate or questionable categories and generates inconsistencies and contradictions. Nevertheless, Hegel's powerful originality and his command of lofty concepts as well as infinite detail are always arresting and inspiring. His vision of an ultimate wholeness achieved through freedom, reason and knowledge makes a profound appeal to intuitions and yearnings that many people experience but that few are able to articulate or express in an intelligible way.

Notes

1. See *Marx* in this book, pp. 110-13.
2. Hegel, *Philosophy of history*, Introduction.
3. Peter Singer, *Hegel* (Oxford University Press, Oxford, 1983), p. 83.

See also in this book

Parmenides, Spinoza, Kant, Marx.

Hegel's major writings

Lectures on the philosophy of history (published posthumously), trans. J. Sibree (Dover, New York, 1956)
The phenomenology of mind (1807), trans. A.V. Miller as *Hegel's phenomenology of spirit* (Oxford University Press, Oxford, 1977)
The science of logic (3 vols, 1812, 1813, 1816), trans. W.H. Johnson and L.G. Struthers (2 vols, Allen and Unwin, London, 1929)
Philosophy of right (1821), trans. T.M. Knox as *Hegel's philosophy of right* (Oxford University Press, Oxford, 1967)
Lectures on aesthetics (published posthumously), trans. T.M. Knox as *Hegel's aesthetics*, (2 vols, Clarendon Press, Oxford, 1975)
The standard edition of Hegel's collected writings in German is *Werke: Vollstandige Ausgabe*, ed. H. Glockner (26 vols, Jubilee Edition, Stuttgart, 1927-40).

Further reading

Brazill, W.J. *The young Hegelians* (Yale University Press, New Haven and London, 1970)

Kaufmann, W. *Hegel: reinterpretation, texts and commentaries* (Weidenfeld and Nicolson, London, 1965)

Norman, R. *Hegel's phenomenology: a philosophical introduction* (Sussex University Press, Brighton, 1976)

Singer, P. *Hegel* (Oxford University Press, Oxford, 1983)

Taylor, C. *Hegel* (Cambridge University Press, Cambridge, 1975)

Arthur Schopenhauer
1788-1860

Schopenhauer has been called 'the philosopher with an obsession for the will'. His philosophy took its impetus from Kant, 'marvellous Kant', as he called him. He maintained that the whole phenomenal world is a manifestation of will. Will is the ungrounded ground of all things and if will is abolished then the world, too, is abolished. This is the dominant theme of all his major works.

Schopenhauer was born in Danzig on 22 February 1788. The family moved to Hamburg in 1793 and he was educated with a view to entering the commercial world, following in the footsteps of his prosperous father. He travelled widely in Europe, developed a tendency to 'brood over the misery of things' and embarked on his business career with reluctance. His father died suddenly in 1805 and after two more years in commerce Schopenhauer resigned his job and began to study Greek and Latin. He then enrolled as a medical student in the University of Göttingen but soon became attracted to philosophy. His doctoral thesis, *The fourfold root of the principle of sufficient reason*, was finished in 1813. His major work, *The world as will and representation*, was published in 1818. He always maintained that his philosophy was 'the real solution of the enigma of the world'. He pursued his philosophical career against the turbulent background of the Napoleonic Wars and within a personal realm that was unstable and erratic. He was brilliant, zestful, lucid and witty, but also lonely, depressive and often bitter. Yet in his last years he experienced the profound pleasure of witnessing the recognition and acclaim of his books.

Schopenhauer advised anyone wishing to understand his thought to look first and with care at his doctoral thesis, *The fourfold root of the principle of sufficient reason*. In it he argues that there are reasons or explanations for everything and that they are of four kinds: hence the description 'the fourfold root'. The four kinds of reasons together constitute the totality of the ways in which we can ordinarily know the world. Thus we have knowledge of physical changes by reference to causality; of connections between concepts by reference to the rules of reasoning, or logic; of mathematical truths by reference to what Schopenhauer describes as 'the pure sensuous intuitions of space and time'; and of ourselves as subjects who will by reference to the laws of motivation.

It is the fourth root, concerning the will, that is especially significant for the development of Schopenhauer's philosophy. His claim is that as a *knowing* subject one can know oneself as a *willing* subject, and that as knower one identifies immediately with oneself as willer. What one wills is explained by motives. Schopenhauer says: 'Without such a motive the action is to us just as inconceivable as is the movement of an inanimate body without a push or pull.'[1]

The pattern of each of the four forms of the root is that of a principle which has its source in a faculty of mind and which operates on what is present to the mind. Thus the faculty of understanding provides the principle or law of causality to explain empirical representations; reason provides the rules for the connection of concepts; sensuous intuitions of space and time the rules for mathematics; and inner self, or self-consciousness, provides the law of motivation that explains what one wills. The whole scheme presupposes a subject–object relationship between each faculty of mind and its appropriate objects. In all this there is a broad general resemblance to Kant.[2] There is a formal similarity between Schopenhauer's fourfold principle of explanation and Kant's pure principles of understanding and both philosophers maintain that the way in which we conceive of the external world is determined by the structures of the human understanding. They are also alike in describing what is present to the mind as 'representations', that is, ideas or mental images. The German word *Vorstellung* is used by both of them and is sometimes translated as 'idea', sometimes as 'representation' in Schopenhauer's writing.

The fourth principle of the fourfold root, in relation to which self knows itself as the willing subject, gives rise to special features. Because to know oneself as willer is to identify immediately with that willing self, the ordinary subject–object relationship is transformed into something which, Schopenhauer says, is mysterious and inexplicable, the key to philosophical truth and 'the knot of the world'.[3] Moreover, the fourth part of the root relates in a special way to the first part; for the representations of the will given to inner sense have a counterpart of events in the external world, and these outer events are present to the faculty of understanding in accordance with the first root's principle of causality. Thus Schopenhauer says that 'motivation is causality seen from within' and that volitions are the inward side of our actions:

The act of will and the action of the body are not two different states objectively known, connected by the bond of causality; they do not stand in the relation of cause and effect, but are one and the same thing, though given in two entirely different ways, first, quite directly, and then in perception by the understanding. The action of the will is nothing but the act of will objectified, i.e. translated into perception.[4]

The double knowledge achieved by the inner knowledge of one's will and the objective knowledge of the actions that are its manifestation is, for Schopenhauer, the clue to complete philosophical understanding. The immediate inner knowledge of one's own will affords one a particular temporal manifestation of will not just in its outward aspects but as a thing-in-itself and it has to be recognised, he maintains, that just as one's body is the objectification of one's own will so are all other phenomena objectifications of will in general. The world as empirical representation is simply the outward face of the world as will: not, however, as a will that has perceptible reasons for its volitions but as one that is a wholly blind and irrational flux of becoming. Schopenhauer argues that whoever has understood the role of the will in the individual

> will recognise that same will not only in those phenomena that are quite similar to his own, in men and animals, but continued reflection will lead him to recognise the force that shoots and vegetates in the plant ... by which the crystal is formed ... that turns the magnet to the North Pole ... all these he will recognise as different only in phenomenon, but the same according to their inner nature.[5]

Will is thus the 'cause' of all things, the striving of each thing to manifest its own nature; and philosophical understanding consists in realising that, cosmically speaking, this is the way things are.

The distinction between the will as a thing-in-itself and the will as it appears to us in its outward aspects is a distinction that has a general application in Schopenhauer's philosophy just as it has in Kant's. It is sometimes referred to as a distinction between noumena and phenomena. Like Kant, Schopenhauer maintained that noumena, or things-in-themselves, cannot be known, but that phenomena, the appearances or representations of things that constitute ordinary experience, are knowable. He differs from

Kant in that he claims that all our particular actions are necessarily manifestations of will and that each action can be explained by a motive. However, for the will-in-itself as a totality there is no motive. It is, for Schopenhauer, absolutely original and originating. He says:

> every man is what he is through his will, and his character is original, for willing is the basis of his inner being. Through the knowledge added to it, he gets to know in the course of experience *what* he is; in other words, he becomes acquainted with his character. Therefore he *knows* himself in consequence of, and in accordance with, the nature of his will, instead of *willing* in consequence of, and according to, his knowing, as in the old view.[6]

In the light of that claim Schopenhauer is able to unfold a sense, denied by Kant, in which one can know the noumenal self. He grants that Kant was right when he said that perception can give us knowledge only of phenomena, but with one exception, 'the single exception of the knowledge everyone has of his own willing'.[7] He believed that in every act of will there is a direct transition of the will-in-itself into the phenomenal world. We *are* our wills and we live out what we are, coming to know what we are through what we do. What we do is done **necessarily** for we already are what we will. The same is true of everything in the world at different levels of consciousness: each thing is what it is in accordance with its own nature and cannot be otherwise.

The consequence of this view is that Schopenhauer did not believe in any personal freedom of the will. He held that the law of causality determines our actions which, under the first part of the fourfold root, are seen as phenomena; and that motives determine our volitions, which are the inward aspect of our actions. However, will-in-itself is not and cannot be determined by anything, for it is the originating source of our actions and of everything that happens

and we cannot therefore probe beyond it. All we can know is that we will our particular acts in consequence of what we are; but can know nothing of how we have come to be what we are. Schopenhauer regards each person and each entity in the world as a fragmentary manifestation of will-in-itself and as striving to exist in its own way, driven by its own nature. He maintains that there is one way of obtaining release from this incessant striving. This is by means of Platonic Ideas through which the individual will may be quieted and released from the treadmill of incessant striving.

The Platonic Idea, in Schopenhauer's scheme of things, differs from the thing-in-itself in virtue of being knowable, though not knowable through any of the forms of the fourfold root. Knowledge of Idea is a kind of pure objectivity, the ideal of all knowing, in which one does not know a particular thing but a universality which Schopenhauer calls 'the eternal form'. And just as knowledge of Idea is not knowledge of an individual thing, so does it require that the knower is not an individual but 'a pure subject of knowing'. To become a pure subject of knowing the will must disappear, since whatever is to be known as Idea must be contemplated without reference to anything one might will in respect of it. In this way the knower becomes one with what is known. The identification of knower and known is achieved either through aesthetic contemplation in which a person, so to speak, inhabits the contemplated object, or when one moves from knowledge of one's own will to a realisation of will in all things.

This kind of knowledge effects a quieting of the individual will. The quieting occurs when a certain state of knowledge is reached. It cannot be brought about by willing nor are one's individual character and propensities altered by it. What is quieted is the will to live so that 'the will now turns away from life; it shudders at the pleasures in which it recognises the affirmation of life. Man attains to the state of voluntary renunciation, resignation, true composure and complete will-lessness.'[8]

Suicide is not the logical consequence of the loss of the will to live, for suicide is an act of will, not of will-lessness. Schopenhauer argues that the consequence of true delivery from the will is that what has hitherto been seen as reality — the medley of desires, pleasures and pains of the phenomenal world of experience — becomes a nothingness. This is because the world of experienced representations is the objectification of the will and when the will goes then that world goes. In its place there is, Schopenhauer says, the state of being of 'those who have overcome the world, in whom the will, having reached complete self-knowledge, has found itself again in everything'.[9] He likens the state to one of 'ecstasy, rapture, illumination, union with God'. At the same time he recognises it as a nothingness since it nullifies the whole of reality as we ordinarily experience it. For those who are full of will the prospect he describes is a nothingness. And for those whose wills are quieted the everyday world is a nothingness.

Schopenhauer's philosophy is packed with stimulating ideas and acute observations that gain significance and importance from the places they are given within his metaphysical scheme. His philosophy exerted a profound influence on the thought of Wittgenstein in that it seems both to have set the scene for Wittgenstein's early struggles to deal with problems about the will and to have provided him with the germ of the solutions he eventually produced.[10] For in his *Notebooks 1914-1916* and his *Tractatus logico-philosophicus* Wittgenstein regards the will as distinct from and other than the actions it somehow seems to generate; he was, in his own phrase, 'held captive' by a picture of the will as a kind of cause that operates to instigate bodily movements. But then, taking impetus from Schopenhauer's many asseverations about the indivisibility of will and body, he develops in his later writings the concept of voluntary action. This new approach recognises the incorrigibility of Schopenhauer's remark that 'I cannot really imagine this will without my body.'

Notes

1. Schopenhauer, *The fourfold root of the principle of sufficient reason*, trans. E.F.J. Payne (Open Court, La Salle, Illinois, 1974), §43.
2. See *Kant* in this book, pp. 89-94.
3. Schopenhauer, *The fourfold root*, §42.
4. Schopenhauer, *The world as will and representation*, trans. E.F.J. Payne (2 vols, Dover Publications, New York, 1966), vol. I, p. 100.
5. Ibid., pp. 109-10.
6. Ibid., pp. 292-3.
7. Ibid., vol. II, p. 196.
8. Ibid., vol. I, p. 379.
9. Ibid., p. 411.
10. See *Wittgenstein* in this book, pp. 145-51.

See also in this book

Berkeley, Kant, Hegel, Nietzsche, Bradley, Wittgenstein.

Schopenhauer's major writings

The fourfold root of the principle of sufficient reason (1813), trans. E.F.J. Payne (Open Court, La Salle, Illinois, 1974)
The world as will and representation (1818), trans. E.F.J. Payne (2 vols, Dover Publications, New York, 1966)
On the freedom of the will (1841) (Bobbs-Merrill, New York, 1960)
Parerga and paralipomena, trans. K. Kolenda (2 vols, Bobbs-Merill, New York, 1960)
Schopenhauer's works in German are in *Sämtliche Werke*, ed. A. Hubscher (7 vols, Brockhause Wiesbaden 1946-50). For a selection in English see *The will to live: selected writings of Arthur Schopenhauer*, ed. R. Taylor (Ungar, New York, 1962).

Further reading

Gardiner, P. *Schopenhauer* (Penguin, Harmondsworth, 1963)
Hamlyn, D.W. *Schopenhauer* (Routledge and Kegan Paul, London, 1980)
Magee, B. *The philosophy of Schopenhauer* (Clarendon Press, Oxford, 1983)
Phillips-Griffiths, A. 'Wittgenstein, Schopenhauer and Ethics' in *Understanding Wittgenstein*, ed. G.N.A. Vesey (Macmillan, London 1974), pp. 96-116

John Stuart Mill
1806-1873

John Stuart Mill is the most eminent of the group of nineteenth-century British philosophers who propounded and developed the doctrine of utilitarianism. He was a social reformer, a defender of personal and political liberty and a philosopher and logician of considerable importance. His essay, *On liberty*, published in 1859, discusses government and legal systems. In the Introduction to it he says 'The only freedom which deserves the name, is that of pursuing our own good in our own way, so long as we do not attempt to deprive others of theirs, or impede their efforts to obtain it.' The starting point for his philosophy was the work of Jeremy Bentham, the radical reformer who first disseminated the idea of 'the greatest happiness of the greatest number' as a moral principle.[1] This became known as the principle of utility. Bentham and James Mill, John Stuart's father, together led the movement that sought to establish the practical, legal and political means of realising it. The term 'utilitarianism', once used to refer to the whole gamut of Bentham's reforming ideas, is now used to refer only to his ethical theory which John Stuart Mill revised and refined in *Utilitarianism*, published in 1861. His major work on logic, *A system of logic*, was first published in 1843. Towards the end of his life he wrote *The subjection of women*, a powerful plea for equality between the sexes.

Mill was born in London in the suburb of Pentonville. His father, who wrote *A History of British India* and was Assistant Examiner at East India House, gave him an exacting education. He was fluent in Greek and Latin before the age of ten when he began logic and he read the proofs of his father's *History* when he was eleven. From his earliest years he was acquainted with Jeremy Bentham and with David Ricardo, the economist, and by the time he was in his mid-teens he was fully involved in all the political and reforming activities his father shared with these men. In 1823 he joined his father as an employee of the East India Company. Before he was twenty he was publishing articles and engaging in high-level discussions and debates. His *Autobiography* gives a full and fascinating account of these early years.

At the age of twenty Mill experienced a severe depression which he attributed to a kind of starvation of his emotions. His recovery began when, finding himself moved to tears by a book he was reading, he realised he had not entirely lost his capacity to feel deeply. With his zest for life revived he was able to work enthusiastically again. He became interested in Thomas Carlyle, Bentham's most censorious critic, and Auguste Comte, the French positivist philosopher. In 1830 he met Mrs Harriet Taylor whom he married in 1850, two years after the death of her first husband. She worked with Mill on many of his projects and they completed *On liberty* together at a time when her health was failing rapidly. Harriet died of tuberculosis at Avignon in 1858 and Mill spent most of the rest of his life there, still working to achieve the aims they had shared. He died at Avignon in 1873.

In *Utilitarianism* Mill develops the principle of utility into a moral theory that provides guidance on how to live virtuously. The creed of utility, he says, 'holds that actions are right in proportion as they tend to promote happiness, wrong as they tend to promote the reverse of happiness'.[2] He points out that the principle is not susceptible of reasoned proof but that 'considerations may be presented capable of determining the intellect ... and this is equivalent to proof'.[3] Happiness, he says, is desirable and the proof of this is that people do desire it: each person's good is a happiness to that person and the general happiness, therefore, a good to the aggregate of all persons. This **argument**, based on psychological **premises**, has become a famous target of copious and detailed criticism.

Mill had to overcome objections made to the Benthamite version of ethical utilitarianism. The Benthamites had maintained that everyone necessarily seeks his or her own pleasure and that pleasure is the greatest good. In consequence they were accused of representing humankind as selfish and base. To counteract this criticism Mill points out that although we all act to obtain pleasure in some sense of that word, it does not follow from this that we always act selfishly, for many people voluntarily perform deeds which manifestly cannot be judged to be selfish. He also revises Bentham's notion of pleasure, rejecting his view that 'push-pin is as good as poetry' by distinguishing between lower and higher pleasures and maintaining that anyone who has experience of both will prefer the higher to the lower pleasures. If there are those who have experienced both but now seek only the lower sort, they do so, Mill says, because they have become incapable of the higher sort.

In the last chapter of *Utilitarianism* Mill tries to deal with a powerful objection to the idea of regarding happiness as the highest moral value. The objection, stated simply, is that happiness cannot be the supreme value because in so many situations we in fact put justice above happiness. In response Mill assembles a formidable array of arguments, all designed to show that although justice is highly important in the hierarchy of human values it is nevertheless one that serves rather than rules the happiness principle. But he does not, in the last analysis, succeed in fully quashing the objection.

Utilitarianism was eagerly adopted by many people in Victorian Britain who were becoming disaffected with Christianity but wanted to establish a clear morality for themselves by means of their own independent thought. Its tenets are still live issues over a hundred years later. The theory has been developed, debated and refined a good deal since Mill established it and it provides a moral doctrine to which many individuals and political and social institutions subscribe wholeheartedly. Two much-discussed versions of utilitarianism are Act-utilitarianism and Rule-utilitarianism. Act-utilitarians, when deciding what is the right thing to do, reflect on which *act* will produce the greatest happiness in a particular situation. Rule-utilitarians resolve the issue by considering the consequences of the proposed act becoming a rule of action for everyone in like circumstances.

Mill's *System of Logic* has been an influential work. In Book I he examines what he calls 'the nature of Assertion'. He distinguishes between general and singular names, between concrete and **abstract** terms and between connotative and non-connotative terms. His major claim here is that terms denote only particulars and that a general term such as 'humankind' does not denote an entity distinct from the individuals that together make up human kind. Book II of the *Logic* deals with syllogistic reasoning.[4] Mill maintains that the nature of the **syllogism** has not been properly understood and that it is wrong to suppose its conclusion is a proof which infers a particular from a general statement. What it actually does, he argues, is to relate **inductive** conclusions to inductive generalisations. He also maintains that the propositions of mathematics are not **analytically** true verbal conventions but are **synthetic** and **empirical**: they are very general truths which we regard as obtaining without exception and we see them as necessarily true only because of a psychological compulsion to do so.

Mill's chief logical interest is in inductive reasoning, which he calls 'Generalisation from Experience.' He is at pains to point out that in induction we infer from the known to the unknown rather than from past events to future events. Thus he says:

> We believe that fire will burn tomorrow because it burned today and yesterday; but we believe, on precisely the same grounds, that it burned before we were born, and that it burns this very day in Cochin China. It is not from the past to the future, as past and future, that we

infer, but from the known to the unknown; from facts observed to facts unobserved.[5]

Mill also maintains that all induction is based on the belief that changes in nature are governed by invariable causal laws and that this fundamental belief is itself an inductive generalisation, though one 'by no means of the obvious kind'. It is 'a great generalisation ... founded on prior generalisations'. He examines causality in some detail, analysing a cause as 'the sum total of the conditions, positive and negative taken together; the whole of the contingencies of every description, which being realised, the consequent inevitably follows'.[6] In Book VI of his *System of logic* he considers the implications of his analysis for what he describes as 'the celebrated controversy concerning the freedom of the will'. The controversy arises because the notion of a universal causality implies that the human will is as much caused, and therefore as necessitated, as any other part of nature and cannot therefore be seen as free. Many of those averting from such a thought had tried to argue that the human will is exempt from causal determination and is therefore free. But Mill, like Hobbes and Hume before him, wants to assent both to a universal causality *and* to freedom of the will. He argues that grave misconceptions have arisen concerning the term 'necessity'. It implies, he says, in its other acceptations, 'irresistibleness'; whereas the causality of the will, like all other causality, 'only means that the given cause will be followed by the effect, subject to all possibilities of counteraction by other causes'.[7] What necessity does not mean, when applied to human action, is that an action is inevitable or uncontrollable. What it does mean is that given that one can know enough of a person's character and disposition then it is possible to predict what that person will do under particular circumstances. Mill says:

When we say that all human actions take place of necessity, we only mean that they

will certainly happen if nothing prevents; when we say that dying of want, to those who cannot get food, is a necessity, we mean that it will certainly happen, whatever may be done to prevent it.[8]

The main theme of the essay *On liberty* which Mill and Harriet Taylor worked on together is that we are justified in interfering with the actions of individuals only if they are harming others. The essay is an extremely lucid piece of writing, advocating open discussion and democratic individualism. Mill deplores the fact that most original opinions 'never blaze out far and wide but smoulder in the narrow circles of thinking and studious persons among whom they originate, without ever lighting up the general affairs of mankind with either a true or a deceptive light'.[9] In *The subjection of women*, which was written in Avignon in the winter of 1860-1 but not published until 1869, Mill argues eloquently that it is because women have been subjected to male dominance that they have developed a certain mode of behaviour and not because they are naturally disposed to such behaviour. It is morally bad, he insists, for a man and woman to engage in a relationship in which only one of them enjoys freedom of choice. Towards the end of the essay he says he will not attempt to describe the marriage that is possible

in the case of two persons of cultivated faculties, identical in opinions and purposes, between whom there exists that best kind of equality, similarity of powers and capacities with reciprocal superiority in them — so that each can enjoy the luxury of looking up to the other, and can have alternately the pleasure of leading and of being led in the path of development ...[10]

He continues: 'To those that can conceive it, there is no need; to those who cannot, it would appear the dream of an enthusiast.' All this is redolent of his relationship with

Harriet. Yet, charged though the essay is with intense feeling, it is still, like everything else he wrote, a work of clarity and order, revealing the fair-mindedness and eagerness to consider every side of a matter that typify almost everything he wrote.

Notes

1. See *Bentham* in this book, pp. 94-6.
2. J.S. Mill, *Utilitarianism*, Ch. 2.
3. Ibid., Ch. 4.
4. For more on syllogism see p. 23 in this book.
5. J.S. Mill, *A system of logic*, Book III, Ch. 3, §1.
6. Ibid., Book III, Ch. 5, §3.
7. Ibid., Book VI, Ch. 2, §3.
8. Ibid.
9. J.S. Mill, *On liberty*, Ch. 2.
10. J.S. Mill, *The subjection of women*, Ch. 4.

See also in this book

Hobbes, Hume, Bentham.

Mill's major writings

A system of logic (1843; 8th edn, 1872)
Principles of political economy (1848; 7th ed, 1871)
On liberty (1859), Everyman Library, no. 482 (J.M. Dent, London, 1929)
Utilitarianism (1861), Everyman Library, no. 482 (J.M. Dent, London, 1929)
Considerations on representative government (1861; 3rd edn, 1865)
The subjection of women (1869), Everyman Library, no. 825 (J.M. Dent, London, 1929)
Autobiography (1873). ed. J.J. Coss (Columbia University Press, New York, 1924 and 1944)
Mill's writings are in *The collected works of John Stuart Mill*, ed. J.M. Robson (21 vols, University of Toronto Press, Toronto and London, 1963-86). There are numerous selections of Mill's writings and some Everyman editions of his major moral and political works.

Further reading

Annas, J. 'Mill and the subjection of women', *Philosophy*, vol. 52 (1977), pp. 179-94
Day, J.P. 'John Stuart Mill' in D.J. O'Connor (ed.), *A critical history of Western philosophy* (The Free Press, New York, 1964; Macmillan, London, 1985)
Gray, J. *Mill on liberty: a defence* (Routledge and Kegan Paul, London 1983)
Robson, M. *The improvement of mankind: the social and political thought of J.S. Mill* (University of Toronto Press, Toronto and London, 1968)
Ryan, A. *J.S. Mill* (Author Guides Series, Routledge and Kegan Paul, London, 1974)
St J. Packe, M. *The life of John Stuart Mill* (Secker and Warburg, London, 1954)
Schneewind, J.B. (ed.) *Mill: a collection of critical essays* (Macmillan, London, 1968)

Soren Kierkegaard
1813-1855

In the history of philosophy Kierkegaard's thought stands as an individualistic reaction to the large abstractions of Hegel. He is regarded, along with Nietzsche, as a major founder and representative of existentialism. He wrote of himself as being 'like a lonely pine tree, egoistically shut off, pointing to the skies' and his own name for himself was 'That individual'. He said: 'The individual is the category through which, from a religious point of view, our age, our race, and its history must pass'.[1] He was passionately Christian but deeply contemptuous of organised religion and of any kind of doctrine that blunted awareness of one's personal existence, remarking that: 'The thinker who can forget in all his thinking also to think that he is an existing individual, will never explain life. He merely makes an attempt to cease to be a human being.'[2] His philosophy embodies a sustained attack on the rational humanism of his time and a plea for a new commitment, a 'leap of faith' in which passion and feeling have as much importance as reason and intellect and in which the inward and personal life of human beings is recognised as the source of meaning and value.

Kierkegaard's writings fall into two main parts. Between 1841 and 1846 he wrote a series of works under a number of different pseudonyms. This period includes *Either-or* (1843), *Fear and trembling* (1843), *Repetition* (1843), *The concept of dread* (1844), *Philosophical fragments* (1844), *Stages on the road of life* (1845) and the *Concluding unscientific postscript* (1846). The second group of writings, produced in the period from 1848 to the year of Kierkegaard's death, 1855, were the outcome of a burgeoning sense of mission towards bringing about profound changes in society. The group includes *Christian discourses* (1848), the second edition of *Either-or* (1849), *The sickness unto death* (1849), *Training in Christianity* (1850), *An edifying discourse* (1850), *Judge for yourself* (1851/2), and a series of articles against Martensen, Bishop of Zealand (1854/5).

Kierkegaard was born in Copenhagen at a time when, although the seat of the Danish government and a centre of learning, it was still a small provincial town supporting a close-knit community. He was a lively child, highly intelligent, animated and often precocious, the youngest of seven children who were the progeny of the second of his father's three marriages. His upbringing was dominated by his father, Michael, with whom he had a profound affinity and from whom he learnt much. But below the surface the family seems to have been affected by a cankerous melancholy. Michael secretly believed that his unfaithfulness to his first wife, who died in childbirth, was to be punished by the operation of an 'infallible law'. This dread seemed to him to be realised when, over a space of ten years, his second wife and five of his children died, leaving, by 1835, only himself, Soren, and an older brother, far gone in melancholy, alive. Soren reacted to all this by giving himself up to dissipation, a phase which ended in 1838 when he and his father were reconciled, shortly before the latter's death. In 1840 Kierkegaard became engaged to Regine Olsen but after much heart-searching and brood; ₃ on his family's story he decided he could not marry her. The engagement ended, as it began, under the watchful eyes of the citizens of Copenhagen.

Thereafter Kierkegaard dedicated himself to writing and to full involvement in the intellectual life of the city and he became a well-known figure. In appearance he was distinctive: he was slight in build and had a malformed spine which gave him an awkward backward-leaning walk; he had a

large head, a mop of fair hair, pale blue eyes and a strong nose and mouth. Those who knew him bore testimony to his immense charm, vivacity and his endearing friendliness. The professor of philosophy at Copenhagen University wrote:

> His smile, and his look, were indescribably expressive. He had a particular way of greeting one at a distance, with a mere look. It was just a little movement of the eyes, and yet it conveyed so much. He could put something infinitely gentle and loving into his gaze, but he could equally goad and tease people to a frenzy.[3]

Yet the inward surface of this demeanour was melancholy and sometimes despair, as Kierkegaard's *Journals* reveal. In March 1836 he wrote:

> I have just returned from a party of which I was the life and soul; wit poured from my lips, everyone laughed and admired me — but I went away — and the dash should be as long as the earth's orbit ____
>
> _____ and wanted to shoot myself.[4]

Kierkegaard objected to Hegel's philosophy because it made concepts and abstractions more important than what is actual and particular. In the Hegelian view the individual realises his or her true nature only in virtue of being an expression or manifestation of an aspect of the current stage of the events of the great **dialectical** process.[5] In opposition, Kierkegaard maintained that the individual human will and the fact of choice are of supreme importance and that to disregard them and to see human beings as merely elements in an inevitable process is not only to be philosophically mistaken but morally wrong as well: it is an abdication of responsibility. His existentialism has the same core as that of later and very different existentialists such as Sartre and Marcel: the notion of undetermined choice.[6] He held that genuine choice is not a matter of invoking criteria, for then one's choice is determined by the criteria, but of making a choice out of doubt and uncertainty. This choice is a leap of faith which affirms the incarnation of God but at the same time recognises it as intellectually and objectively a kind of absurdity. The affirmation, or leap of faith, must be made without reference to the experience or advice of others: it involves a recognition of one's complete individual separateness and responsibility for oneself. It is the only way to achieve the 'ethical reality that should mean more to a person then "heaven and earth and all that therein is", more than the six thousand years of human history'.[7] Making this leap is what it means to be a human being. Moreover, it is not something that is done for ever, for ethical reality requires continuity and must be perpetually renewed: 'The goal of movement for an existing individual is to arrive at a decision and renew it.'[8] In the *Concluding unscientific postscript* Kierkegaard wrote:

> Through having willed in this manner, through having ventured to take a decisive step in the utmost intensity of subjective passion and with full consciousness of one's eternal responsibility (which is within the capacity of every human being), one learns something else about life, and learns that it is quite a different thing from being engaged, year in and year out, in piecing together something for a system.[9]

The developments of Kierkegaard's own life are reflected in the three stages of development he sees as possible for human beings. In *Either-or* he contrasts the aesthetic with the ethical. At the aesthetic stage a person tries to escape boredom and life's pains by a romantic pursuit of a whole range of pleasures, but without ever achieving the living personal experience that is desired. The result is a despair that may eventually motivate one to a commitment of ethical values. Fulfilment is then sought at a further stage by means of a dedication to duty and obedience to the dictates of an objective morality. But once again the experience lacks personal meaning and fails to validate one's individual existence. A transformation occurs only if one progresses to the religious stage, by choosing to acknowledge one's mortality and sinfulness, the inadequacy of objective ethics to furnish a meaning for oneself and the dread of utter emptiness that underlies all our aesthetic and ethical seekings. To make the leap of faith and then to make it again and again is the activity of the religious stage: 'Man only begins to exist in faith' and there can never be a cut-and-dried system or formula for an authentic life but only the active and perpetual inhabiting of one's situation of groundless choice; for 'life must be lived forward, but understood backwards'. In an entry in the *Journals* Kierkegaard wrote, 'The thing is to find a truth which is true *for me*, to find *the idea for which I can live and die.*'[10]

Kierkegaard was a brilliant writer whose perspicacity and passion are evident in almost everything he wrote. Although his philosophy is bound into and, indeed, springs from his own life and personal experience, it nevertheless embodies points of view and intuitions constitutive of common human experience. His concern with subjectivity opened the way to a new kind of philosophical sensibility and a new consideration of the value of the human individual. But the same concern with subjectivity also produced some dubious although deeply interesting implications, for Kierkegaard believed that truth is truth for a subject; otherwise it is empty. This seems to obliterate any distinction between how things seem to be and how they may be in reality.

Notes

1. Kierkegaard, *The journals of Kierkegaard 1834-1854*, trans. A. Dru (Fontana/Collins, London, 1958), p. 133.
2. Kierkegaard, *Concluding unscientific postscript* (Princeton University Press, Princeton, 1941), p. 85.
3. Quoted in *The journals*, Introduction, p. 9.
4. Kierkegaard, *Journals*, pp. 50-1.

5. See *Hegel* in this book, pp. 96-100.
6. See *Sartre* in this book, pp. 157-63.
7. Kierkegaard, *Concluding unscientific postscript*, p. 305.
8. Ibid., p. 284.
9. Ibid.
10. Kierkegaard, *Journals*, p. 44.

See also in this book

Hegel, Nietzsche, Heidegger, Sartre.

Kierkegaard's major writings

Either-or, vols. I and II (1843)
Fear and trembling (1843)
Philosophical fragments (1844)
The concept of dread (1844)
Concluding unscientific postscript (1846)
Christian discourses (1848)
The sickness unto death (1849)
An edifying discourse (1850)
All the above works are published by Princeton University Press and are also available in paperback. See also *A Kierkegaard anthology*, ed. R. Bretall (Princeton University Press, Princeton, 1946).

Further reading

Blackham, H.J. *Six existentialist thinkers* (Routledge and Kegan Paul London, 1961), Ch. 1
Hannay, A. *Kierkegaard* (Routledge and Kegan Paul, London, 1982)
Lowrie, W. *A short life of Kierkegaard* (Princeton University Press, Princeton, 1942)

Karl Marx   1818-1883

Marx is a profound and pervasive influence in twentieth-century life. His thought affects the lives of millions and has impacted on many aspects of modern society, in particular on history, sociology, economics, philosophy and the arts. Many of his ideas, like those of Freud, are now part of our cultural inheritance.

He was born in the German Rhineland, at Trier, in 1818 and was of Jewish origin. He became a law student at the University of Bonn when he was 17, behaved rather wildly and transferred, at his father's injunction, to the University of Berlin. At Berlin he turned to philosophy and began to work seriously on a doctoral thesis after his father's death forced him to consider his financial and career prospects. The thesis was accepted in 1841 but did not lead to the university lectureship he had hoped for. He turned to journalism, did well in writing on political and social issues and in 1842 became editor of the *Rhenish Gazette*. But the job did not last. The Prussian government suppressed the paper and in 1843 Marx, newly married, took his young wife Jenny with him to Paris where he began writing for the *German-French annals*. Again the venture was a failure and, because of the *Annals'* revolutionary ideas, the Prussians issued warrants for the arrest of its editors. This meant that Marx was unable to return to Prussia. He stayed in France, developing his political and philosophical ideas, and began his friendship and collaboration with Friedrich Engels. In 1847 he went to London to attend the Congress of a new organisation, the Communist League, and was commissioned, together with Engels, to write a simple declaration of the League's doctrine. This declaration, the *Communist manifesto*, was published in 1848.

By now Marx was in political disrepute at home, in France and in Belgium and in 1849 he settled his family in London where he lived for the rest of his life. For a while everything was difficult and harsh, not only because of a lack of money but because two of the Marxes' children died in infancy and a third, Edgar, when he was eight years old. Nevertheless, Marx worked intensively, writing many articles as well as a draft of his book *Capital* and engaging in all kinds of political debate and controversy.

By the time he was in his fifties his ideas were becoming established. *Capital* was translated into Russian in 1872 and became widely read and Marx, by then well known, enjoyed regular contact with like-minded theorists all over Europe. His last years were made deeply unhappy by deaths in his family. Several of his grandchildren died in infancy. In 1881 his wife died after a wretchedly long illness and this loss was followed a year later by the death of one of his daughters. Marx himself died on 14 March 1883.

When Marx first began to formulate his ideas in the late 1830s the philosophy of G.W.F. Hegel was dominant at the University of Berlin.[1] Hegel had posited the existence of Mind as a universal spirit. He maintained that particular individual minds are parts of the universal Mind but are unaware of this ultimate oneness, so that Mind is estranged or alienated from itself. It nevertheless develops, and necessarily must develop, towards a condition of greater and greater freedom by gradually recognising its own unity. This self-knowledge is brought about by a process of dialectic. Hegelian dialectic is a kind of dynamic and progressive opposition in which an initial notion, the thesis, is countered by a contrary one, the antithesis. This opposition culminates in a synthesis which preserves and combines what is rational in the first two positions and then forms the basis of a new thesis. And so the dialectic proceeds.

The followers of Hegel, the Young Hegelians, were not comfortable with the thought that Mind was the ultimate reality. Nevertheless, they wanted to abolish what they saw as self-alienation and to liberate humanity through the historical and dialectical process of self-knowledge. Moreover, they saw religion as a form of **alienation** through which humankind had attributed all the goodness and wisdom of which it was capable to a remote God instead of recognising them as essentially human capacities. This was the breeding ground of Marxian thought. Following the ideas of Feuerbach, Marx rejected the Hegelian concept of the Absolute and of Mind as the true reality and instead placed human beings and human consciousness at the centre of his philosophy. Gradually he came to see the social relations that develop in connection with work, production, bargaining and money as the determining forces in human history. The social relations that obtain at a particular time correspond, he says, to a stage of development of the material powers of production and this whole complex of related forces constitutes the economic structure of society. He writes:

> The mode of production in material life determines the general character of the social, political and spiritual processes of life. It is not the consciousness of men that determines their existence, but, on the contrary, their social existence determines their consciousness.[2]

Marx maintains that as development proceeds there comes a point when the material forces of production enter into conflict with the existing relations of production, with the result that what was once development becomes bonds and fetters for people. This produces a period of social revolution although, he says, 'No social order ever disappears before all the productive forces, for which there is room in it, have been developed; and new higher relations of production never appear before the material conditions of existence have matured in the womb of the old society.'[3] What he is suggesting here is that productive forces such as manual labour, tools, machinery and raw materials give rise to 'relations of production' between the people who deploy and those who are deployed within the productive system. Relations of production are those obtaining between landowner and labourer, factory owner and factory worker and so on. They compose a society's economic structure and are the support of its political, moral and spiritual superstructure. Thus Marx's claim amounts to saying that economic forces determine every aspect of life and this is probably the most contentious claim in his whole doctrine. Just as Hegel believed in a necessary progress of Mind towards greater self-consciousness so Marx believed in the necessary development of human material life and human nature towards a unity and harmony in their controlling forces.

Once his attention was focused on a material and physical reality rather than a spiritual one, Marx quickly singled out the working class, or proletariat, as a force that was of supreme importance in virtue of its profound impoverishment, its ubiquity and, above all, its utter self-alienation. In a process of material dialetic it was unambiguously cast in the role of a powerful antithesis to the thesis of private ownership of property, thus playing a vital part in the dialectical advance of humanity's redemption of itself. Human labour and its concomitant economics were to be the material content of the formal structure of Marx's dialectic. He believed that it was of the essence of human beings that they should actively make things, though not within a production system they did not control or which exploited their ability to work and set them in competition against each other. Such conditions, which Marx saw as prevailing almost everywhere, could be changed, he insisted, only by the abolition of private property, wages and the work system that exploited people's labour. These measures would liberate people from having to see everything in terms of market value; they would allow people to enjoy the look and the presence of objects rather than seeing them as bargaining tools. Moreover, he believed that all this must and would come about, for the materialist dialectic, like Hegel's non-materialist one, proceeded inevitably along a path of historical necessity. It was not consciously shaped by those who participated in it. In *The holy family* Marx wrote:

> It is not a question of what this or that proletarian or even the whole proletarian movement momentarily *imagines* to be the aim. It is a question of *what* the proletariat *is* and what it consequently is historically compelled to do. Its aim and historical action is prescribed irrevocably and obviously, in its own situation in life as well as in the entire organisation of contemporary civil society.[4]

Marx developed his economic theory in *Capital*. He tries to show that capitalism carries within itself the seeds of its own destruction. He argues that capitalists make their profits by exacting a surplus from their workers but that since capital is always increasing, the ratio of labour to capital gradually decreases. This means that eventually the rate of profit must fall and that capitalism will therefore end. Economists have been severely critical of this theory, largely because, contrary to Marx's claims, it is not endorsed by scientific testing and is not substantiated by events. In the end it is as much a **metaphysical** doctrine as Hegel's doctrine of spirit was. But this does not mean that Marx's work is without value and importance. It offered a detailed and original critique of capitalism and new perspectives on the social, political and economic dimensions of society. Moreover it raised profound questions about human nature and human freedom, thereby radically affecting the conceptions and aspirations human beings have of themselves. Numerous 'philosophies' have been developed from it, although Marx himself would never have wanted his thought to be regarded as philosophy. He saw most philosophy as a manifestation of the alienation he wanted to overcome and as something that would disappear as a consequence of the social revolution he predicted: its phantom concepts of justice and reason would, he believed, be transformed into material reality. But many of Marx's followers, building upon his ideas and, eager to develop all they could out of every one of them, have constructed a whole range of systems from his work, elaborating Marxist views on ethics, aesthetics, theology, metaphysics and **epistemology** as well as on the whole range of political, social and economic concerns which Marx himself dealt with at considerable length. Even though many of these systems show themselves to be incompatible with one another they are nevertheless testimony to the generative properties of Marx's critique of human society.

Marx's written output was prodigious. An edition of his collected works, now in preparation in East Germany, is likely to fill a hundred volumes. Commentaries, critiques and expositions of his work are proportionately copious, filling many thousands of books. The sheer quantity of writing about Marx is indicative of the massive shift of attitude which his ideas have brought about, a shift from a stance of experiencing life from the point of view of an individual agent to the stance of an observer of that experience. When Marx was buried in Highgate Cemetery, Hampstead, Frederich Engels delivered a funeral address that included the following words:

> His mission in life was to contribute in one way or another to the overthrow of capitalist society ... to contribute to the liberation of the present-day proletariat which he was the first to make conscious of its own position and its needs, of the conditions under which it could win its freedom. Fighting was his element. And he fought with a passion, a tenacity and a success which few could rival ... and consequently was the best-hated and most calumniated man of his time ... he died, beloved, revered and mourned by millions of revolutionary fellow workers from the mines of Siberia to the coasts of California ... his name and his work will endure through the ages.[5]

Notes

1. See *Hegel* in this book, pp. 96-100.
2. K. Marx, *A contribution to the critique of political economy*, Preface.
3. Ibid.
4. K. Marx, *The holy family* in D. McLellan (ed.), *Karl Marx: selected writings* (Oxford University Press, Oxford, 1977), pp. 134-5.
5. F. Engels, quoted in I. Berlin, *Karl Marx: his life and environment* (Oxford University Press, Oxford, 1978), p. 206.

See also in this book

Hegel, Mill, Nietzsche.

Marx's major writings

The poverty of philosophy (1847), trans. H. Quelch (Twentieth-Century Press, London, 1900)
The Communist manifesto (1848), ed. A.J.P. Taylor (Penguin, Harmondsworth, 1967)
Grundrisse (1857-8) The Introduction to the next item (Penguin, Harmondsworth, 1967)
A contribution to the critique of political economy (1859), trans. N.I. Stone (University of Chicago Press, Chicago, 1904)
Capital (1867 onwards), (3 vols. vol. I, Penguin, Harmondsworth, 1967)
Marx's writings in German are in preparation in East Germany and are expected to fill about 100 volumes. A *Collected works* in English is in the process of publication (Lawrence and Wishart, London, 1975-). There is a good selection of his writings in *Karl Marx: selected writings*, ed. D. McLellan (Oxford University Press, Oxford, 1977) and an 8-volume Marx Library is published by Penguin.

Further reading

Adams, H.P. *Karl Marx in his earlier writings* (Allen and Unwin, London, 1940)
McLellan, D. *The Young Hegelians and Karl Marx* (Macmillan, London, 1969)
— *Karl Marx: his life and thought* (Macmillan, London, 1973)
Ollman, B. *Alienation: Marx's conception of man in capitalist society*, 2nd edn. (Cambridge Univeristy Press, Cambridge, 1977)
Singer, P. *Marx* (Oxford University Press, Oxford, 1980).
Tucker, R. *Philosophy and myth in Karl Marx* (Cambridge University Press, Cambridge, 1961)

Charles Sanders Peirce 1839-1914

Peirce was the founder of pragmatism, which he described as 'a method of determining the meanings of hard words and abstract conceptions'. The mainstream of pragmatism developed from an obscurely expressed but famous maxim Peirce produced in 1878: 'Consider what effects, that might conceivably have practical bearings, we conceive the object of our conceptions to have. Then, our conception of these effects is the whole of our conception of the object.'[1] He was a highly original thinker in a number of philosophical areas: in symbolic logic, ethics, aesthetics and religion as well as **epistemology** and **metaphysics**. He devised several Logical Algebras. These are sets of symbols governed by transformation rules which, when applied, generate further sets of symbols which can be used to represent the relationships holding between certain principles of logic, thus exhibiting those relationships with clarity. The general notion Peirce derives from this algebraic work is that any sign, in order to have meaning, must be capable of development in terms of other signs. This notion, in one form or another, underlies not only his mathematical and logical work but his wider philosophising as well.

Peirce was born in 1839 in Cambridge, Massachusetts. His father, Benjamin Peirce, was a professor of mathematics and astronomy at Harvard University. He instructed his son in mathematics and taught him to conduct laboratory experiments, thereby developing the boy's precocious talent for science. Peirce entered Harvard when he was 16 and graduated four years later. For thirty years he was employed by the United States Coastal and Geodesic Survey but intermittently also gave lectures on logic and the history of science at Harvard. In 1891 he gave up his work on the Survey and turned his whole attention to logic and philosophy, intending to organise and write up the results of years of philosophical reflection. But lack of money forced him to write popular articles for cash and the books he meant to write did not materialise. He became something of a recluse as he grew older, eccentric in his habits, solitary, impecunious and irascible. Yet he commanded profound respect in academic circles. William James wrote of him: 'I yield to no one in admiration of his genius, but he is paradoxical and unsociable of intellect, and hates to *make connexion* with anyone he is with.'[2] When Peirce fell ill in the last years of his life James generously helped to support him. Peirce died without completing any of the books he had planned but he had written over a hundred papers and a hundred and fifty reviews of scientific and philosophical books. After his death his unpublished manuscripts were bought by the Philosophical Department at Harvard and between 1931 and 1958 appeared in a series of volumes known as his *Collected papers*.

The main ideas of pragmatism appear to have been formulated at the meetings of a Harvard group calling themselves the Metaphysical Club. The club's members, several of whom were scientists, critically scrutinised metaphysical theories and discussed the nature of belief. Peirce's best-known exposition of pragmatism is contained in a paper, 'How to make our ideas clear', written in 1878. What he offers is a method or technique for solving philosophical problems. He says: 'If one can define accurately all the conceivable experimental phenomena which the affirmation or denial of a concept could imply, one will have therein a complete definition of the concept.' This 'pragmatic significance' of a concept, belief or idea constitutes its meaning. Peirce uses the categorical statement 'This is hard' to provide an example of his method. The pragmatic meaning of the statement is obtained by translating it into a hypothetical statement such as 'If one were to try to scratch this, one would not succeed.' If no such translation can be be given then the initial categorical statement, 'This is hard' has no meaning. Thus he says: 'Our idea of anything *is* our idea of its sensible effects; and if we fancy that we have any other we deceive ourselves ... It is absurd to say that thought has any meaning unrelated to its only function.'[3] He regards thought as something in which we engage in order to move from doubt to belief. Genuine doubt, he says, is something that simply occurs and that cannot be intellectually provoked; it is an uneasy state that triggers off a search for belief which is then pursued by means of thought. The assuagement of doubt through thought results in beliefs which produce habits, or rules of action, and a rule of action reveals the significance of the belief from which it derives. Rules or habits, in turn, are distinguished by the actions they generate. He says:

Thus we come down to what is tangible and conceivably practical, as the root of every real distinction of thought, no matter how subtle it may be; and there is no distinction of meaning so fine as to consist in anything but a possible difference of practice.[4]

Peirce's somewhat awkward descriptions of pragmatism have sometimes been misunderstood. His method requires that we consider what 'practical bearings' a concept might conceivably have and that the effects so conceived shall be expressible in the type of conditional statement cited in discussing the concept 'hard' above. In claiming that our conception of an object is our conception of its sensible or practical effects he is not, as some have thought, saying that we have secured the meaning of a concept once we have observed its practical effects in particular instances. Pragmatism, he says, is 'a method of ascertaining the meanings, not of all ideas, but ... "intellectual concepts", that is to say, of those upon the structure of which, arguments concerning objective fact may hinge'.[5] It can show where words are being used imprecisely or ambiguously, thereby revealing that 'supposed problems are not real problems'. It is a method for making our beliefs clear and for showing the justifications it is possible to offer for them.

'How to make our ideas clear' made no noticeable impact when it was first published in 1878. But twenty years later pragmatism was adopted, adapted and disseminated by William James. Pragmatism as expounded by Peirce is a doctrine about how to establish empirical meanings. In the hands of William James it became a theory of both meaning and truth. Peirce eventually, in 1905, tried to separate his own theory from James's, renaming it 'pragmaticism', a word which he decided was 'ugly enough to be safe from kidnappers'. Nevertheless, he had the utmost respect and admiration for James. He wrote: 'He is so concrete, so living; I a mere table of contents, so abstract, a very snare of twine.'[6]

Peirce's work on logical relations led him to propound an evolutionary **cosmology**

which he called synechism. Briefly, synechism is the view that there is in the universe a comprehensive tendency towards an ever-developing continuity and uniformity. As an example of this tendency Peirce cites the continuous connections between past and present that are the conditions of memory. Similarly, our habits of action are acquired by means of the connections thought makes between feelings and actions. At a cosmic level, natural laws are the equivalents of human habits. Peirce suggests that 'at present, the course of events is approximately determined by law. In the past that approximation was less perfect; in the future it will be more perfect. The tendency to obey laws has always been and always will be growing.'[7] This means that at some time in the distant past everything was more or less indeterminate. But even then, according to Peirce, the tendency to move towards some kind of regularity and uniformity was present in that 'in every conceivable real object, there is a greater probability of acting as on a former like occasion than otherwise'.[8] However, in the state of primal chaos it is chance that at first dominates and then diminishes as law-like activity develops and increases. The thought occurs that the slow but comprehensive movement from chaos to order is the cosmic equivalent of human progress from doubt to belief. Certainly, Peirce spoke of everything as coming, in an infinitely distant future, to a 'concrete reasonableness', that is, a condition in which human beings would have perceived the laws and all their inter-connections within the universe and so would reach a state of rational and physical harmony with all things. He felt that if contemplation and study of the physico-psychical universe 'can imbue a man with principles of conduct analogous to the influence of a great man's works or conversation' then that is to understand something of what is meant by 'God'.

Notes

1. C.S. Peirce, 'How to make our ideas clear' in *Popular Science Monthly*, vol. 12 (January 1878), pp. 286-302. Also in *Collected papers of Charles Sanders Peirce* (see Further reading below).
2. Quoted in W.B. Gallie *Peirce and pragmatism* (Penguin, Harmondsworth, 1952), p. 38.
3. Peirce, 'How to make our ideas clear'.
4. Ibid.
5. See Gallie, *Peirce and pragmatism*, p. 11.
6. Quoted in J. Passmore, *A hundred years of philosophy* (Penguin, Harmondsworth, 1968), p. 102.
7. From a fragment dated 1890 and quoted in Gallie, *Peirce and pragmatism*, p. 218.
8. Ibid.

See also in this book

James, Frege, Bergson.

Peirce's major writings

Collected papers of Charles Sanders Peirce (8 vols., 1931-58), vols. 1-6 ed. C. Hartshorne and P. Weiss; vols. 7, 8 ed. A. Burks, (Harvard University Press, Cambridge, Mass., 1958)
A good selection of Peirce's writings is also available in J. Buchler (ed.), *The philosophy of Peirce* (Routledge and Kegan Paul, London, 1940).

Further reading

Ayer, A.J. *The origins of pragmatism: studies in the philosophy of Charles Sanders Peirce and William James* (Blackwell, Oxford, 1968)
Gallie, W.B. *Peirce and pragmatism* (Penguin, Harmondsworth, 1952)
Thayer, H.S. 'Pragmatism' in D.J. O'Connor (ed.), *A critical history of Western philosophy* (The Free Press, New York, 1964; Macmillan, London, 1985)
White, M. *Pragmatism and the American mind* (Oxford University Press, Oxford, 1973)

William James
1842-1910

William James was the major American philosopher of his day. He adopted and developed the philosophy of pragmatism, first expounded by his fellow American Charles Sanders Peirce. At the heart of his thought is an acceptance of the plurality, flux and indefiniteness of all things and a candid, common-sense attitude towards every aspect of ordinary human experience. This never makes James's philosophy prosaic and

mundane; indeed, it is remarkable for its vivid, lively and often inspirational quality. He maintained that if an idea 'works' it is a true idea; in so far as it makes a difference to life it is meaningful. Truth, for him, is not a fixed and unchanging absolute that is independent of human cognition of it but is invented or created by means of human activity. Moreover, truth and goodness are closely connected: what is true turns out to be what is good. James's ultimate concern is a moral one. He wants to proclaim a philosophical method for living well as the beings we manifestly are.

James was born in New York City, the son of Mary Robertson Walsh James and Henry James senior, the Swedenborgian theologian. He was the oldest of five children and had one sister and three brothers, one of whom, Henry James, achieved fame as an outstanding novelist. The family was a gifted, unconventional and lively one. James's formal education was irregular. His real schooling took place in the family home where intelligent and learned friends frequently came to engage in discussions on a wide range of topics. He attended schools in Switzerland, Germany, France and England, and became especially interested in the natural sciences and in painting. In 1860 he started formal training as a painter but the venture convinced him that this was not his vocation. A year later he entered the Laurence Scientific School at Harvard, and transferred to the medical school there in 1864. On an expedition to Brazil in 1865 he fell ill with smallpox and thereafter suffered recurring bouts of ill health through much of his life. He received his medical degree in 1869 and after a period of illness and recuperation began teaching at Harvard; first, anatomy and physiology, then psychology and, eventually in 1879, philosophy. He remained associated with Harvard until 1907. After his marriage in 1878 both his health and temperament seemed to achieve a rather more even keel. He lectured, taught, travelled and became widely known, giving and receiving tremendous intellectual stimulation within a circle of eminent and scholarly friends and colleagues. His lively style of speaking and writing made him extremely popular at every level. In 1899 James was climbing in the mountains near his home in New Hampshire and lost his way. The rigours of this ordeal affected his heart, already diagnosed as suffering impairment, and for the next two years he was virtually an invalid. Then, to his own surprise, he recovered and was able to return to Harvard and his busy life of lecturing. He eventually retired from the university in 1907 and in 1909 published *A pluralistic universe*, in which he brilliantly discusses the work of Hegel, Fechner and Bergson. A few months later his heart again began to give trouble and he died in his New Hampshire home on 26 August 1910.

James held that the individual's personal viewpoint and attitude are of major importance in philosophy. His own writings reveal how brilliantly gifted he was in articulating with clarity and grace the precise 'feel' of inward experiences. His large and famous work, the *Principles of psychology*, published in 1890, amply exhibits his conviction that it is experience rather than theory, abstractions and traditional philosophy that is the key to a practical understanding of ourselves and the world. In the *Principles* he gives an account of mental states, maintaining that they are engendered by physical states but that they also effect physical changes. He refused to subscribe to a traditional **dualism** of the physical and mental but at the same time would not allow that the mental was reducible to the physical. He maintained that the mind must be seen as an instrument for realising purposes. Throughout the *Principles* his aim is to give a full description by means of introspective observation of mental states and activities. A famous chapter, 'The stream of thought', establishes as 'the first and foremost concrete fact which everyone will affirm' that consciousness of some sort goes on'. Analysis of thought, or consciousness, James says, shows that every mental state belongs with a personal consciousness; that thought is continuous in the sense that even though one may sleep or lose consciousness one's waking consciousness links back to one's pre-sleep consciousness; that thought is always changing in the sense that there are no identical recurring states; and that consciousness is able to be selective of its objects. These claims are backed up by descriptions which are wonderfully perspicuous, apt and detailed. Consider, for example, the following:

Suppose we try to recall a forgotton name. The state of our consciousness is peculiar. There is a gap therein; but no mere gap. It is a gap that is intensely active. A sort of wraith of the name is in it, beckoning us in a given direction, making us at moments tingle with the sense of our closeness, and then letting us sink back without the longed-for term. If wrong names are proposed to us, this singularly definite gap acts immediately so as to negate them. They do not fit into its mould. And the gap of one word does not feel like the gap of another ... When I vainly try to recall the name of Spalding, my consciousness is far removed from what it is when I vainly try to recall the name of Bowles.[1]

James writes with equal penetration and perception on 'the Self'. In the *Principles* it is psychology he is writing and so he is not immediately concerned to establish philosophical grounds for the concept of the self. But he does discuss, in Chapters 6 and 10, the matter of a philosophical basis for the self and in the condensed version of the *Principles*, the *Briefer course* (known to students as 'the Jimmy' because the *Principles* was called 'the James') he summarises his view by saying that 'states of consciousness are all that psychology needs to do her work with. **Metaphysics** or theology may prove the soul to exist; but for psychology the **hypothesis** of such a substantial principle of unity is superfluous.'[2] In the *Principles* he distinguishes between the I and the Me, saying with typical succinctness that the I 'is that which at any given moment *is* conscious, whereas the Me is only one of the things which it is conscious of'.[3] He classifies the constituents of the Me under three headings: the material me, the social me, and the spiritual me. He points out that there is rivalry and conflict between the different Mes, and that most of us are haunted by 'the sense of an ideal spectator' who judges what we make of ourselves through these interactions.

Pragmatism, published in 1907, consists of eight essays in which James sets out his philosophical position. The opening essay spells out a contrast in terms that have since become famous between the tough-minded and tender-minded temperaments in philosophy; between the **empiricists** who are 'pessimistic', 'irreligious', 'sceptical' and 'pluralistic', and the **rationalists** who are 'idealistic', 'optimistic', '**monistic**' and 'dogmatical'. James maintains that these traditional attitudes do little to satisfy the philosophical needs of the ordinary person for facts, science *and* religion; but pragmatism can satisfy those needs in that it offers a method that has appeal to all temperaments, rejects neither religion nor facts and takes account of subjectivity as an important element in philosophy. His pragmatism differs from that of C.S. Peirce in that he sees it as a theory of both meaning and truth, whereas Peirce's pragmatism was concerned only with meaning.[4] From his psychological studies he concludes that the primary function of thought is to enable us to relate to the world and the people around us; its purpose is to 'carry us prosperously from any one part of our experience to any other part'. The meanings of the ideas, beliefs and theories involved in thought are discerned by asking what difference they make to our lives; and they are true if living by them produces 'satisfactory relations with other parts of our experience'. The pragmatist has

to ask: 'What, in short, is the truth's cash value in experiential terms?' He or she concludes that true ideas are those that we can assimilate, validate, corroborate and verify; false ideas are those that we cannot Thus James does not claim, in expounding the pragmatic theory of truth, that an idea i. true merely in virtue of appealing at whim to an individual. He maintains that when the pragmatic method is applied to metaphysica. questions it shows up the poverty of a great deal of philosophical speculation. For example, our accounts of a concept such as substance, thought of as an underlying reality that supports the perceived world, add nothing to what we actually know of the world and therefore make no practical difference to our lives. He held that metaphysica. problems are, at root, moral or religious issues and that pragmatism will reveal these issues and so enable them to be understood and resolved.

For William James, experience meant experience of every kind and of everything; it was, in all its aspects, the condition and the stuff of human life. In expounding the method of pragmatism James believed he was simply articulating the ways in which we all, with varying abilities, engage in the activity of living in the world. He conceived of the universe as a huge natural system in which many pluralities coexist and within which human beings are continually reshaping their activities and strategies in relation to everything they encounter. Evolutionary change and development never cease; there is nothing fixed and unchanging that awaits discovery, but there are unlimited possibilities to consider and a perpetual challenge to be joyfully confronted.

Notes

1. W. James, 'The stream of thought' in *The principles of psychology*, vol. I.
2. W. James, *Psychology: the briefer course*, Ch. 10.
3. W. James, 'The consciousness of self' in the *Principles*, vol. I.
4. See *Peirce* in this book, pp. 113-16.

See also in this book

Mill, Peirce, Bergson.

James's major writings

The principles of psychology (1890) (2 vols, Macmillan, London, 1890; Dover Publications, New York, 1950)
Psychology: the briefer course (1892) (Holt, New York, 1920)
The will to believe and other essays in popular philosophy (1897) (Longman, New York, 1897; 2nd edn., Dover Publications, New York, 1956)
The varieties of religious experience: a study in human nature (1902) (Longman, New York, 1902)
Pragmatism: a new name for some old ways of thinking (1907) (Longman, New York, 1907; Meridian Books, New York, 1955)
A pluralistic universe (1909) (Longman, New York, 1909)
James's writings are collected in *The works of William James*, general ed. F.H. Burkhardt (13 vols., Harvard University Press, Cambridge, Mass., 1975-).

Further reading

Ayer, A.J. *The origins of pragmatism* (Macmillan, London, 1968)
Knight, M. *William James* (Penguin, Harmondsworth, 1950)
Mellor, D.H. (ed.) *Prospects for pragmatism* (Cambridge University Press, Cambridge, 1980)
Moore, G.E. 'William James's "Pragmatism"' in *Philosophical studies* (Routledge and Kegan Paul, London, 1960)
Perry, R.B. *The thought and character of William James* (2 vols., Oxford University Press, Oxford, 1935)

Friedrich Nietzsche
1844-1900

Nietzsche was a radical and highly original thinker. He was prophetic, poetic and profoundly critical of philosophy as he found it. Much of his own philosophy is a sustained attack on the belief that there is an objective world structure that is independent of any human apprehension of it. The arresting style and intensity of his writing have made his ideas attractive in a popular and sometimes superficial way so that the intellectual quality of his thought has sometimes been overlooked.

He was born of Lutheran parents at Röcken, near Leipzig, on 15 October 1844 and received his early education at the Schulpforta, a famous school established during the Reformation in a former Cistercian monastery and renowned for the quality of its teaching. Nietzsche was an exemplary pupil and in 1864 he went to the University of Bonn and then to the University of Leipzig. In 1869, at the age of 25, he was appointed to a professorship at the University of Basle and in 1872 took Swiss citizenship. In the Leipzig years he read and was deeply influenced by Schopenhauer's *The world as will and representation* and he became a close friend of Richard Wagner, the composer, and his wife, Cosima. For several years he regarded Wagner as the creative genius who, through his music dramas, would bring German culture to a glory comparable with that achieved by the dramatic tragedies of early Greece. He gradually became disillusioned with Wagner and his eventual disgust at the composer's nationalism as well as with his anti-Semitism and overweening arrogance resulted in *Nietzsche contra Wagner*, published in 1888.

Nietzsche's health was always poor and in 1878 he resigned his post at Basle on grounds of illness. During the next ten years he wrote copiously, struggling against chronic ill health and much unhappiness. In 1889 he became insane and thereafter was cared for by his sister, Elizabeth, who took charge of all his manuscripts, apparently suppressing, modifying and promulgating them as she chose and often distorting their emphases and meanings. But by the time Nietzsche died in 1900 his reputation was established. The popular image of him is of someone who advocated a ruthless and passionate pursuit of power, yet in his private life he was gentle, courteous and considerate. He is often associated, again in popular conceptions of his thought, with Nazism and Hitlerism, and there is no doubt that many of his ideas were entirely apt for exploitation by those movements. His sister, in her old age, regarded Hitler as the embodiment of the Ubermensch, or Superman, eulogised by Nietzsche.

Nietzsche's opposition to the view that there is an underlying objective and unchanging reality generates philosophical problems. In place of a belief in a deep reality he urges a reliance on sense and common sense as the most useful means of understanding the world. It is not, he maintains, that a common sense view gives the correct version of how things are, for there is no such thing as a correct view. But common sense supplies the perspective by which we live and is not merely a superstructure concealing a true underlying reality. He says, 'The apparent world is the only one: the "real world" is merely a lie.[1] There would, he insists, be no real world laid bare before us were we able to subtract our 'interpretations'. Common sense is therefore to be defended, not because it is true but because it is the way in which we in fact deal with the world. He says:

> We have arranged for ourselves a world in which we can live — with the acceptance of bodies, lines, surfaces, causes and effects, motion and rest, form and content. Without these articles of faith no one now would be able to live. But this by no means constitutes a proof. Life is no argument. Amongst the conditions of life, error might be one.[2]

The problems become clearly apparent when we ponder the question: if there is no underlying and fixed reality, and if the common sense view, although useful, is always false, does Nietzsche leave himself any intelligible way of speaking about the world? He condemns all conceptualisation and linguistic organisation of experience and yet uses that very language to articulate his condemnation and to imply that there is indeed a true state of affairs that would be, or is, discernible once we free ourselves from all the known modes of discernment. A.C. Danto has asked of Nietzsche:

> How are we to understand a theory when the structure of our understanding itself is

called in question by that theory? And when we have succeeded in understanding it, in our own terms, it would automatically follow that we had misunderstood it, for our own terms are the wrong ones.[3]

Nietzsche is also acutely critical of the idea of the self as an entity or **substance**. He argues that we mistakenly infer, through the general notions of causality and action, that there must be an agent which exercises the will in order to bring about actions. But this, he says, is 'false causality': 'A thought comes when "it" will, not when "I" will',[4] and the concept of the will is not the clear and simple one that philosophers often take it to be. Once again he is insisting that our beliefs about laws such as those of causality and necessity are simply useful devices for giving broad and unrefined accounts of the world, enabling us to communicate with and understand each other but telling us nothing of how matters really stand.

There is a close affinity between some of Nietzsche's ideas and existentialism. Like the existentialists, he maintains that we make rather than discover values and meanings and that this making is brought about through actions which, in the last analysis, are not and cannot be justified or grounded in reasons and which are expressions of personal authenticity.[5] We have to separate ourselves from the meaningless flux of things and demand of ourselves that we create new ideals and new values by rejecting existing conventions and accepted 'truths' and by exerting a 'will to power' that embraces suffering as a means to richer experience and fulfils the yearnings of the heart rather than the dictates of reason. This does not mean that Nietzsche is without respect for reason; indeed, he esteems it highly. But he regards the work of reason as well as the acquisition of scientific knowledge as a means to the supremely important matter of ascribing values and creating fresh perspectives. He urges his readers to work to *understand* how accepted values become firmly established; how, for instance, the practices of fasting and celibacy became so important in Christianity and how a trans-valuation of these values might come about through the actions of those with a will to power who can simply command change in the words, 'It shall be thus.' Such persons will be beyond their own time and therefore, in spite of their strength, will be lonely, abused and misunderstood by many. They will realise that there is no God but will affirm existence and will embrace and welcome its every pain as well as its joy.

In connection with the affirmation of existence Nietzsche propounded a doctrine of eternal recurrence. This states that whatever happens has happened infinitely many times already and will go on happening infinitely many times in exactly the way it is now happening. The problems raised by the doctrine are manifold. What, for example, are we to think of the idea of a law of eternal recurrence in the light of Nietzsche's rejection of all law-like explanations of reality? And what is the point of advocating super-human exertions of the will if what takes place is simply an exact repetition of what has already occurred an infinite number of times? It is not clear how such questions can be effectively answered but what is plain is that the doctrine of eternal recurrence was extremely important for Nietzsche's thought. For him it meant that the life one has now is the only life one has, and that one has it for ever. He says, 'I come eternally again to this same life, in what is greatest and what is smallest, and teach again the eternal recurrence of all things.'[6]

Nietzsche's first book, *The birth of tragedy*, was a highly original analysis of Greek tragedy and contains his famous discussion of the Apollonian and the Dionysian. He contrasts the Dionysian spirit of excess, frenzy and savage abandon with Apollonian restraint, order and harmony, and points out that in Greek tragedy the powerful Dionysian chaos is magnificently ordered and deployed by Apollonian quali-

ties. Between 1873 and 1876 Nietzsche published four 'untimely meditations' and between 1878 and 1886 five books written largely in aphoristic style. The last of these five was *Thus spake Zarathustra*, now widely regarded as his masterpiece, even though it contains very little sustained argument. *Beyond good and evil* appeared in 1886. It is aphoristic in style, apart from the poem at its conclusion, and touches on the whole range of Nietzsche's philosophical interests. It was followed in 1878 by *Toward a genealogy of morals* and in 1888 by five other short books. Nietzsche also wrote a brilliantly cynical review, *Ecce homo*, of his own work, but it was withheld by his sister until 1908. The last book he completed was *Nietzsche contra Wagner*, the short work in which he finally severed his connection with Richard Wagner. Other writings were assembled and edited by his sister, but the extent of the alterations she made is difficult to judge.

Nietzsche's concept of the Ubermensch, or Superman, permeates much of his work. His conception of such a person, who might be female or male, is not so much of someone who is in some sense superior in breeding and endowment, but of a person who confronts all the possible terrors and wretchedness of life and still joyously affirms it. Nietzsche advocated rigorous self-discipline and a voluntary exposure to suffering in order to exercise the will to power that could overcome the kind of submissive mediocrity he saw as characteristic of most people's lives. He regarded the will to power as the very essence of human existence, the source of all our strivings and of the cruelty that is a necessary though never an admirable component of any life. Moreover, the will to power as exercised by the Ubermensch was not simply a pitting of oneself against the pain and bitterness of life in order to preserve oneself but an effort to master all adversity and continually make a new and higher density for oneself. In Nietzsche's universe God is dead and there is no limit to what humankind alone might set itself to achieve. His advice is to follow one's highest ideals and to act on them at each moment, since what one does now will recur repeatedly through all eternity.

Nietzsche's brilliant and powerful prose style is perhaps his chief claim to fame. His short sentences have a poetic intensity that forces one to dwell on them and a vitality that is almost a physical presence on the page. He has been called the philosopher's philosopher and also the non-philosopher's philosopher. His influence on European literature, both prose and poetry, has been profound and numerous philosophers have written books on him.

Notes

1. Nietzsche, *Twilight of the idols*, Ch. 3 aph. 2.
2. *The gay science*, aph. 121.
3. A.C. Danto, 'Nietzsche' in D.J. O'Connor (ed.), *A critical history of Western philosophy* (The Free Press, New York, 1964; Macmillan, London, 1985).
4. Nietzsche, *Beyond good and evil*, aph. 17.
5. See *Sartre* in this book, pp. 157-63.
6. Nietzsche, *Thus spake Zarathustra*, III, 'The recurrence'.

See also in this book

Hegel, Schopenhauer, Marx, Heidegger, Sartre.

Nietzsche's major writings

The birth of tragedy out of the spirit of music (1872), trans. W. Kaufmann (Vintage Books, New York, 1967)
Untimely meditations (1873-6)
Human, all too-human (1878), trans. J.E. Hollingdale (Cambridge University Press, Cambridge, 1986)
The gay science (1882), trans. W. Kaufmann (Random House, New York, 1974)
Thus spake Zarathustra (1883-5), trans W. Kaufmann in *The portable Nietzsche* (The Viking Press, New York, 1954)
Beyond good and evil (1886), trans. W. Kaufmann (Vintage Books, New York, 1967)
Toward a genealogy of morals (1878), trans. W. Kaufmann (Vintage Books, New York, 1967)
Nietzsche contra Wagner (1895), trans. W. Kaufmann in *The portable Nietzsche* (The Viking Press, New York, 1954)
Nietzsche's collected works in German are in *Nietzsche: Werke in drei Bänden*, ed. K. Schlekta (Carl Hanser, Munich, 1954-6). They are translated into English in *The complete works of Friedrich Nietzsche*, ed. Oscar Levy (18 vols, T.N. Foulis, Edinburgh and London, 1909-13).

A wide selection of his writing is available in *The portable Nietzsche* (Viking Press, New York, 1954). A more recent edition in German is *Werke: Kritische Gesamtausgabe*, ed. Giorgio Colli and Mazzino Montinari (de Gruyter, Berlin, 1967-78).

Further reading

Crane, B. *Nietzsche* (Harvard University Press, Cambridge, Mass., 1941)
Danto, *Nietzsche as Philosopher* (Macmillan, London and New York, 1965)
Hollingdale, R.J. *Nietzsche* (Author Guides, Routledge and Kegan Paul, London, 1973)
Schact, R. *Nietzsche* (Routledge and Kegan Paul, London, 1983)

Francis Herbert Bradley
1846-1924

Bradley is the most formidable representative of that group of philosophers known as the British Idealists. The group held to the broadly Hegelian view that everything that exists is an aspect of one Mind. Bradley developed his own version of idealism, using terms such as 'the Absolute' and 'the Whole' to refer to the undivided totality of the one Mind. He maintained that the Absolute cannot be thought but is nevertheless knowable in that we can form some idea of 'an absolute experience in which phenomenal distinctions are merged'. He mounted a sustained and frequently caustic attack on empirical philosophy and especially on the **empiricism** and utilitarian ethics of John Stuart Mill. His writing is critical, rebarbative and eloquent. T.S. Eliot regarded his style as a model of English prose.

Bradley was born at Clapham, London, the son of the Reverend Charles Bradley, an Evangelical preacher whose two marriages produced twenty children. After schooling at Cheltenham and Marlborough, Bradley went to University College, Oxford, obtaining a First in classics and then a Second in *literae humaniores*. He was awarded a fellowship at Merton College in 1870, tenable for so long as he remained unmarried, and stayed at Merton for the rest of his life except for short periods spent abroad for the sake of chronically poor health. He had an impressive appearance and manner, was sociable, talkative and opinionated and well liked by those close to him. All his books are dedicated to 'E.R.', an American woman whom he met abroad and to whom he wrote letters in which he set out his ideas on **metaphysics**. He wrote chiefly on ethics, logic and metaphysics. Both Bertrand Russell and G.E. Moore attributed their early adherence to idealism to Bradley's influence and it was against his views that they rebelled, at the turn of the century, with what Russell called 'a sense of emancipation'.[1]

Much of the importance of Bradley's *Principles of logic*, published in 1883, stems from its critique of the empiricist approach to logic. That approach was based on the study of the contents of the human mind, generally conceived of as ideas combining together in various ways, and the elucidation of the various types of relations that might hold between the ideas. Bradley strongly opposes this view of logic. Judgement, he argues, does not consist in a psychological connecting of ideas but in the referring of an idea, or ideal content, to reality. He also rejects the empiricist view that the meaning of an idea is somehow bound into the content or constituents of the idea. He maintains instead that meaning is not a property of an idea or image but is something given to the idea in its use: symbolism is conventional rather than natural in character. He is profoundly critical of Mill's adherence to the **inductive** method of arguing from **particulars** to **universals**.[2] For, he said, it is only by a theory or universalising principle of some kind that particulars can be legitimately grouped together; any such grouping therefore presupposes a universal or ideal as its basis. Knowledge accordingly has its foundation in universals rather than in particulars.

When he turned his attention to the older, traditional logic Bradley expressed criticisms that rapidly gained complete acceptance. He points out that universal affirmative judgements are hypothetical, not categorical; that

the grammatical subject of a statement is not necessarily identical with its logical subject; that not every proposition is of subject–predicate form, as is presupposed by the **syllogism**; and that the syllogism cannot take account of relational arguments. Contemporaneously with Bradley's rejection of a psychologically grounded logic and of important aspects of traditional logic, another kind of rejection of established logical methods, equally radical and destined to be more influential, was being made by Gottlob Frege at the University of Jena.[3]

Bradley made his criticisms of logic not so much to advance logic itself as to support his main metaphysical thesis. That thesis is expounded in his major work, *Appearance and Reality*, published in 1893. It is Bradley's contention that our ordinary metaphysical views, derived largely from science and religion, do not stand up to any scrutiny that questions whether they could form the first principles of a theory of human experience. Even though views such as that everything can be accounted for in terms of primary and secondary qualities, or that an adequate description of reality is one given in terms of objects in space and time, may serve as acceptable descriptions of the appearances of things, they cannot, he claims, satisfy us as accounts of ultimate reality. He argues that upon close examination they collapse into contradictions and cannot therefore tell us anything about reality because 'ultimate reality is such that it does not contradict itself'. Bradley's arguments for this claim are extended and not easy to follow. Briefly, they are based on his account of what he calls 'feeling', a fundamental and primitive sense of the wholeness of all things which is an 'ultimate fact' for him and the starting point of his metaphysics. He writes:

In the beginning there is nothing beyond what is presented, what is and is felt, or rather is felt simply. There is no memory or imagination or hope or fear or thought or will, and no perception of difference or likeness. There are, in short, no relations and no feelings, only feeling.[4]

Although it is primary, feeling, he says, becomes worked on and broken up by thought which, even as it separates and discriminates every detail in a search for knowledge, aims thereby to reconstitute everything in a comprehensible and single whole. That single whole in which everything is coherently related is the Absolute. The Absolute is not a different realm, separate from everyday appearances; it is precisely those appearances, but understood as a totality; it is 'everything that is the case seen as constituting a single self-differentiating system'. But it is not simply the thought sum of appearances; for, rather as feeling is prior to thought, so is comprehension of the Absolute beyond and on the far side of thought, transcending it and all its contradictions. The nature of thought is such that it cannot but fragment the unitariness with which feeling is acquainted; but system, Bradley maintains, can restore unitariness. Here his logic and metaphysics are mutually supportive to the highest degree. His metaphysics asserts the interdependence of all things; his logic propounds a doctrine of 'internal relations' in which all the relations in which an object stands are essential relations, making the object what it uniquely is. From such considerations of internal relations one moves towards the concept of the Absolute as the necessary system that both contains and transcends all such relations.

Bradley's first well-known book, *Ethical studies*, is regarded as the most Hegelian of his writings. Once again, the tone is one of sharp criticism. He inveighs against Kant as well as John Stuart Mill, objecting to the formal nature of Kant's ethics, the hedonism of Mill's and the abstract nature of both systems. His own starting point is the morality of ordinary people from which he derives a famous doctrine which he calls 'My Station and its Duties'. It is a doctrine that is consistent with his account of reality as a unitary manifold in which everything is interdependent and internally related. He maintains that morality consists in a self-realisation that is worked out in the context of life in a community of persons and not from the standpoint of the isolated individual; any person 'is what he is ... so far as he is what others also are'.[5] However, he did not regard the establishing of one's station and duties as the whole of morality, for both station and duties could be surpassed and a person need not be confined to either. Nor did he think it was the task of the moral philosopher to formulate rules of ethical conduct. With ethics, as with the sciences, history, religion, aesthetics and politics, the task of philosophy, he said, was to understand.

Notes

1. See *Russell* in this book, pp. 134-8.
2. See *Mill* in this book, pp. 104-7.
3. See *Frege* in this book, pp. 125-8.
4. Bradley, *Collected essays* (Clarendon Press, Oxford, 1935), p. 216.
5. Bradley, *Ethical studies*, 2nd edn. (Oxford University Press, London, 1962), p. 167.

See also in this book

Hegel, Mill, Frege, Russell, Moore.

Bradley's major writings

Ethical studies (1876), 2nd edn., 1927 (Oxford University Press, London, 1962)
Principles of logic (1883), 2nd edn., 1922 (Clarendon Press, Oxford, 1922)
Appearance and reality (1893), 2nd edn., 1897 (Clarendon Press, Oxford, 1930)
Essays on truth and reality (1914) (Clarendon Press, Oxford, 1914)
Collected essays (1935) (Clarendon Press, Oxford, 1935)

Further reading

Eliot, T.S. *Knowledge and experience in the philosophy of F.H. Bradley* (Faber and Faber, London, 1964)
Manser, A. *Bradley's logic* (Blackwell, Oxford, 1983)
Moore, G.E. *Some main problems of philosophy* (Allen and Unwin, London, 1953), Chs. 11, 12, 16
Walsh, R. 'F.H. Bradley' in D.J. O'Connor (ed.), *A critical history of Western philosophy* (The Free Press, New York, 1964; Macmillan, London, 1985)
Wollheim, R. *F.H. Bradley* (Penguin, Harmondsworth, 1959)

Gottlob Frege   1848-1925

When Frege died in 1925, having taught at the University of Jena for thirty years, he was scarcely known outside a small circle of professional mathematicians and philosophers. In the late twentieth century he is recognised as someone who laid the foundations for modern philosophy of language and for modern logic, and who showed the affinity of logic with mathematics. Although similar attributions may be made to Bertrand Russell, Russell and Frege worked largely independently of each other and Frege's work is now regarded by some to be more exact and penetrating. His influence is clear in the work of the logical positivists of the early twentieth century and in much of Ludwig Wittgenstein's philosophy. As a consequence of the discovery of flaws in some aspects of his work, by the early 1920s Frege had lost confidence in his derivation of mathematics from logic and he began to consider geometry as the fundamental mathematical theory but did not publish the result of his investigations. A full understanding of the significance of his ideas requires a grasp of the technical language of mathematics and logic, but some of its main directions can be made plain without that.

Frege regarded logic as the foundation for philosophy. In doing so he instigated a radical change in the stance of the majority of Western philosophers whose main preoccupation since the time of Descartes, in the early part of the seventeenth century, had been with the nature of knowledge rather than with logic. Following Frege, Wittgenstein adopted the same attitude to philosophy in the *Tractatus* and thereafter philosophy moved rapidly into a new era.[1] Frege's *Foundations of arithmetic*, published in 1884, was a starting point for these innovations. It asks two major questions: What are numbers? What is arithmetic truth? In dealing with these questions Frege demolishes most of his predecessors' answers to them. Numbers, he argues, are neither Platonic perfections, existing inviolate in a separate realm, nor are they, as J.S. Mill had held, **abstractions** from experiences of varying groups of entities. He suggests that numbers 'belong' to concepts and that a number is made determinate only by being ascribed to a concept. He writes:

> If I say that 'Venus has 0 moons', there simply does not exist any moon or agglomeration of moons for nothing to be asserted of; but what happens is that a property is ascribed to the *concept* 'moon of Venus', namely that of including nothing under it.[2]

Numbers, he maintains, are objects, and just as the 'is' in an assertion such as 'Aristotle is the author of *De anima*' asserts the identity of 'Aristotle' and 'the author of *De anima*', so should the 'four' in 'the number of Jupiter's moons is four' be seen as identical with 'the number of Jupiter's moons'. Frege defines the concept 'having the same number as' by means of logical rather than arithmetical terms, using the logical notions of class and extension. He then goes on to define the series of numbers entirely in logical terms and thus derives arithmetic from logic. Zero, for example, is defined as the number which belongs to the concept 'not identical with itself' since, he argues, there is nothing that belongs with that concept. Once he had defined arithmetical procedures in terms of logic Frege had shown, he thought, that arithmetical truths are *analytic* in that all the laws of number are analytic: they are, he said, 'objects given directly to our reason and, as its nearest kin, utterly transparent to it'.[3] He believed in the existence of real abstract entities awaiting discovery by the reasoning of mathematicians. Rationality enables us to have insight into the laws of mathematics just as it does into the laws of logic.

Frege's derivation of arithmetic from logic was a brilliant achievement but it produced intractable problems. Bertrand Russell discovered a paradox that impaired the status of its logical element, which was the cause of Frege's eventual doubts about the derivation. Then, in 1931, a theorem produced by Kurt Gödel demonstrated that in certain important systems of mathematics consistency is not compatible with completeness since such systems, when consistent, are **necessarily** incomplete. This showed that some mathematical truths are in principle unprovable and that logic cannot account entirely for mathematics in the way Frege had hoped. In spite of these difficulties the influence of his work and the esteem in which it is held remain undiminished. Indeed, the problems connected with it have only produced a keener interest and more assiduous efforts towards its further development and application.

Frege's philosophy of language accrues largely from his philosophy of mathematics. Its dominant concern is with meaning and a number of issues connected with that concern are discussed in a famous paper written by Frege in 1892 called 'Sense and reference'. In the paper he works out a distinction between sense (*Sinn*) and reference (*Bedeutung*) by means of the following considerations.

If we ask what might be taken to be the meaning of the singular term 'the Morning Star', many might answer that the term means the planet to which it refers, or that it has meaning in virtue of the associations we make between the term and the planet. It could therefore be said that, generally speaking, the meaning of the term is taken to be that to which it refers, its referent. Frege, however, has objections to this view. He reminds us that the planet that was at one time known as 'the Morning Star' was later found to be identical with the planet called 'the Evening Star': it was realised that the two names referred to one planet. He points out that if our understanding of a name consisted in *knowing* what it referred to then any person who had previously understood the two terms would have known what they stood for and so would have known that it

was one thing. There would accordingly have been no later discovery of that fact. And what this makes clear is that the two terms 'the Morning Star' and 'the Evening Star' differ in sense although they have the same referent. The distinction between sense and reference shows how we are able to make use of different expressions for the same object. When he considers the meaning of sentences Frege decides that we can change the 'thought' of a sentence without changing its reference and that the 'thought' of a sentence must therefore be its sense. For example, 'the morning star is a body illuminated by the sun' has a different 'thought' from 'the evening star is a body illuminated by the sun', but refers to the same object. Frege concludes that the role of reference is to determine the **truth-value** of sentences rather than their meanings, and that the sense of an expression determines the referent of the expression. He writes of the sense of a name as indicating a route to its referent and of different names providing different routes to the same referent. The sense or 'thought' of a sentence is not a private or subjective matter, for it comprises the conditions which make a sentence true. Thus, if we say that 'Aristotle is wise' or 'the Morning Star is bright', we suppose that certain conditions obtain in virtue of which those sentences are true. Frege's conclusion is that when we understand a sentence what we understand is the conditions that make a sentence true, or a relation among truth-values. Using the principle that every term stands for its extension, that is, for the entity or entities to which it applies, he constructed a symbolic logic of the relations between sentences, using the mathematical notion of a function to refer to predicates and to yield truth or falsehood according to the objects to which they are attached. This mathematical type of logic has ousted the old Aristotelian logic. Moreover, Frege's view that truth is fundamental to language, carrying as it does an assumption that there is an objective truth that is the determinant of sense, has generated many debates within the philosophy of language and **metaphysics**.

It has been widely held that Frege took meaning to consist in both sense and reference, but in a book called *Frege: philosophy of language* Michael Dummett has argued against this view. He points out that Frege distinguishes three things: sense, tone and force, variations of which, in sentences, affect the meanings of those sentences. This is not to say that reference has nothing to do with meaning, but only that it is not an ingredient of it; rather, it is a *consequence* of meaning, in that it is determined by sense. Dummett argues that a theory of meaning is a theory of understanding. Such a theory has to give an account of 'what a person knows when he knows what a word or expression means, that is, when he understands it'.[4] The account must state what understanding consists in and, he says, 'To claim that reference is not an ingredient in meaning is, therefore, to claim that our understanding a word or expression never consists, even in part, merely with our associating something in the world with that word or expression.'[5] Dummett maintains that this is in 'complete consonance with Frege's views'. He also discusses some problems that relate to the notion of sense. Since the sense of an expression is not clear-cut the question arises whether sense is subjective and therefore not, like reference, shared between the speakers of the language. Dummett's response to this is to point out that an individual's means of determining a reference cannot rest on some knowledge possessed by him alone. He says:

Only what is known about the referent of an expression, and is taken by the individual to be reliable information about it, can enter into the sense attached by that individual to the expression; and only what is more or less common knowledge will normally be taken as part of that sense.[6]

He cites a connection made by Frege between sense and information, reminding us that what we find acceptable or unacceptable in the sense of an expression depends on a continual revision and supplementation of information that enables us to fix definite senses to expressions and so establish the grounds of statements in which they occur. In doing this we both recognise and refine established practices; but Dummett's point is that this activity is one of systematising our linguistic practices. In doing so it makes the sense of a statement something for which an objective justification may be sought. Frege's discussion of sense errs, he says, in regarding the nuances and flexibility of natural language as defects in it and in wanting a language in which each logically simple expression is definable in some way. On Dummett's view, sense does not have to be thus artificially fixed, since our linguistic practices already provide the conditions for objectivity.

Although there are many idioms of natural languages that his system of logic cannot encompass, Frege's work has been the starting point or basis for many attempts to extend the logical analysis of ordinary language. In the later philosophy of Wittgenstein the Fregean conception of language as analysable in terms of rules that yield truth-values is found questionable in the light of Wittgenstein's view that linguistic understanding depends on membership of a community within which there is agreement concerning the language used. This agreement, Wittgenstein believed, was at root an agreement not simply about definitions of words but in our reactions to life and the world.

Notes

1. See *Wittgenstein* in this book, pp. 145-51.
2. Frege, *Foundations of arithmetic*, trans. J.L. Austin (Blackwell, Oxford, 1950), p. 69e.
3. Ibid., p. 115e.
4. Michael Dummett, 'Sense and reference' in T. Honderich (ed.), *Philosophy through its past* (Penguin, Harmondsworth, 1984), p. 447. (This is Ch. 5 of Dummett's *Frege: philosophy of language* cited in

Further reading below.
    5. Ibid.
    6. Ibid., p. 458.

See also in this book

Bradley, Russell, Wittgenstein, Carnap.

Frege's major writings

'Begriffsschrift' (1879)
'Function and concept' (1891)
'On concept and object' (1892)
'On sense and reference' (1892)
'What is a function?' (1904)
The five items listed above are available in P. Geach and M. Black, *Translations from the philosophical writings of Gottlob Frege* (Blackwell, Oxford, 1952).
The foundations of arithmetic (1884), trans. J.L. Austin (Blackwell, Oxford, 1950)
'The thought: a logical inquiry', trans. A.M. Quinton and M. Quinton, *Mind*, vol. 65 (1956), pp. 289-311, reprinted in P.F. Strawson (ed.), *Philosophical logic* (Oxford University Press, Oxford, 1967), pp. 17-38

Further reading

Anscombe, E. and Geach, P. *Three philosophers* (Blackwell, Oxford, 1961)
Dummett, M. *Frege: philosophy of language* (Duckworth, London, 1981)
— *The interpretation of Frege's philosophy* (Duckworth, London, 1981)
Kneale, W. and Kneale, M. *The development of logic* (Clarendon Press, Oxford, 1962), Chs. 7 and 8
Passmore, J. *A hundred years of philosophy* (Penguin, Harmondsworth, 1968), Ch. 6
Walker, J. *A study of Frege* (Blackwell, Oxford, 1965)

Edmund Husserl   1859-1938

Husserl dedicated himself to a search for what he called 'the Archimedean point': the foundation of human knowledge. He maintained that a philosopher should never take anything for granted and should always be ready to abandon what he has done and to start all over again. Acting on his own advice, he paid careful attention to Frege's criticisms of his early attempts to analyse mathematical concepts in psychological terms and produced a sequel that treated logic and mathematics as sciences that are independent of experience and therefore quite distinct from psychology. He developed 'pure phenomenology', a procedure based on the examination of the contents of one's own consciousness. His method requires the exclusion of all assumptions about the external causes and results of those contents. Its aim is to discern the essential nature of mental acts and, thereby, the truths that are the sources of human knowledge.

Husserl was born at Prossnitz in Moravia. He studied mathematics at Berlin and then psychology with Franz Brentano at Vienna. In 1887 he became a *Privatdozent* (an instructor) at Berlin. In 1900 he was appointed professor of philosophy at Göttingen and in 1916 moved to a professorship at Freiburg where his teaching, as described by his pupil, Martin Heidegger, consisted in a step-by-step training in phenomenological 'seeing' which at the same time demanded that one relinquish the untested use of philosophical knowledge. He taught at Freiburg until 1929 and lived there for the rest of his life, unhappily subject to anxieties and strictures imposed on him because he was of Jewish descent.

In the nineteenth century and earlier the term 'phenomenology' had a wide range of uses. Since Husserl's employment of it early in the twentieth century it has been used to describe both the phenomenological method of doing philosophy and any descriptive method of studying a given topic. Husserl's phenomenology owes a good deal to the influence of Franz Brentano, his teacher at the University of Vienna. Brentano had argued that it was the distinguishing mark of mental phenomena that they include 'an object intentionally within themselves' and that such an object may or may not refer to any material reality. There are interesting and complicated logical considerations attached to this notion of an intentional object but for Brentano and his pupils it was the actual phenomenon, the mental experience of an intentional object, that was the focus of attention. Husserl's phenomenological method is set out and exemplified in Part I of his *Ideas: general introduction to pure phenomenology*, published in 1913. He maintains that the method is descriptive but that it is nevertheless distinct from psychological description. It requires that one holds in suspension, or 'brackets', what he calls 'the natural attitude'. Our first outlook, he says, is from a natural standpoint from which we are aware of the world 'spread out in space endlessly, and in time becoming and become, without end'. All the things of the world are there, whether one attends to them or not. They are, Husserl says, 'partly pervaded, partly girt about with a *dimly apprehended depth or fringe of indeterminate reality*'.[1] We sometimes bring some of them into focus but more generally they remain within the 'zone of indeterminacy'. Similarly with the world regarded temporally, there is a horizon, 'infinite in both directions'. Husserl writes:

> I can shift my standpoint in space and time, look this way and that ... I can provide for myself constantly new and more or less clear and meaningful perceptions and representations ... in which I make intuitable to myself whatever can possibly exist really or supposedly in the steadfast order of space and time.[2]

Moreover, this world, he says, which is continually 'present' for me, is not merely a world of facts but also a world of values that are as constitutive of it and as immediately given as its factuality. This natural world remains in some sense 'present' even if I focus attention on some different sphere, on arithmetic and number, for example, and so adopt 'an arithmetical standpoint'. When I contemplate mathematics thus, the natural standpoint 'is now the background for my consciousness as act, but it is *not the encircling sphere within which an arithmetical world finds its true and proper place*'.[3] Both worlds, the natural and the arithmetical, are present; both are related to my ego, but are distinct from each other. This type of structure of experience, Husserl maintains, is the same for everyone. Its content varies for each person in that 'each has his place whence he sees the things that are present, and each

enjoys accordingly different appearances of things'.[4] At the same time we have a common understanding of the objective spatio-temporal world to which we belong. The characterisation he has given, Husserl says, is 'a piece of pure description *prior to all theories*'; it is a general description of the way in which we inhabit and relate to the world, the particular contents of which are the objects of study for the sciences of the natural standpoint.

Husserl's aim is to perform a 'phenomenological reduction' of the natural standpoint. This is done by 'bracketing' off or putting to one side our belief in the totality of objects and things we engage with from the natural standpoint and attending instead to our *experiencings* of them. To 'bracket' things in this way is not so much a matter of doubting their existence but of disconnecting from them; it is 'a certain refraining from judgement which is compatible with the unshaken and unshakable because self-evidencing conviction of Truth'.[5] It is simply to make no use of what one 'brackets', even though one knows exactly what it is that is thereby put aside. This is the first step in the reduction. The second is to describe the structures of what remains after 'bracketing' has taken place. It is these structures or forms of consciousness which 'constrain psychic existence' and which constitute the possibilities for mental experiences. They have to be described just as they declare themselves to consciousness.

Husserl believes that in addition to considering one's experiencings of other people and other things by means of a phenomenological reduction, one can also discover one's own 'transcendental ego'. In doing so, the Archimedean point is reached; the real task of phenomenology begins with the recognition of the undeniable existence of the ego that is a pure consciousness quite distinct from the 'psychical self' that is of interest to psychology.

Husserl's views on the transcendental ego provoked many philosophical misgivings in the minds of other phenomenologists. Chiefly, they doubted whether there were mental phenomena, descriptions of which could support his contentions. But Husserl, by and large, held to his views, although in his later writings he posited the idea that the transcendental ego was correlative to the world rather than the 'absolute' to which all else is relative. After his death in 1938 the phenomenological movement became less unified but nevertheless found powerful exponents in Jean Paul Sartre and Martin Heidegger, both of whom developed highly individual lines of thought that included phenomenological procedures. Heidegger, in his paper 'My way to phenomenology', describes his early puzzlement with the method of phenomenology and recounts how that puzzlement was gradually dispelled in being taught by Husserl at Freiburg. Husserl's influence was a profound and enduring one. Heidegger wrote:

> I remained so fascinated by Husserl's work that I read it again and again in the years to follow without gaining sufficient insight into what fascinated me. The spell emanating from the work extended to the outer appearance of the sentence structure and the title page ...[6]

Notes

1. Husserl, *Ideas for a pure phenomenology*, Second Section, First Chapter, §27.
2. Ibid.
3. Ibid., §28.
4. Ibid., §29.
5. Ibid., §31.
6. Walter Biemel, *Martin Heidegger* (Routledge and Kegan Paul, London, 1977), p. 10.

See also in this book

Descartes, Frege, Heidegger, Sartre.

Husserl's major writings

Logical investigations (1900-1), trans. J.N. Findlay (2 vols, London, 1970)
Ideas: general introduction to pure phenomenology

(1913), trans. W.R. Boyce Gibson (Allen and Unwin, London 1931; Collier Books, New York, 1962)
Cartesian meditations (1929), trans. D. Cairns (The Hague, 1960)
Husserl's writings in German are collected in *Husserliana, Gesammelte Werke* (The Hague, 1950-). For a range of works in English see E. Husserl, *Shorter works* (Harvester Press, Brighton, 1981).

Further reading

Farber, M. (ed.) *Philosophical essays in memory of Edmund Husserl* (Harvard University Press, Cambridge, Mass., 1940)
Kolakowski, L. *Husserl and the search for certitude* (Yale University Press, New Haven, 1975)
Passmore, J. *A hundred years of philosophy* (Penguin, Harmondsworth, 1968), Ch. 8
Pivcevic, E. (ed.) *Phenomenology and philosophical understanding* (Cambridge University Press, Cambridge, 1975)

Henri Bergson 1859-1941

The concept of time is central in Bergson's philosophy. He distinguished between scientific time as measured by clocks and other devices, and pure time, a flowing sequence of continuous events which we experience immediately and within which it is sometimes possible, he claims, to act freely and authentically. He posited a vital impulse, *élan vital*, which is the fundamental reality through which cosmic power is experienced and he was opposed to all points of view that regarded intellect, rationality and science as superior. Many of his ideas have a close affinity with those of William James who described Bergson as advising us to

> dive back into the flux itself ... if you want to *know* reality, that flux which Platonism, in its strange belief that only the immutable is excellent, has always spurned: turn your face towards sensation, that flesh-bound thing which rationalism has always loaded with abuse.[1]

Bergson was born in Paris of Anglo-Polish parents. He attended the Lycée Condorcet there and then the Ecole Normale from which he graduated in 1881. In succeeding years he taught philosophy in

Angers and Clermont-Ferrand and then returned to Paris, teaching in several lycées and then at the Ecole Normale. In 1900 he was awarded a Chair at the Collège de France. By this time he was beginning to publish his work: *Laughter* in 1900 followed by *Creative evolution* in 1907. In 1911 he visited England and gave lectures in Birmingham and Oxford. *Creative evolution* had given him an international reputation and was extremely popular; in 1914 he was elected to membership of the Académie Française. In the same year some of his books were put on the Index of books prohibited by the Holy Office at Rome because his anti-intellectualism was thought to be harmful to Roman Catholicism. But his philosophy continued to be widely read and admired and its influence on other thinkers was profound. In 1919 a collection of his essays, *Mind-energy*, was published and in 1922 *Durée et simultanéité*, a discussion with Einstein about relativity. Bergson retired from his professorship at the Collège de France in 1921 because of poor health. He was awarded the Nobel Prize for Literature in 1927. In the years after World War One he gave close attention to international politics and worked to promote collaboration and peaceful co-existence between nations. Soon after the outbreak of World War Two, when he was living in occupied Paris, he was required to register as a Jew. He queued for several hours in cold conditions to fulfil this requirement and subsequently developed a pneumonia from which he died on 3 January 1941.

It was *Creative evolution*, published in 1907 and translated into English in 1911, that established Bergson's importance; but in *Time and free will*, published in 1889, he had already elaborated the contrast between time as deployed in the sciences, where it is thought of as some sort of homogeneous medium regularly punctuated by marks of division such as minutes and hours, and time as a dynamic, active and ever-changing stream of events: the flow of life itself. It is,

he maintains, the intellect that operates with the first sense of time, organising and conceptualising everything into distinct entities or sequences or states and thereby giving reality a neat and orderly aspect which it does not in fact possess. He allows that this intellectualism has practical uses, enabling us to survive capably, but at the same time insists that it leads to philosophical error in that it gives a false picture of what is really taking place. In reality there are none of the 'identical situations' that our words and intellectual classifications lead us to believe in but, instead, a flux of shifting experiences that are always different and fleeting. This is what real time, or 'duration', is. It does not extend through space like an unrolling ball of string and is not measured by any kind of chronometer. It exists as duration only because we ourselves observe it. Bergson says:

> the interval of the *durée* exists only for us, and because of the mutual penetration of our conscious states; outside us one would find nothing but space, and thus simultaneities, of which one may not even say that they objectively succeed each other.[2]

This conception of the nature of reality has implications for ideas of human freedom. Bergson thinks of the essential core of a person, 'the profound self' that we live rather than conceptualise, as not co-ordinate with our bodily movements. Freedom belongs with our direct, non-spatial experience of reality. It is felt but is not explicable and it is exercised, he says, only when one's action derives from the totality of one's being. Thus he writes: 'We are free when our acts emanate from the whole of our personality, when they express it and when they have this kind of indefinable resemblance to it that we see sometimes between a work and the artist.'[3] There is no objective *proof* of this kind of freedom because each person's freedom is exclusive to that person and cannot be directly experienced by anyone else. Bergson maintains that human beings do not exercise their full freedom as much as they might.

In *Creative evolution* Bergson develops his anti-intellectualism and engages in **metaphysics**. He rejects **materialist** and mechanist accounts of reality along with theories that describe it in terms of movement towards some goal or purpose. He rejects also the view that some kind of individual purpose controls the functioning of each organism. His own view is that the life-force, the *élan vital*, brings about the creative evolution of everything. This basic energy has no specified or specifiable goal; it is a creative and originating force which produces endless variations of forms against which it then has to contend in order to create further variations. Its activity increases freedom by overcoming the disintegration and inertia characteristic of matter. At one point in *Creative evolution* Bergson speaks of the *élan vital* as God. He writes: 'Thus defined, God has nothing of the ready-made, he is uninterrupted life, action, freedom. And the creation, so conceived, is not a mystery; we experience it in ourselves when we act freely.'[4] There seems to be more than a hint of **pantheism** in this conception of God as apparently identical with the *élan vital* and as experienced directly in our actions. But in letters to Joseph de Tonquédec Bergson maintained that he regarded God as a free creator, the generator of life and matter but distinct from them. Thus he nullifies any imputations of pantheism one might be tempted to make. What he does maintain, however, is that human life is part of a great and unfragmented whole which is recognised as such when we rely on our direct **intuitive** apprehension of, and participation in, the seamless flow of real time. The intuitive faculty that enables us to do this is something quite different from the intellect which artificially immobilises and fragments reality. Intuition, Bergson maintains, is nonconceptual. Directed on to the outer world it enables one to be transported into the interior of an object 'in order to coincide with

what there is unique and consequently inexpressible about it'. In contrast, intellect can only observe from the outside, using symbols to refer to its object, and it can sometimes produce **paradox** and falsification. Bergson regarded Zeno's 'paradoxes' as examples of ways in which attempts to conceptualise and explain motion have produced error and puzzlement. It is, he holds, incorrect to try to analyse motion by breaking up the passage of an object into sections or stoppages. Only the intuitive attitude can yield a knowledge that is undistorted and pure. Intellect immobilises everything in its attempt to circumscribe and be exact; the result is that the concepts it uses in making that attempt come to seem more real than what they refer to.[5] Intuition, derived as it is from instinct — it is instinct become conscious and objective — is able to participate in the living nature of things. However, it is not the case, according to Bergson, that intellect is without value and therefore to be disregarded. Indeed, it is essential in the creative evolution generated by the *élan vital* for it is deployed in combination with instinct to develop the capacity of intuition for more profound and more sustained insights. We are not to think of this creative progress as a warring of two distinct and entirely opposing substances but rather as a bifurcation of something original and primary that is the common source of both. Here Bergson freely mixes his metaphysical and scientific theories. He maintains that the *élan vital* originally diverted primitive living systems into several different directions of development, thus producing plants, insects and vertebrates, representing stability, instinct and intelligence. Thereafter, matter and consciousness have interacted to evolve not, Bergson insists, in accordance with a predetermined plan but nevertheless in such a way that progress and improvement continually take place on a cosmic scale: the *élan vital* operates throughout the universe and has, no doubt, produced other beings on other planets.

In his later years Bergson became increasingly religious and mystical in outlook. In *The two sources of morality and religion*, written 25 years after *Creative evolution*, he attempts a philosophical examination of anthropological and sociological answers to questions about the origins of morality and religion. For Bergson, the springs of such phenomena are to be found once again in a coming together of the human mind with the *élan vital*; and the mind most able to effect this union is the mind of the mystic. The ordinary morality of communities and societies serves numerous practical ends, binding people together and furthering easy coexistence, but beyond this limited and limiting system is another kind of morality, perceived by the more visionary mind which embraces all humanity. The mundane and partial morality of separate communities arises from the need to preserve societal life, but the universal morality is inspired by a religious perception of a higher and finer ideal of a community in which the dignity of every human being is recognised. Nevertheless, the morality of ordinary social life is the necessary condition of the imaginative and spiritual qualities of the universal morality.

Bergson's flamboyant and inspirational style of philosophising attracted severe criticism as well as admiration. Chief among his critics was Julien Benda, who regarded him as a supreme example of a general cultural and philosophical decline that had abandoned analytical and scientific thinking in favour of emotionalism, indeterminacy and a passive, feminine attitude. The American philosopher, Charles Sanders Peirce, felt himself maligned when his fellow philosopher, William James, pointed to what he saw as resemblances between Bergson's and Peirce's views. Strong critical opposition came, too, from several Roman Catholic philosophers in France and especially from Jacques Maritain, who felt that Bergson's anti-intellectualism threatened the traditional Catholic faith. At the same time, a modernist movement in Roman Catholicism that was questioning those very traditions of acquies-cence to authority and urging the significance and importance of personal religious experience was sympathetic to Bergson's philosophy. Bergson himself, as he grew older, drew close to the Catholic faith and declared that were it not for his wish to affirm his solidarity with the persecuted Jewish race he would have sought baptism into the Church. Manifestly, it was not his intention to undermine a faith he wished to espouse: no doubt it was his conviction that philosophical illumination could, in the end, only purify and enhance any religious doctrine.

A cogent objection to Bergson's condemnation of the devitalising rigidity of words and concepts is that he has to use them in order to articulate that condemnation and so vitiates the very perception he wants to communicate to us. To this accusation he might reply by reminding us that creative evolution moves towards something not unlike a Hegelian synthesis, in which intelligence and instinct combine to produce richer intuitive activity; and that in his philosophy he has effected, in his use of the language, a part of that creative advance.

Notes

1. See J. Passmore, *A hundred years of philosophy* (Penguin, Harmondsworth, 1968), p. 106.
2. H. Bergson, *Time and free will*, quoted in L. Kolakowski, *Bergson* (Past Masters, Oxford University Press, Oxford, 1985), p. 16.
3. Ibid., p. 129.
4. Bergson, *Creative evolution*, quoted in Kolakowski, *Bergson*, p. 61.
5. See *Zeno* in this book, pp. 13-15.

See also in this book

Zeno, Augustine, Peirce, James, Bradley.

Bergson's major writings

Time and free will: an essay on the immediate data of consciousness (1889), trans. F.L. Pogson (Allen and Unwin, London, 1971)
Matter and memory (1896), trans. N.M. Paul and W. Scott Palmer (Allen and Unwin, London 1970)
Laughter (1900), trans. C. Brereton and F. Rothwell (Macmillan, London, 1911)

Creative evolution (1907), trans. A. Mitchell (Greenwood Press, London, 1976; University Press of America, 1984)
An introduction to metaphysics, trans. T.E. Hulme (Macmillan, London, 1913)
The two sources of morality and religion (1932), trans. R.A. Andre and C. Brereton (Doubleday, New York, 1954; University of Notre Dame Press, 1977)
Bergson's writings are collected in *Oeuvres*, ed. André Robinet (Presses Universitaires de France, Paris, 1970).

Further reading

Kolakowski, L. *Bergson* (Oxford University Press, Oxford, 1965)
Lindsay, A.D. *The philosophy of Bergson* (Dent, London, 1911)
Maritain, J. *Bergsonian philosophy and Thomism* (Greenwood, London, 1955, 1968)
Pilkington, A.E. *Bergson and his influence: a reassessment* (Oxford University Press, Oxford, 1976)

Bertrand Russell   1872-1970

Russell's work has been profoundly influential in the development of philosophy in the twentieth century. His most important contributions have been to mathematical logic and the philosophy of logic but he also had a polymathic grasp not only of numerous philosophical topics but of the natural and social sciences and politics and throughout his life he engaged in public debate on countless social and political issues. With Alfred North Whitehead he wrote *Principia mathematica*, in which is propounded a system of logic that generates mathematics, thereby reducing mathematics to logic. He developed two theories, the Theory of Types and the Theory of Descriptions, and tackled problems relating to truth, meaning and belief. His well-known book, *The problems of philosophy*, is widely regarded as a classic introduction to philosophy and philosophising. In 1924 he described his philosophical position as that of logical atomism, which maintains that all complex entities are, upon analysis, reducible to simple particulars that can be denoted by logically proper names. The first of his lectures on logical atomism opens with the declaration that 'the world contains facts, which are what they are what-ever we may choose to think about them'. Although he later modified his doctrine of logical atomism it remained the basis of his conception of reality throughout the rest of his philosophical development. He was a **sceptic** concerning arguments for the existence of God, saying that he saw no reason to believe in a deity, and in a book called *Why I am not a Christian*, published in 1927, he systematically examines and criticises the arguments for God's existence. He was equally critical of Christian theology and practices. Politically he favoured a form of Guild Socialism, the chief concern of which was to balance the interests of producers and consumers for the widest possible benefit of the community as a whole. He regarded nationalism as a profound folly and danger and advocated a world government, even though he recognised the near-impossibility of bringing it into being. He was a leading influence in the Campaign for Nuclear Disarmament and in numerous peace initiatives until his death in 1970.

Russell was born one year before the death of John Stuart Mill, who was his secular godfather. His mother was the daughter of Lord Stanley of Alderly; his father, Viscount Amberley, was the eldest son of Lord John Russell, the Whig politician who introduced the 1832 Reform Bill. Both parents died before Russell was four years old and thereafter he was brought up by a formidable grandmother and educated privately until he went to Trinity College, Cambridge, with a scholarship in mathematics. His intellectual flourishing began immediately. He gradually moved from mathematics to philosophy and stayed on for a fourth year at Trinity in order to read for part two of the Moral Science Tripos. In 1895 he obtained a Fellowship at Trinity. In July 1900, at a Philosophy Congress in Paris, he met the Italian logician, Peano, and through an exchange of ideas with him developed his thoughts on the possible identity of mathematics and logic. The eventual outcome of this was his collaboration with A.N.

Whitehead, who had examined him for his Trinity scholarship, to produce *Principia mathematica.* The detailed work of the book consisted largely in the laborious writing out of theorems and this was undertaken by Russell. In his book on Russell, A.J. Ayer has related that from 1907 to 1910 Russell worked on the book for about eight months in each year, from ten to twelve hours a day. Ayer continues:

> When the book was completed, the Syndics of the Cambridge University Press estimated that its publication would involve them in a loss of £600 of which they were not willing to bear more than half. The Royal Society, of which Russell and Whitehead were both Fellows, Russell having been elected in 1908, agreed to contribute £200, but the authors had to find the remaining £100. Thus, their financial reward for this masterpiece, which had cost them ten years' work, was minus £50 apiece.[1]

In the years succeeding the publication of *Principia* Russell expanded his philosophical interests and also became involved in numerous social and political issues. He became a pacifist in 1901, stood unsuccessfully for Parliament in 1907 and championed the cause of women's suffrage. He was an agnostic and a freethinker and a bold flouter of authority. He was therefore continually engaged in a whole variety of disputes and conflicts and was frequently in the public eye. In 1918 he was sent to prison for six months for an alleged libel of the American Army and used the time of his sentence to write his *Introduction to mathematical philosophy.* Around this time the influence of Ludwig Wittgenstein,[2] who had arrived in Cambridge in 1912, was beginning to be felt in philosophy. Russell admired him greatly but ultimately diverged from his philosophical views. In the next few years he wrote prolifically, producing *Analysis of mind* in 1921 and following it with a series of short books dealing with relativity, atomic theory,

scientific and educational topics, religion, marriage and morals. On his brother's death in 1931 he became Earl Russell. He lived somewhat precariously and was largely dependent on teaching and lecture tours in the USA for his income. In 1932 his second marriage ended, obliging him to pay alimony. He was frequently abused and rejected by the respectable establishments where he sought work. In 1940 the offer to him of a professorship at the City College of New York provoked an outcry that culminated in a taxpayer's suit demanding the annulment of the appointment. As a result Russell was unable to take up the post. Ten years later, after being awarded a Nobel prize for literature, he returned to New York to give a lecture and was received with rapture. In 1944 he was invited to return to Trinity as a Fellow of the College. His *History of Western philosophy*, probably his best-known book, was published in 1945 and his *Human knowledge: its scope and limits* in 1948. A third marriage broke up in 1949 and in 1952 he married again. From 1955 to the end of his life he lived in North Wales, taking an ever-increasing interest in politics and peace initiatives and engaging in discussion and negotiation at the very highest level. In 1964 he established the Bertrand Russell Peace Foundation, supporting it with funds derived from the sale of his own archives. Two years later he set up an International War Crimes Tribunal of which the French philosopher, Jean-Paul Sartre, was a prominent member. Three days before his death at the age of 98 he dictated a condemnation of Israel's conduct in the Israeli–Arab war: the 'Message from Bertrand Russell to the International Conference of Parliamentarians in Cairo'.

Russell's earliest philosophical work was produced under the influence of the **idealism** of Hegel and Bradley, both of whom maintained that reality is one and that it is wholly mind. Partly through his work on Leibniz, partly through the exchange of ideas with G.E. Moore, his contemporary at Trinity, Russell became critical of the implications of this doctrine.[3] It saw everything as inter-related and thereby, according to Russell, made mathematics impossible, since in mathematics it is required that each unit must be identified and known before its relations with other units can be considered. Russell therefore propounded a realist and atomic view that recognised a plurality of things that were not mind-dependent and not internally related as in the Hegelian system. On this atomic view the meaningful use of a name depended on there being a constituent of the world corresponding to the name and a given fact could be considered and affirmed without having to think of that fact in relation to every other part of the whole. Russell was supported and inspired in the development of this thesis by the work of G.E. Moore, who in 1903 published an influential paper called 'The refutation of idealism'. A difficulty with the new realism was that along with the externality of relations went a picture of the world as a teeming mass of real entities, some of which were indiscernible although required as the referents of meaningful discourse. Russell therefore invoked Ockham's Razor,[4] the maxim which states that 'Entities are not to be multiplied without necessity' and devised a method of logical analysis in which constructions out of known entities replaced inferences to unknown entities. The result was a sturdy logical **empiricism** which in one form or another characterises the whole of Russell's work, although he never aimed to produce anything like a coherent system of philosophy. Indeed, he consciously rejected systematisation and advocated a piecemeal approach in which problems are treated one by one, using the analytic method.

The Theory of Descriptions amply illustrates Russell's method. It was designed to meet the difficulty of seeing how a certain kind of description may be seen as meaningful. For example, in the sentence 'The present king of France is bald' the denoting phrase 'The present king of France' refers to a non-existent person. If it is held, as Russell

held, that meaningful discourse must have referents, then the sentence is meaningless: it cannot be said to be either true or false. Russell therefore analyses a sentence of this kind in the following way. He divides it into two parts that are connected by a conjunction, thus: 'There is a unique individual ruling France, and if someone rules France then he is bald.' This renders the sentence meaningful by disposing of the reference to a non-existent entity. The claim that 'there is a unique individual ruling France' is a false claim, and because a sentence containing a conjunction is false if either of its parts are false, the whole sentence is accordingly false and therefore meaningful.

Russell starts his first chapter of *The problems of philosophy* with a question: 'Is there any knowledge in the world which is so certain that no reasonable man could doubt it?' To answer the question he examines and describes the way in which we perceive the world. He introduces the term 'sense-data' for 'such things as colours, smells, hardnesses, roughnesses and so on' and calls our awareness of a sense-datum a sensation. He distinguishes between what he calls 'knowledge by acquaintance' and 'knowledge by description'. Where knowledge of things is concerned, he maintains, we can have direct acquaintance only with sense-data, our selves and our mental states. He argues that we are not directly acquainted with physical objects but infer to objects such as tables, trees, dogs, houses and people from sense-data, the objects being the causes of the sense-data. The difficulty here is that of seeing how inferences are made from sense-data to an entity satisfying a common-sense account of a physical object. Russell eventually decided that physics could do without physical objects and that it should adhere to the maxim that 'whenever possible logical constructions are to be substituted for inferred entities'. He also came to the conclusion that we are not directly acquainted with a self but nevertheless are able to be acquainted with mental facts such as willing, believing and wishing. He maintained a distinction between such mental facts and sense-data, the latter being what is willed, believed, wished for and, in general, experienced.

Propositions about belief present Russell with a problem. He distinguishes two kinds of propositions, atomic and molecular, the truth or falsity of a molecular proposition being determined by the truth or falsity of the atomic propositions into which it is analysable, while the truth of an atomic proposition is determined by reference to the fact it depicts. But it is difficult to assign propositions about mental facts to either of these categories. The proposition 'He believes that p is q' appears to be molecular, consisting of 'He believes' and 'p is q'; but on examination it is clear that the truth or falsity of 'p is q' has no bearing on the truth of the whole proposition 'He believes that p is q' and cannot therefore be assigned a truth value appropriate to the form 'x and y'. When Russell wrote *The analysis of mind* he tried to resolve this difficulty along **behaviourist** lines by reformulating propositions about belief. For if one reformulates a proposition such as 'I believe that Alsatian dogs are dangerous' as 'When I see an Alsatian dog coming I keep out of the way', then beliefs and other 'mental facts' no longer have to be regarded as requiring a logic of their own.

Russell continued to develop and revise his views. He was always ready to recognise flaws and inadequacies in doctrines he had argued for and always ready to rethink and reformulate his ideas. The philosopher Charlie Broad, Professor of Moral Philosophy at Cambridge from 1933 to 1953, remarked that Russell produced a brand-new philosophy every few years. Notwithstanding such remarks Russell himself, in his intellectual autobiography, *My philosophical development*, asserts a coherent development in his work in spite of his avowed piecemeal approach to particular philosophical problems, and he admits to only one radical change of direction, namely his early move

from Hegelianism to the espousal of Peano's logic and logical atomism. His allegiance to the principle of Ockham's Razor and his indebtedness to G.E. Moore — although this latter influence was often rejected — are always apparent in his work. But the presiding eminence at all times is science and the demand to find a justification for its general propositions. Physics requires the existence of continuing physical objects; but this, in turn, requires a notion such as that of **substance** and this notion is a major difficulty for a philosophy that eventually wanted to see everything in terms of qualities rather than in terms of substances that support qualities. Russell eventually argues that there are certain principles, such as the permanence of things and **inductive** reasoning, that have to be adopted for the foundations of science even though they cannot be verified by experience. He held that they are somehow extracted by us from experience.

It is sometimes said that Russell's philosophical achievements are underestimated. If they are, one reason for such undervaluing may be the decisive swing, in the mid twentieth century, away from science-grounded philosophising to enquiries into the significance of language and the analysis of ordinary discourse, once described by Russell as 'the different ways in which silly people can say silly things'. Another, more trivial, reason may be the pontificating and opinionated tone of much of Russell's writing. Even his most lucidly and economically expressed arguments manage frequently to impart a flavour of authoritarianism and a petulant intolerance of any equivocation. A short browse in his *History of Western philosophy* amply exemplifies this characteristic. But such considerations should not affect a cool judgement of Russell. In his case we have to ponder an observation of Goethe's:

> With narrow-minded persons and those in a condition of mental darkness, we find conceit. With men of intellectual lucidity and high endowment we never find it. In

the latter cases there is generally a feeling of joyful strength; and since this strength is a reality, their feeling is not conceit, but something else.

Notes

1. A.J. Ayer, *Russell* (The Woburn Press, London, 1974), pp. 16, 17.
2. See *Wittgenstein* in this book, pp. 145-51.
3. See *Hegel*, pp. 96-100, *Bradley*, pp. 122-4, and *Moore*, pp. 138-42, in this book.
4. See *Ockham* in this book, pp. 39-41.

See also in this book

Ockham, Hegel, Bradley, Moore, Wittgenstein.

Russell's major writings

A critical exposition of the philosophy of Leibniz (1900) (Allen and Unwin, London, 1937)
The principles of mathematics (1903), 2nd edn., (Allen and Unwin, London, 1937)
Principia mathematica, with A.N. Whitehead (3 vols. Cambridge University Press, Cambridge, 1910, 1912, 1913)
The problems of philosophy (1912) (Oxford University Press, Oxford, 1973)
Our knowledge of the external world (1914), 3rd edn. (Allen and Unwin, London, 1926)
An inquiry into meaning and truth (1940) (Allen and Unwin, London, 1940)
History of Western philosophy (1945) (Allen and Unwin, London, 1945)
Logic and knowledge (1956) (Allen and Unwin, London, 1956)
Autobiography (3 vols., Allen and Unwin, London, 1967, 1968, 1969)

Further reading

Ayer, A.J. *Russell* (The Woburn Press, London, 1974)
Clark, R.W. *The life of Bertrand Russell* (Penguin, Harmondsworth, 1975)
Eames, E.R. *Bertrand Russell's theory of knowledge* (Allen and Unwin, London, 1969)
Kilminster, C.W. *Russell* (Harvester Press, Hassocks, Sussex, 1986)
Pears, D.F. *Bertrand Russell and the British tradition in philosophy*, 2nd edn. (Fontana, London, 1968)
Schilpp, P. (ed.) *The philosophy of Bertrand Russell* (Cambridge University Press, Cambridge, 1944)
Watling, J. *Bertrand Russell* (Oliver and Boyd, Edinburgh, 1970)

George Edward Moore
1873-1958

In the story of twentieth-century British philosophy the name of G.E. Moore is linked with that of Bertrand Russell. Both men were at Trinity College, Cambridge, in the mid-1890s and it was Russell who inspired Moore to forsake his classical studies and read moral sciences for the third year of his tripos. Thereafter Moore took the lead in rebelling against the **idealism**, derived from Hegel and Bradley, that was the prevailing philosophical orthodoxy. His essay, *The refutation of idealism*, was published in 1903 and sets the tone of scrupulous common-sense enquiry that characterises all his work. He designated three main areas of concern for philosophy: the first concern is with giving 'a general description of the *whole* of this universe, mentioning all the most important kinds of things which we *know* to be in it'; the second is with examining the ways in which we can have knowledge of things; the third is with ethics. Moore's influential book, *Principia ethica*, propounds the view that goodness is indefinable and unanalysable and so incapable of proof or disproof. In reply to his own question, what are 'the most valuable things we can know or imagine'?, he answers that they are 'certain states of consciousness which may be roughly described as the pleasures of human intercourse and the enjoyment of beautiful objects'.[1] His philosophical importance rests largely on the method of linguistic analysis by which he sought to elucidate meanings and on his allegiance to the deliverances of ordinary language.

Moore was born in the London suburb of Upper Norwood. He attended Dulwich College and in 1892 entered Trinity College to read classics, changing to moral sciences for his third year. He was elected to a fellowship at Trinity in 1896 and thereafter wrote numerous papers and *Principia ethica* and engaged regularly in discussion with Bertrand Russell. He left Cambridge when his fellowship ended in 1904 but was invited to return in 1911 as a lecturer and in 1925 was appointed to a chair of mental philosophy and logic. He retired in 1939 but remained in

Cambridge and continued to philosophise into his eighties, having exercised a strong and benign influence on Cambridge pupils and colleagues for the greater part of an otherwise uneventful academic life. Together with Bertrand Russell and Ludwig Wittgenstein he was a source of major changes in British philosophy. It has been remarked that Wittgenstein's early philosophy is Russellian, his later Mooreian.

When Moore rejected the idealist thesis that everything is Mind he adopted the common-sense view that there is a world of physical objects of which we become aware in acts of perception. He maintained, against idealism, that because awareness is mental it does not thereby follow that what one is aware of is also mental. Many idealists, he says, have thought that yellow is identical with the sensation one has of yellow. His own analysis points out that to have a sensation is to have a sensation *of* something; it is 'to know something which is as really and truly not a part of *my* experience, as anything which I can ever know'. He argues that we do not need to provide evidence for the existence of external objects because it is something we know already. In a paper called 'Proof of an external world' he writes:

I can prove now that two human hands exist. How? By holding up the two hands, and saying, as I make a certain gesture with the right hand, 'Here is one hand', and adding, as I make a certain gesture with the left hand 'and here is the other.'[2]

The bland simplicity of that declaration is at once salutary and enraging; salutary because it draws any speculative thinker back to the centre of common experience, but enraging because it seems to beg the very question that is being asked, namely, Can we *know* if there is external world? It is also entirely characteristic of Moore's approach to philosophy and exemplifies the ingenuous candour with which he customarily responded to the elaborate and tortuous intellectual constructions that some of his

fellow philosophers were wont to provide in order to justify what he himself saw as transparently self-evident truths. It is consonant, too, with something he wrote later in some autobiographical notes:

I do not think that the world or the sciences would ever have suggested to me any philosophical problems. What has suggested philosophical problems to me is things which other philosophers have said about the world or the sciences ...[3]

Moore does not claim infallibility for the assumptions of common sense, nor does he accept every such assumption uncritically. But in critically examining common-sense assumptions he gives full weight to such considerations as that most of them are universally accepted, that they are extremely difficult to deny in the sense that we cannot help holding and living by them, and that the attempt at their denial often produces inconsistencies elsewhere in our system of beliefs. These considerations provide a body of reasons which incline us to assent to common-sense beliefs and, Moore maintains, they produce a more forceful argument for accepting common-sense beliefs than do reasons adduced for denying them.

Moore's analytic method did much to influence the way philosophy developed in the hands of his younger contemporaries. He held that a close and detailed scrutiny of linguistic terms, and in particular of the concepts we use, can reveal unclarities and ambiguities that are the source of philosophical problems and of what he regards as the sometimes unlikely solutions proposed for them. Thus his whole tendency is not so much to provide answers to questions as to endeavour to understand the questions being asked. His analyses are directed to discovering the meanings of ordinary expressions by distinguishing the various parts into which a concept can be separated and by seeing the relationship in which those parts stand to each other. In *Principia ethica* Moore declares that previous systems of ethics have failed because the questions of ethics have been formulated imprecisely. He identifies two questions which he says have 'almost always been confused both with one another and with other questions'. The first question is: What kind of things ought to exist for their own sakes? The second is: What kind of actions ought we to perform?[4] He distinguishes between intrinsic and extrinsic good, intrinsic good being a property of the kind of things which ought to exist for their own sake, extrinsic good belonging with things which are good because they are means to what is intrinsically good. When he examines intrinsic goodness Moore finds it to be unanalysable: 'good', in its adjectival sense, he maintains, refers to a simple, unanalysable property. He writes: 'My point is that "good" is a simple notion, just as "yellow" is a simple notion; that, just as you cannot, by any manner of means, explain to anyone who does not already know it, what yellow is, so you cannot explain what good is.'[5] Moreover, it is, he says, 'non-natural'; that is, it cannot be defined in terms of any natural property. The non-definability of good follows from its characterisation as simple and unanalysable but in emphasising that it is not equivalent to any natural property such as that of being pleasant Moore is wanting to prevent the commission of what he calls 'the naturalistic fallacy'. Natural properties are, of course, part of nature but good is non-natural and so not a property to be classified among the objects of natural science. It is therefore fallacious, he argues, to think that natural properties such as those of being pleasant or desirable, although they may be additional properties of something we describe as 'good', are *definitive* of good. Moreover, that such properties are not definitive of good is clearly apparent when we realise that we can meaningfully ask of something that is pleasant whether it is also good; for in asking that question we are not merely asking whether what is pleasant is pleasurable. However, if 'good' were definable in terms of what is pleasant, then we would be asking

just that **tautologous** question. If we ask how it is recognised what things are good, Moore's reply is that ethical propositions asserting goodness are intuitions. In the Preface to *Principia ethica* he writes, 'I would wish it observed that, when I call such propositions "Intuitions" I mean *merely* to assert that they are incapable of proof; I imply nothing whatever as to the manner or origin of our cognition of them.'[6] What he is anxious to deny here is something maintained by 'the Intuitionist proper', namely, that propositions which assert that a certain action is right, or is a duty, are incapable of proof or disproof. Still less, he says, does he want to imply that such propositions should be regarded as true simply in virtue of being cognised intuitively.

Moore does not want to say that '*the* good', as distinct from good understood as a property, is unanalysable. Concerning this distinction he says:

I must try to explain the difference between these two. I suppose it may be granted that 'good' is an adjective. Well, 'the good, that which is good,' must therefore be the substantive to which the adjective 'good' will apply: it must be the whole of that to which the adjective will apply, and the adjective must *always* truly apply to it. But if it is that to which the adjective will apply, it must be something different from that adjective itself; and the whole of that something different, whatever it is, will be our definition of *the* good.[7]

Moore maintains that the states of consciousness he has identified as supremely valuable, namely 'the pleasures of human intercourse and the enjoyment of beautiful objects', are wholes, and that it is such wholes that we should aim for rather than their individual constituents. The greatest good, he argues, is that of personal affection, since it includes the aesthetic pleasure experienced in appreciating the admirable mental qualities of other persons who, in turn, are appreciating yet other persons. He holds that the true beauty of anything depends on 'the *objective* question whether the whole in question is or is not truly good, and does not depend upon the question whether it would or would not excite particular feelings in particular persons'.[8] In discussing wholes he introduces the idea of 'organic unities', pointing out that a collection of individually good things does not necessarily result in a good whole and that no whole, however composed, necessarily produces a goodness or badness that is proportional to the goodness or badness of its parts. For example, two evils such as a crime and its punishment may together constitute a better whole than one of the two evils on its own can make. In a similar manner, an object which in itself is both good and beautiful has little value except in relation to a pleasurable consciousness of it. Thus any estimate of the good of a whole must take into account the organic relationship of its parts.

One of Moore's most cogent criticisms is of a version of ethical subjectivism that maintains that a judgement such as 'This is good' is the equivalent of saying 'I approve of this,' thereby analysing the judgement as an expression merely of subjective approval and disposing of the difficulty of giving an account of what 'good' objectively might be. Moore points out that if one person says 'This is good' of an object and another person says 'This is bad' of the same object then, on a subjective theory, there is no disagreement between these two people and this is quite contrary to our common-sense understanding of what has been said. Once again, the inadequacy of an explanation is brought out by appeal to our ordinary understanding of terms and concepts. He was equally critical of ethical theories based on the notion of a supersensible reality, insisting that although 'good' is a non-natural property it is nevertheless not a supernatural one. And he points out that the belief that good belongs solely to an absolutely Perfect Being precludes the possibility of any human

endeavour making a difference to that condition.

Although Moore used and advocated analysis as a method, he did not believe it was the only way of doing philosophy. He never rejected the view that philosophers should also be concerned with large questions about the nature of things and indeed his own attention to the question of what *the* good substantively is displays just such a concern. Although the conclusions of his analyses are for the most part unacceptable to English-speaking philosophers in the late twentieth century, the method and practice of detailed analysis have become their indispensable tool. His ideas influenced the Bloomsbury circle, which included Virginia and Leonard Woolf, Lytton Strachey, Desmond MacCarthy and J.M. Keynes. In a *Memoir*, Keynes wrote of the 'beauty of the literalness of Moore's mind, the pure and passionate intensity of his vision, *un*fanciful and *un*dressed-up' and said of him that 'even when he was awake, he could not distinguish love and beauty and truth from the furniture'.[9]

Notes

1. G.E. Moore, *Principia ethica* (Cambridge University Press, Cambridge, 1962), Ch. 6, §113.
2. G.E. Moore, 'A proof of an external world' in *Philosophical* papers, (Macmillan, New York, 1962).
3. In *The philosophy of G.E. Moore*, ed. P. Schilpp (Northwestern University Press, Evanston, 1942).
4. Moore, *Principia ethica*, Preface, p. viii.
5. Ibid., p. 7.
6. Ibid., Preface, p. x.
7. Ibid., Ch. 1, §9.
8. Ibid., Ch. 6, §121.
9. J.M. Keynes, *Two memoirs* (Hart-Davis, London, 1949), p. 94.

See also in this book

Hegel, Bradley, Russell, Wittgenstein.

Moore's major writings

Principia ethica (1903) (Cambridge University Press, Cambridge, 1903, 1959)
Some main problems of philosophy, lectures written in 1910 and 1911 (Allen and Unwin, London, 1953)

Ethics (1912) (Oxford University Press, Oxford, 1966)
Philosophical studies (1922) (Routledge and Kegan Paul, London, 1960)
Commonplace book (1919-53), ed. C. Lewy (Allen and Unwin, London, 1963)

Further reading

Passmore, J. *A hundred years of philosophy* (Penguin, Harmondsworth, 1968), Ch. 9
Urmson, J.O. *Philosophical analysis* (Clarendon Press, Oxford, 1956)
White, A.R. *G.E. Moore: a critical exposition* (Blackwell, Oxford, 1958)

Moritz Schlick   1882-1936

Schlick was a founder member of the Vienna Circle, that group of twentieth-century scientists, mathematicians and philosophers who formulated the philosophy known as 'logical positivism' or 'logical empiricism'. He shared Ludwig Wittgenstein's view that philosophy is not a body of doctrine but an activity. Inspired by the analyses of Ernst Mach, who became Professor of the Philosophy of Science at Vienna in 1895, Schlick adopted a critical approach to the concepts that formed the bases of the individual sciences. His aim was to understand the meanings of those concepts and, thereby, to understand what can count as knowledge. With other members of the Vienna Circle he was responsible for the formulation and refinement of its famous verification principle which states that 'the meaning of a proposition is the method of its verification'. He likened his philosophical method to the Socratic quest for the clarification of concepts.

Schlick was born in Berlin. His family was one of the few families of the Czech Protestant nobility that had survived the oppression of the Habsburg dynasty. When he was 18 he entered the University of Berlin and studied physics under Max Planck. His doctoral thesis, which he presented in 1904, dealt with the reflection of light. He held a lectureship and then became an associate professor at the University of Rostock from 1911 to 1917. In 1922 he became Professor of the Philosophy of the Inductive Sciences at the University of Vienna and it was then that the Vienna Circle was formed under his leadership. He greatly admired Ludwig Wittgenstein whose *Tractatus logico-philosophicus* was carefully studied by the Circle at its meetings in the years 1924 to 1926. Wittgenstein never became a member of the Circle for he did not entirely share its views, but he formed an enduring friendship with Schlick and it was Schlick who persuaded him, in 1927, to return to the philosophical work he had abandoned. During his Vienna years Schlick went to the United States twice as a visiting professor. He published a series of papers and, in 1930, a book, *The problems of ethics*. In June 1936, when he was on his way to give a lecture, he was murdered by an insane student who had made an earlier attempt on his life. The meetings of the Vienna Circle then ended, not only because of Schlick's death but also as a consequence of the Austrian Ministry of Culture's policy of refusing philosophy professorships to scientific and analytically minded candidates. Most of the members of the Vienna Circle emigrated to England and the United States of America, thereby ensuring further dissemination of their views. In England logical positivism was already known through the work of A.J. Ayer, the Oxford philosopher whose lucid account of it first appeared in *Language, truth and logic*, published in January 1936.

Much of Schlick's work is concentrated on establishing and clarifying the details of verificationism. The verification principle identifies the meaning of a statement with the method of its verification. That method of verification is empirical: we understand the meaning of a statement if we know what kind of observations verify it. Thus, if someone declares that 'The post has arrived' we understand the meaning of the statement when we know what kinds of observations — inspection of the doormat or the letterbox in the front door, for example — can demonstrate its truth or falsity. In a paper in which he discusses the principle Schlick maintains that it is not a theory; that is, it is not a **hypothesis** about meaning because, he says, we must presuppose meaning in order to formulate any hypothesis. He argues that any explanation of the meaning of sentences depends on pre-established connections between 'the words and the rest of the world'. If I do not understand the connections then I must be taught them by undergoing experiences that make the connections plain. Schlick says: 'All your future understanding will be by virtue of these experiences. In this way all meaning is essentially referred to experience.'[1] Concerning the principle itself he writes:

> We have not made any assumptions, we have done nothing but formulate the rules which everybody always follows whenever he tries to explain his own meaning and whenever he wants to understand other people's meaning ... In establishing the identity of meaning and manner of verification we are not making any wonderful discovery, but are pointing to a mere truism.[2]

It follows from the verification principle that where there is no method of verification for a statement, the statement has no meaning. Consequently, **metaphysical** statements that seem to be describing the nature of reality as a whole, or the existence of the soul or free will, if subjected to the criterion of meaningfulness entailed by the principle of verification, are shown to be meaningless, since there are no empirical observations relevant to establishing their truth or falsity. Schlick maintains that so-called questions of metaphysics are unanswerable because they are actually not questions; that so-called problems of metaphysics are insoluble 'not because they pass the power of our understanding, but simply because they are not problems'.[3] They are, he says, attempts to express content. But content, in his view, is incommunicable and subjective; only structure is objective. He writes: 'All the different

individuals communicate to each other the structural forms, the patterns, and they can all agree about these, but ... about the ineffable content they can neither agree nor disagree.'[4] What he is pointing out here is that it does not make sense to think that one could take one's experience of something such as a colour from one's own consciousness and put it into someone's else's; yet this is just what is being attempted, he believes, in metaphysical utterances. Structure, by contrast, seems to be objective in that it can somehow be seen to correspond with facts; but the exact nature of that correspondence is not clear and it proved to be a source of difficulty for philosophers seeking to establish the grounds of verificationism.

The severance of metaphysics from philosophy was a major aim of the advocates of logical positivism. In defending the ascription of meaninglessness to statements of metaphysics A.J. Ayer has pointed out that they are regarded as *factually* meaningless, with emphasis on the word 'factually'. He writes:

> It is not denied that language has other uses besides that of imparting factual information. Nor is it maintained that these other uses are unimportant, or that metaphysical statements may not serve them. They may, for example, express an interesting and challenging attitude to life. All that is claimed is that they are not capable of stating facts.[5]

What the Vienna Circle could not and did not want to deny was the meaningfulness of the statements of mathematics and logic. The members of the Circle held to Frege's view that mathematics is derived from logic.[6] They maintained that statements of mathematics are **necessarily** true because they are true by definition, and that they are **tautologies** in that they say nothing about how things are in the world. But statements of value, ethical and aesthetic, when taken as descriptive of a value realm distinct from the natural world are found meaningless when assessed by the verificationist criterion. When Schlick wrote his *Problems of ethics* he treated ethical statements as empirical. His first chapter opens thus:

> If there are ethical questions which have meaning, and are therefore capable of being answered, then ethics is a science. For the correct answers to its questions will constitute a system of true propositions, and a system of true propositions concerning an object is the 'science' of that object.[7]

The object of ethics, he says, has many names, among them 'morality', 'the morally "valuable"', and 'good'; and ethics seeks to understand this object but not to produce or establish morality. He rejects the ideas of attempting merely to define 'good', of positing a special 'moral sense' that enables us to discern it, and of limiting our account of it as Kant did to a statement of a purely formal property. Kant's belief that the concept of moral good is completely exhausted by describing it as 'what should be' is, he says, 'one of the worst errors of ethical thought'.[8] His own empirical approach is to elucidate a hierarchy of norms or rules by a method which is no different from the method of the sciences. The method simply observes and records what things actually are valued and held to be morally good and uses its findings as the basis for establishing norms or rules by which to make further moral judgements. Such judgements are justified in virtue of corresponding to the established norms. Within the hierarchy, lower norms are seen as valid in relation to higher norms but the question of the justification of ultimate values is, according to Schlick, 'senseless, because there is nothing higher to which these could be referred'.[9] He regards the formulation of questions about ultimate values as meaningless and remarks: 'Such norms as are recognised as the ultimate norms, or highest values, must be derived from human nature and life as facts.' And a page later he writes: 'Foreign to us is the pride of those philosophers who hold the questions of ethics to be the most noble and elevated of questions just because they do not refer to the common *is* but concern the pure *ought*.'[10]

Schlick distinguishes between an investigation into what the norms of conduct are and an investigation into the causes of their being what they are. He calls the latter investigation 'explanatory ethics' and regards it as the proper task of ethics. It seeks the natural law governing behaviour in general in order to learn what is peculiar to moral action. Thus, for Schlick, the central problem of ethics is the causal explanation of moral conduct and the method of ethics is a psychological one. This conclusion is consistent with the Vienna Circle's aim of unifying the sciences rather than generating new, distinct disciplines. Schlick says of the true philosopher that 'there is for him only *one* reality and *one* science'.[11]

Another member of the Vienna Circle, Rudolf Carnap, in his short 'Autobiography' has pointed out that Schlick's philosophical work has not found the attention it deserves. He testifies to Schlick's personal qualities in the following words:

> The congenial atmosphere in the Circle meetings was due above all to Schlick's personality, his unfailing kindness, tolerance and modesty. Both by his personal inclination towards clarity and by his training in physics, he was thoroughly imbued with the scientific way of thinking ... By his clear, sober and realistic way of thinking, Schlick often exerted a sound moderating influence on the discussions of the Circle. Sometimes he warned against an exaggerated thesis or against an explication that appeared too artificial, and he appealed to what might be called a scientifically refined common sense.[12]

Notes

1. In O. Hanfling (ed.), *Essential readings in logical positivism* (Basil Blackwell, Oxford, 1981), p. 34.

2. Ibid.
3. Ibid., p. 36.
4. Ibid., p. 97.
5. A.J. Ayer, 'The Vienna Circle' in *The revolution in philosophy* (Macmillan, London, 1956), p. 74.
6. See *Frege* in this book, pp. 125-8.
7. In Hanfling, *Essential readings*, p. 207.
8. Ibid., p. 213.
9. Ibid., p. 217.
10. Ibid., pp. 218, 219.
11. Ibid., p. 224.
12. Rudolf Carnap, *The philosophy of Rudolf Carnap*, ed. P.A. Schilp (Open Court, La Salle, Ill., 1962). See pp. 20-9.

See also in this book

Hume, Bradley, Frege, Wittgenstein, Carnap.

Schlick's major writings

Collected papers 1926-36, ed. H. Mulder and B. Van der V-Schlick (Reidel, Dordrecht, 1978, 1979)
Problems of ethics (1939) (Dover Publications, New York, 1962)
Philosophy of nature, trans. A. Von Zeppelin (Greenwood Press, London, 1949)

Further reading

Ayer, A.J. *Language, truth and logic* (1936), 2nd edn. (Gollancz, London, 1951)
Feigl, H. and Sellars, W. (eds.) *Readings in philosophical analysis* (Appleton-Century-Crofts, New York, 1949)
Hanfling, O. *Logical positivism* (Basil Blackwell, Oxford, 1981)
—— (ed.) *Essential readings in logical positivism* (Basil Blackwell, Oxford, 1981)
Kraft, V. *The Vienna Circle* (Greenwood Press, London, 1953)
Popper, K.R. *The logic of scientific discovery* (Hutchinson, London, 1958)
Urmson, J.O. *Philosophical analysis* (Oxford University Press, Oxford, 1956)

Ludwig Wittgenstein 1889-1951

Wittgenstein was, unquestionably, a genius. He produced two distinct philosophies, both of which have been and still are profoundly influential. His earlier philosophy is embodied in a short book, the *Tractatus logico-philosophicus*, first published in 1921 and introduced to English-speaking readers in 1922 by Bertrand Russell who said of it that it 'deserves, by its breadth and scope and profundity, to be considered an important event in the philosophical world'. The *Tractatus* rests on the view that the structure of reality determines the structure of language. Wittgenstein's later philosophy rejects that view and explores instead the idea that it is our language that gives us our conception of reality; that there is not a uniform structure to language but that it has various forms that exhibit only loose interconnections. Thus both his philosophies are concerned with language and its limits. But the earlier philosophy is a coherent and orderly whole while the later is piecemeal and written as series of remarks, descriptions, questions and conjectures that invite the reader to engage in working towards an understanding that is not dominated by any guiding theory. What emerges from this later work is a conception of philosophy that sees it as quite distinct from the systematised procedures of science and as an activity of clarification rather than the exemplification of a thesis or theory. In the *Philosophical investigations* Wittgenstein remarks that philosophical problems are:

not empirical problems; they are solved, rather, by looking into the workings of our language, and that in such a way as to make us recognise those workings: *in despite of* an urge to misunderstand them. The problems are solved, not by giving new information, but by arranging what we have always known. Philosophy is a battle against the bewitchment of our intelligence by means of language.[1]

Wittgenstein was born in Vienna and was the youngest of eight children. He had four brothers and three sisters, all of whom were talented, particularly in music. Early in life he developed an interest in machinery. He studied engineering in Berlin and then, in 1908, went as a research student to Manchester where he designed a jet-reaction engine and a propellor. While there he read Bertrand Russell's *The principles of mathematics* and, after meeting the mathematician Frege in 1911, resolved to study with Russell who was then at Trinity College, Cambridge. He was admitted to Trinity in 1912 and spent five terms there engaging frequently in discussions with Russell, G.E. Moore and J.M. Keynes. In World War One he served in the Austrian army, was several times decorated for bravery and was eventually taken prisoner by the Italian army in the southern Tyrol. During all this time he kept philosophical notebooks, many of which he destroyed shortly before his death but out of which developed the *Tractatus logico-philosophicus* which was sent to Russell from the prison camp at Monte Cassino where Wittgenstein was held. After his release he returned to Vienna, gave his sisters the fortune he had inherited from his father and trained as a teacher. For a while he taught at a village school but he was profoundly unhappy, sometimes suicidal, and felt a total failure. In 1926 he gave up schoolteaching and worked for a while as a gardener. He spent two years designing a house for his sister and during this time became acquainted with Moritz Schlick, Professor of Philosophy at the University of Vienna, and other philosophers and mathematicians. The outcome of this renewed philosophical activity was that he returned to Cambridge as a research student and submitted the *Tractatus* as his PhD thesis. Russell and Moore were the examiners for the thesis and Wittgenstein was given a research fellowship at Trinity. In Vienna, where he spent his vacations, the philosophical movement of logical positivism was being developed under the leadership of Moritz Schlick by the group known as the Vienna Circle.[2] The Circle members had acclaimed the doctrine of the *Tractatus* but Wittgenstein, in spite of close affinities with the Circle's views, did not join it. He was already at work on new ideas of his own in mathematics and the philosophy of mind and he was writing at length on both topics. His lectures at Cambridge were wholly idiosyncratic in style, content and presentation, and

were becoming famous. He gave them in his room in Trinity, sitting in a deckchair and wearing an open-necked shirt, flannels and a leather jacket. Georg von Wright, in his biographical sketch of Wittgenstein, has written that:

> He had no manuscript or notes. He *thought* before the class. The impression was of tremendous concentration. The exposition usually led to a question, to which the audience were supposed to suggest an answer. The answers in turn became starting points for new thoughts leading to new questions.[3]

Two sets of notes that Wittgenstein dictated to his philosophy classes between 1933 and 1935 have become known respectively as *The blue book* and *The brown book*. They show the direction of his interest towards philosophy of mind, treating of concepts such as sensation, imagination and voluntary action. In 1935 he visited the Soviet Union and then Norway where he lived in a hut he had built for himself on an earlier visit. There he worked on his *Philosophical investigations*, which has become his best-known book. In 1939 he was appointed to the chair of Philosophy at Cambridge, previously occupied by G.E. Moore, but war broke out before he could take up the appointment. He served as a medical orderly during the war, eventually taking up his professorship in 1945. After two years he resigned, having found life as a professional philosopher intolerably artificial, and he lived for a while in Ireland. He then visited a friend, Norman Malcolm, in the United States but returned to England in 1949, weakened by an illness which was found to be cancer. He spent the last two years of his life staying with friends in Oxford and Cambridge and died in Cambridge, in the house of his physician, Dr Bevan, on 29 April 1951. He worked at philosophy as often as he could until shortly before his death and the writing of his last months was published in 1969 under the title *On certainty*. Wittgenstein's literary executors have, since his death, been arranging and gradually publishing his work. Although some has been lost and some destroyed at his own request, there is now a substantial body of his philosophy in print. His life and personality have exerted almost as much fascination as his thought. Numerous former pupils, friends and colleagues have testified to his charm, irascibility, magnetism and intellectual brilliance; anecdotes about his musical prowess and memory, his originality, rudeness, generosity and eccentricity abound in written recollections of encounters with him. He loved American films and would go to the cinema to ease his mind of philosophy. Norman Malcolm relates that Wittgenstein was frequently exhausted and revolted by lecturing. In a *Memoir* of Wittgenstein he writes:

> Often he would rush off to a cinema immediately after a class ended. As the members of the class began to move their chairs out of the room he might look imploringly at a friend and say in a low tone, 'Could you go to a flick?' On the way to the cinema Wittgenstein would buy a bun or cold pork pie and munch it while he watched the film. He insisted on sitting in the very first row of seats, so that the screen would occupy his entire field of vision, and his mind would be turned away from the thoughts of the lecture and his feelings of revulsion.[4]

In the Preface to the *Tractatus* Wittgenstein states that 'the book deals with the problems of philosophy, and shows, I believe, that the reason why these problems are posed is that the logic of our language is misunderstood'. He believed the *Tractatus* contained truths that were 'unassailable and definitive' and that in stating them he had found 'the final solution of the problems'. Whereas Frege and Russell had regarded logic as the science of the laws of thought, Wittgenstein saw it as the form of reality itself. The problems of philosophy, he thought, would be solved by showing that the structure of reality determined the scope of meaningful language and that the task of logic was to mirror the universe. Logic was therefore not just a science that is among or alongside other sciences, but one that had an absolute and ultimate character. This is the starting point from which the *Tractatus* unfolds.

It consists of seven numbered sections. The first six sections have subdivisions that are indicated by means of decimal numbers. The thesis of the first main section is that propositions are pictures: they represent facts pictorially. The second main thesis is that the elementary propositions into which all meaningful propositions are ultimately analysable are composed of names which are logically proper names; that is, names which cannot fail to refer to the things that bear them. The third main thesis is a consequence of the second. It states that the world consists of simple objects which are unanalysable and which are the bearers of the logically proper names so arranged as to constitute facts. The fourth main thesis asserts that all propositions are truth-functions of the elementary propositions that are composed of logically proper names so configured as to picture a possible configuration of simple objects. The fifth main thesis is that the propositions of logic are tautologies, that is, are empty of content in that they say nothing about how things are in the world. The sixth thesis is that many of our utterances that we take to be significant are in fact not so but are 'unsayable' in that they are not analysable as logical pictures of simple objects. Such utterances include remarks about what is good or bad and the propositions — now to be thought of as pseudo-propositions — of philosophy, including the claims of the *Tractatus* itself. The seventh section consists of only one remark: 'What we cannot speak about we must pass over in silence.'

The facts that propositions represent are *possible* facts. Wittgenstein describes such possibilities as 'atomic facts'. Atomic facts are what make propositions true or false. A proposition is true if certain atomic facts obtain, and false if they do not obtain. Logic is therefore concerned with all possible facts: a logical picture contains the possibility of the situation it represents and is then found true or false by being compared with reality. The truth of a compound proposition depends on the truth of its elementary components except in the case of tautologies such as 'Either it is raining or it is not raining,' which are true under all possible conditions, or in the case of contradictions such as 'It is raining but it is not raining,' which are false under all conditions. In both these sorts of cases we do not need to test the propositions against reality. At 4.462 in the *Tractatus* Wittgenstein writes: 'Tautologies and contradictions are not pictures of reality. They do not represent any possible situations. For the former admit *all* possible situations, and the latter *none.*'

Wittgenstein describes tautologies and contradictions as 'senseless' because there is no point in reality to which they attach. He describes the propositions of ethics, aesthetics, religion and **metaphysics** as 'nonsensical' because they use language in an attempt to transcend the limits of language, trying to go beyond what meaningfully can be said: they attempt to speak of matters that the final remark of the *Tractatus* abjures us to 'pass over in silence'. 'What can be said' consists of the propositions of natural science. Towards the end of the *Tractatus* Wittgenstein writes:

> The correct method in philosophy would really be the following: to say nothing except what can be said, i.e. propositions of natural science — i.e. something that has nothing to do with philosophy — and then, whenever someone else wanted to say something metaphysical, to demonstrate to him that he had failed to give a meaning to certain signs in his propositions.[5]

Because Wittgenstein described ethical, aesthetic and religious discourse as 'nonsensical' it was thought by some that he regarded all such talk as unimportant and worthless. But this was not the case. In a letter to Paul Engelmann he wrote that the point of the *Tractatus* was an ethical one and that the more important part of it was the part that he did not write. In making a fundamental distinction between, on the one hand, the language of natural science and, on the other, that of ethics, aesthetics and religion he saves the latter from any sort of reduction to or translation into the former. Moreover, his remarks in the sixth section of the *Tractatus* at no point suggest that he regards ethical, aesthetic and religious discourse as nonsensical in any ordinary sense of that term. At 6.52 he says: 'We feel that even when *all possible* scientific questions have been answered, the problems of life remain completely untouched.' And at 6.42: 'it is impossible for there to be propositions of ethics. Propositions can express nothing that is higher.' It is clear from these remarks that what is regarded as, in a logical sense, nonsensical, is also judged to be 'higher'. Concerning the pronouncements of philosophy, which are also excluded from the category of the sayable, he says:

> My propositions serve as elucidations in the following way: anyone who understands me eventually recognises them as nonsensical, when he has used them — as steps — to climb up beyond them. (He must, so to speak, throw away the ladder after he has climbed up it.)[6]

A gap of about ten years separates the *Tractatus*, which Wittgenstein completed in 1918, from his resumption of sustained philosophical work. *Philosophical investigations*, published in 1953, clearly exemplifies the differences between his earlier and his later work, but also exhibits a continuity between them; for in the *Investigations* Wittgenstein is as much concerned with language as he was in the *Tractatus*, although the nature of the concern is different. Whereas the *Tractatus* was cryptic and aphoristic in style, the *Investigations* is discursive and reveals no obvious structure and no presuppositions about the relationship between language and the world. Whereas the *Tractatus* deals with the nature of propositions the *Investigations* concentrates largely on those propositions that describe mental life. In the *Tractatus* Wittgenstein bases everything on the idea that meaning and lack of meaning depend on the formal relationship in which a proposition stands to reality. In the *Investigations* meaning is seen as a function of how we use words: human purposes and the forms of life in which human beings engage are what give language its meanings. There is no final analysis of propositions into logically proper names that are the names of the simple objects of the world. Instead, language is seen as a natural human phenomenon and philosophy's task that of assembling reminders of our actual use of language in order to abolish the puzzlement it sometimes produces. Philosophy 'simply puts everything before us, and neither explains nor deduces anything'; its results 'are the uncovering of one or another piece of plain nonsense'; philosophical problems are solved 'not by giving new information, but by arranging what we have always known'.[7] And Wittgenstein maintains that 'the philosopher's treatment of a question is like the treatment of an illness'; that is, the philosophical treatment does not have the form of question-plus-answer but, as with an illness, when the problem is treated properly, it goes away.[8]

A brief comparison of the ways in which Wittgenstein deals with difficulties about the will in his earlier and later philosophy shows something of the changes that took place in his thinking. The doctrine of the *Tractatus*, as we have seen, is that the world is the totality of facts in logical space; and the world, Wittgenstein argues, 'is independent of my will'.[9] In the *Notebooks 1914-16*, which contain much of his preparatory work for the *Tractatus*, he wrote 'I will call "will" first and foremost the bearer of good and evil.'[10] The

will is therefore inseparable from ethical matters and propositions about the will accordingly fall into the category of 'what cannot be said'. But the presuppositions of the *Tractatus*, in establishing a sharp bifurcation between will and world, produce a philosophical problem. For although the will is, from the point of view of the *Tractatus*, somehow 'outside' the world, Wittgenstein is acutely aware that will 'penetrates the world' and that on any ordinary understanding of will it is regarded as active in the world. Yet the consequences of seeing that the will is distinct from the facts of world are that 'I cannot bend the happenings of the world to my will: I am completely powerless.'[11] Held captive by his own account of how things are, he writes in the *Notebooks*: 'It is clear, so to speak, that we need a foothold for the will in the world.'[12] He struggles to give an account of will that conceives of it as — perhaps — 'an attitude towards the world', but is profoundly dissatisfied with the results of this struggle; for, once again, will is characteristically manifested *in* the world, in bodily movements and in the bringing about of changes in states of affairs rather than in some kind of detached stance towards the world.

In all this it is important to notice that Wittgenstein speaks of 'the will' and of 'willing' in a very broad and general sense. Later he developed the view that it is just this tendency to generalise that so often leads us astray. In the *Blue book* he writes of 'our craving for generality' and says 'I could also have said "the contemptuous attitude towards the particular case".'[13] He links this with our preoccupation with the method of science, a preoccupation that leads us to attempt to explain as much as possible through the smallest possible number of natural laws. This tendency, he says, is 'the real source of metaphysics, and leads the philosopher into complete darkness'.[14] It is a turning away from generality to a consideration of particular cases that characterises the shift from a *Tractatus* conception of the will to its conception in the later philosophy. In fact, Wittgenstein almost effected the transition in the *Notebooks* where he does consider a particular willed action and concludes that: 'The act of will is not the cause of the action but is the action itself. One cannot will without acting.'[15] But he cannot break away, in those earlier writings, from his dichotomous picture of the will and the world, and seems not to have recognised the possibilities of this new approach. It is only in the *Brown book* (pp. 150-5) and then in the *Philosophical investigations* (I, 611-28) that he succeeds in dismantling the metaphysical structure that had generated the problems about the will and, indeed, a whole range of connected problems in the philosophy of mind, and turns wholeheartedly to an examination of how words are actually used in particular cases. The examination releases us from the conception of the will as some kind of distinct entity or power that somehow operates levers to produce change, or is a kind of 'attitude' towards the physical realm. If we think of actual instances of voluntary action we begin to see in most of them there is nothing that is distinguishable as 'an act of will' and which consequently qualifies the willed acts as 'voluntary': in the case, for example, of a person who 'finds himself getting up' in the morning, there is no 'act of volition'; he just gets up. There is a whole range of situations to which the term 'voluntary action' is applicable but we mistakenly tend to isolate the experience of muscular effort as a prototype of willing and then into difficulty. Here again, in the search for a yardstick by which to judge the voluntariness or otherwise of actions is a manifestation of our 'craving for generality' and our 'contempt for the particular case'. Wittgenstein presses home the view that it is circumstances of varying kinds, rather than one type of mental state, that characterise voluntary actions. In the *Philosophical investigations* the point is made that 'willing' is not the name of an action, not one stage in a process; nor is it that which constitutes an abiding core of self in a person. Willing is the action itself. In examining particular cases Wittgenstein turns away from presuppositions about the structure of reality and from the attempt to see all language as conforming to that structure. Instead, he looks at what we say and do, resisting the temptation to infer underlying structures from the surface appearance of our discourse and recognising the incorrigibility of claims such as Schopenhauer's 'I cannot really imagine the will without my body.'[16] Wittgenstein's sustained development of this approach has resulted in a most formidable achievement the influence of which has been profound, generating a mode of philosophising that rejects theorising and works to resolve philosophical difficulties by 'arranging what we have always known'.

In his early philosophy Wittgenstein strove to uproot the deeply entrenched traditions of thought. In his later philosophy he accepts, uses and transforms them. Much of his greatness as a philosopher consists in his doing that.

Notes

1. Wittgenstein, *Philosophical investigations*, 109.
2. See *Schlick* and *Carnap* in this book, pp. 142-5 and 154-7.
3. Georg von Wright, 'A biographical sketch', reprinted in N. Malcolm's *Memoir* cited in note 4 below.
4. Norman Malcolm, *Ludwig Wittgenstein: a memoir* (Oxford University Press, London, 1958; paperback, 1962), p. 28.
5. Wittgenstein, *Tractatus logico-philosophicus*, 6.53.
6. Ibid., 6.54.
7. Wittgenstein, *Philosophical investigations*, 126, 119, 109.
8. Ibid., 225.
9. Wittgenstein, *Tractatus*, 6.373.
10. Wittgenstein, *Notebooks*, 21.7.16.
11. Ibid., 11.6.16.
12. Ibid., 4.11.16.
13. Wittgenstein, *Blue and brown books*, pp. 17, 18.
14. Ibid.
15. Ibid.
16. See *Schopenhauer* in this book, pp. 100-3.

See also in this book

Frege, Russell, Moore, Schlick, Carnap.

Wittgenstein's major writings

Notebooks 1914-1916 (1969), trans. G.E.M. Anscombe (Blackwell, Oxford, 1969)
Tractatus logico-philosophicus (1921), trans. D.F. Pears and B.F. McGuiness (Routledge and Kegan Paul, London, 1961)
Philosophical investigations (1953), trans. G.E.M. Anscombe (Blackwell, Oxford, 1953)
Remarks on the foundations of mathematics (1956), trans. G.E.M. Anscombe, 3rd edn (Blackwell, Oxford, 1978)
The blue and brown books (1958), 2nd edn (Blackwell, Oxford, 1969)
Zettel (1967), trans. G.E.M. Anscombe (Blackwell, Oxford, 1967)
On certainty (1969), trans D. Paul and G.E.M. Anscombe (Basil Blackwell, Oxford, 1969)

Further reading

Fann, K.T. *Wittgenstein's conception of philosophy* (Blackwell, Oxford, 1969)
Hacker, P.M.S. *Insight and illusion* (Clarendon Press, Oxford, 1972)
Kenny, A. *Wittgenstein* (Penguin, Harmondsworth, 1973)
Passmore, J. *A hundred years of philosophy* (Penguin, Hardmondsworth, 1975)
Pears, D. *Wittgenstein* (Fontana/Collins, London, 1971)
Stenius, E. *Wittgenstein's Tractatus, a critical exposition of its main lines of thought* (Blackwell, Oxford, 1960)
Zemach, E. 'Wittgenstein's philosophy of the mystical' in *Essays on Wittgenstein's Tractatus*, ed. I.M. Copi and R.W. Beard (Routledge and Kegan Paul, London, 1966)

Martin Heidegger   1889-1976

Heidegger described his philosophy as the Quest for Being. He is classed with and is inseparable from the existentialists although he steadfastly disavowed this connection, maintaining that it is Being as such rather than personal existence that is his main concern. His work is dominated by a search for some sort of meaning lying at the heart of the astonishing fact that 'there are things in being'. It owes a good deal to Kierkegaard and to Heidegger's teacher, Edmund Husserl. Heidegger in turn exerted a strong influence on Sartre. He employs the term *Dasein* to describe the mode of existence of a human being and argues that human life is radically different from other forms of life because it is able to be aware of

itself and to reflect on its Being. Human beings, he holds, may choose to live authentically, having a full sense of their situation in the world, or inauthentically as near-automatons, unthinkingly conforming to established routines and patterns. His major philosophical work is *Being and time*, first published in 1927.

Heidegger was born at Baden in Germany. He studied philosophy at Freiburg University, where Husserl taught from 1916 to 1929, and became a teacher there before moving to a professorship at Marburg in 1923. He returned to Freiburg as a professor in 1928 and became rector of the university in 1933. In his inaugural address he enthusiastically acclaimed National Socialism, unequivocally aligning himself with the Nazi movement and advocating a fusion of the language of current politics with his own philosophical language. But ten months later he resigned the rectorship, recognising that he had been gravely mistaken, and withdrew from active engagement in politics. In September 1966, in an interview with *Der Spiegel*, Heidegger responded to reproaches that had been levelled at him over thirty years but forbade publication of the interview until after his death. It was eventually printed on 31 May 1976, five days after his death. In the interview Heidegger states that he had hoped to preserve the self-determination of the German university but that it was clear to him that he 'would not see it through without some compromises'. At the same time, he says, he also saw in National Socialism the possibility that 'here is something new, here is a new dawn'. In 1933 he had adjured students: 'Do not let doctrines and ideas be the rules of your Being. The *Fuhrer* himself and he alone *is* the present and future German reality and its rule.' In the interview he says, 'I would today no longer write the sentences which you cite. Even by 1934 I no longer said such things.'

In *Being and time* Heidegger gives his analysis of human existence. He regards the analysis as the pathway to an understanding of Being itself. His method is that of pheno-menology, learned from Husserl.[1] Its aim is to indicate and describe the data of immedi-ate experience just as they are, without superimposing organising concepts upon them and without abstracting from them. From the phenomenological point of view the world is the condition we engage with and inhabit; it is constitutive of our lives. We are not to see the world simply as a physical object against which we are set as individual thinking subjects; rather, we are 'beings-in-the-world' and *Dasein*, our human reality or mode of being, is that multitude of ways in which we inhabit life; that is, by 'having to do with something, producing something, attending to something and looking after it, making use of something, giving something up and letting it go, undertaking, accomp-lishing, evincing, interrogating, considering, discussing, determining ...'[2] Heidegger writes of the human 'encountering' of the world and of the 'mood' in which we encounter it as placing a value on the world. We find ourselves occupying the world, in the sense of inhabiting our own perspectives on life and using what we find around us, and this is our facticity. He speaks also of each person's appropriation of the world, the grasp of one's situation in the world and the understanding that one can attempt to become and do what one envisages rather than be carried along by the surge of events. But this very engagement with the life of the world produces a tension between one's self-realisation and the unthinking communal practices of the 'they' of the world. I can become depersonalised, an object for the use of others, by succumbing to the mechanical habits and conventions of everyday exist-ence, conforming to what is average, unsur-prising and often banal. Heidegger describes such a person as 'the anonymous one', a human being become alienated from her or his true self; someone lacking authenticity. Yet it is not the case that, if I am authentic, I will necessarily behave in startling or out-landish ways, but that my actions, whether

outlandish or mundane, originate from my own perspective rather than from external factors.

Heidegger uses the term '*Sorge*', trans-lated as 'care', to describe the prevailing attitude of *Dasein*. A human being is, as it were, 'thrown' into an already existing world and thereafter has to be responsible for itself and involve itself in a concerned way in the world it finds. Thus, care, or concern, characterises our ceaseless interaction with everything we find or use or become involved with. It is the structure of the way in which we inhabit life: the active relationship, the constitutive and indispensable condition of *Dasein*. Heidegger's emphasis on and elucidation of this interdependence of the human being and the world reinforce his rejection of the traditional distinction between the thinking subject and an exterior objective world, and of the consequent prob-lems of demonstrating the existence and true nature of the latter. He argues that the distinction is a false one and that a correct phenomenological account of how things are reveals that the beings who set out to construct a proof of the existence of the external world are already parts of that world. They are 'being-in-the-world', not isolated and distinct from it. However, Heidegger is not attempting to accommodate our rational constructions concerning phys-ical objects and the space and time of theor-etical science within a comprehensive phenomenological account. A utensil of the world such as a hammer can, he says, be regarded as something 'ready-to-hand', as 'in-use', and as an element in my present activity of being in the world; or it can be seen as a given object that is 'at-hand', avail-able in the world. These are simply different perspectives on the hammer. What is incor-rect is to see the scientific conception as superior to the practical one and as declar-ative of a fundamental and superior truth about the nature of reality.

Connected with 'care' is the concept of anxiety, or dread, a dominant theme in existentialist philosophy. Like Kierkegaard, Heidegger distinguishes between 'anxiety' and 'fear' by pointing out that fear is fear of some object while 'that in the face of which one has anxiety is characterized by the fact that what threatens is *nowhere*'.[3] Anxiety is a recognition of the being of the world; it is experienced as an overwhelming sense of the inescapable presence and utter meaninglessness of being. It forces one to a vivid awareness of one's own existence and, above all, to a contemplation of the possibilities there are for oneself in the future. Thus care is characteristic of this whole experience: one concerns oneself with the present situation, with the future that is open before one and with the way in which one relates to others and to things. Human beings, Heidegger maintains, are constantly turning away from this experience of their freedom and responsibility, hiding themselves in the anonymity of an unreflective communal life. And this is the inescapable situation that is *Dasein*: we exist not only as parts of the community but as isolated individuals. Both modes of existence are constitutive of the human way of being in the world. They are its universal structure. The experience of anxiety, or dread, reveals to us that we may choose ourselves if we so wish; it also reveals to us that we can evade the responsibility of making that perpetual choice.

Heidegger maintains that realisation of one's death is the key to authenticity. By recognising that death renders everything meaningless and ends all possibilities, we come to see, he says, that we can either confront this fact or seek distraction from it. To accept it fully is not to reject participation in the life of the world. It is simply to see the activities of the world within the context of an awareness of death and to confront the absurdity of finding oneself inhabiting a life that was preceded by nothing and will be succeeded by nothing. It is this realisation that can make a person accept responsibility for his or her existence. What is understood, with the clarity of a revelation, is that the nothingness that surrounds one's existence renders everything meaningless and that meanings and values can be bestowed only by oneself. One has to take what is there as if one had willed it to be as it is, and then make something of it. In all this Heidegger is not wanting to urge that the authentic life is morally superior to the inauthentic. His claim is that he is setting out the structure of *Dasein* and that he does so as a necessary preliminary to the understanding of Being as a whole. It is temporality that binds a personal existence into a whole, he argues, since a person is not simply someone existing *in* time but is a temporal being; that is, a being with a past, a present and a future which are in perpetual interaction and recreation to constitute a personal existence. The temporal structure of this existence is the condition of self-consciousness and action and also of being able to posit the larger world and all other existents concerning which one can ask why there is such Being as a whole. Temporality is the condition of history, too, and an understanding of Being, according to Heidegger, depends on a perception of the kind of movement characteristic of historical movement. It is the task of the historian to discern these larger movements. An authentic life is one lived not only from a sense of self-awareness and personal temporality but within a framework of historicity and destiny.

Heidegger's writings are generally held to be extremely obscure. It is not just that his thought tries to penetrate ultimate and abstract matters but also that he uses language in a highly idiosyncratic way. John Macquarrie, a translator of *Being and time*, describes, in the Preface to the book, how Heidegger uses words in unusual ways, produces his own vocabulary and exploits the German language's capacity for constructing new compound words. Macquarrie writes:

Adverbs, prepositions, pronouns, conjunctions are made to do service as nouns; words which have undergone a long history of semantical change are used afresh in their older senses; specialised modern idioms are generalised far beyond the limits within which they would ordinarily be applicable. Puns are by no means uncommon and frequently a key-word may be used in several senses, successively or simultaneously.[4]

Heidegger's later writings are even more difficult than his earlier works, oracular in tone, cryptic and terse in style. In consequence he has come to be regarded by many with a mixture of irritation and reverence. His output is considerable and covers a wide range of topics: logic, philosophy of science, philosophy of history, ontology, metaphysics, language, technology, poetry, Greek philosophy and mathematics. In spite of the abstruseness of his ideas his influence has spread very wide. He saw himself as a philosopher with a mission to redeem a civilisation that had sold out to technology, science and a calculating rationality; that had 'fallen out of Being' and that must be recalled and made once again 'at home' in Being. The intensity with which he consistently expounds and proclaims this theme is remarkable. In a paper called 'Martin Heidegger at eighty' Hannah Arendt wrote: 'Heidegger never thinks "about" something. He thinks something.'[5]

Notes

1. See *Husserl* in this book, pp. 128-30.
2. Heidegger, *Being and time*, trans. John Macquarrie and Edward Robinson (Blackwell, Oxford, 1962), p. 83 (Part One, Division I, II).
3. Ibid., p. 231.
4. Ibid., Translators' Preface, p. 14.
5. Hannah Arendt, 'Martin Heidegger at eighty' in *Heidegger and modern philosophy*, ed. M. Murray (Yale University Press, New Haven and London, 1978), p. 296.

See also in this book

Duns Scotus, Kierkegaard, Husserl, Sartre.

Heidegger's major writings

Being and time (1927), trans. John Macquarrie and

Edward Robinson (Blackwell, Oxford, 1962; Harper and Row, New York, 1962)
What is metaphysics? (1929), trans. William Kluback and Jean T. Wilde, German/English text (Twayne Publishers, New York, 1958; Vision Press, London, 1958)
An introduction to metaphysics (1953), trans. Ralph Manheim (Doubleday, New York, 1961)
What is called thinking? (1952), trans. Fred D. Wieck and J. Glenn Gray (Harper and Row, New York, 1968)
The origin of the work of art (1956), trans. Albert Hofstadter in A. Hofstadter and R. Khuns (eds.) *Philosophies of Art and Beauty* (Random House, New York, 1964)

Further reading

Biemel, W. *Martin Heidegger* (Routledge and Kegan Paul, London, 1977)
Blackham, H.J. 'Martin Heidegger' in *Six existentialist thinkers* (Routledge and Kegan Paul, London, 1961)
Macquarrie, J. *Existentialism* (Penguin, Harmondsworth, 1973)
Mehta, J.L. *The philosophy of Martin Heidegger* (Harper and Row, New York, 1971)
Murray, M. (ed.) *Heidegger and modern philosophy* (Yale University Press, New Haven and London, 1978)
Steiner, G. *Heidegger* (Harvester Press, Hassocks, Sussex, 1978)

Rudolf Carnap 1891-1970

Carnap is the most eminent member of the Vienna Circle, that group of scientists, philosophers and mathematicians who, in the 1930s, formulated and developed the philosophy of logical positivism. He believed it was possible to bring about a 'unified science' by applying a method of logical analysis to the **empirical** data of all the sciences. Like all the members of the Vienna Circle he held that statements are meaningful only if they are empirically verifiable in some way and that **metaphysical** statements, when subjected to that criterion, are shown not to have factual meaning. He worked extensively on the foundations of logic and mathematics and, in his later years, on **induction** and probability.

Carnap was born at Ronsdorf in Germany. He studied physics, mathematics and philosophy at the universities of Freiburg and Jena and at the latter was taught by Gottlob Frege, whose influence is apparent in his work. He served in the army in World War One and then returned to Jena to complete his doctorate in the philosophy of science. His doctoral thesis, a comparative study of the concepts of space used in physics, mathematics and philosophy, emphasised the importance of giving logical analyses of concepts. In 1926 Moritz Schlick, then Professor of the Philosophy of Inductive Sciences at the University of Vienna, invited Carnap to a post as Privatdozent (instructor) at Vienna. Carnap soon became a leading figure in the Vienna Circle and in 1929 published *The logical construction of the world.* In the same year, with Otto Neurath and Hans Hahn, he produced *The Vienna Circle: the scientific conception of the world,* a statement of the Circle's aims and methods. With Hans Reichenbach he founded *Erkenntnis,* a journal devoted to scientific philosophy and in 1931 he was appointed to a chair of natural philosophy at the German University in Prague. While there his *Logical syntax of language* was published. He left the German University at the end of 1935, finding it difficult to work there as Nazism developed, and went to the United States where within a few months he was given an appointment at the University of Chicago. He taught there until 1952, developing his interest in logical syntax and semantics and editing, with Charles Morris, the *International encyclopaedia of unified science.* He then spent two years at the Institute for Advanced Study in Princeton and in 1954 moved to a chair of philosophy at the University of California, Los Angeles. He retired from full-time teaching in 1961 and died in 1970.

The philosophy of logical positivism, or logical empiricism, the latter often being its preferred title, has David Hume as its ancestor. Hume had rejected claims to knowledge of metaphysical matters such as the existence of God or the immortality of the soul because the ideas on which such claims are based cannot be traced back to simple sense impressions which, he held,

must be their source if they are to count as knowledge.[1] In a comparable way, the members of the Vienna Circle rejected as meaningless any statement that was not empirically verifiable. By that criterion of verifiability they found metaphysical statements meaningless. In the Circle's manifesto, *The Vienna Circle: the scientific conception of the world,* we read:

If anyone asserts 'There is a God', 'The primary cause of the world is the Unconscious', 'There is an entelechy which is the leading principle in living beings', we do not say 'What you say is false'; rather, we ask him 'What do you mean by your statements?' It then appears that there is a sharp division between two types of statements. One of the types includes statements as they are made in empirical science; their meaning can be determined by logical analysis, or, more precisely, by reduction to simple sentences about the empirically given. The other statements, including those mentioned above, show themselves to be completely meaningless, if we take them as the metaphysician intends them.'[2]

The early formulations of the criterion for determining meaningfulness led to difficulties that provoked disagreement as well as extensive discussion in the Vienna Circle. The 'simple sentences about the empirically given' referred to in the quotation above were at first thought of as being themselves verified by a person's having experiences of whatever was described in such simple sentences. But this view invites the objection that people have different experiences and that a sentence might therefore have different meanings for different people: its meaning would depend entirely on one's private experiences. Moritz Schlick tried to solve this problem by distinguishing the content of experience from its form. Content, he maintained, was private, but the words used and their logical ordering are demonstrable and these latter, formal features are all that are necessary for logical analysis. Carnap shared this view for a time but then rejected it on the grounds that the words used to describe the formal features are as much dependent on private experience as the words used to describe content. In the *Unity of science* he works out a way in which the observation statements required for verification are not private to the observer.

His solution of the difficulty is to say that a statement is verifiable if it stands in a certain logical relation to a set of observation statements. This shows the logical possibility of verifying the statement. He calls the observation statements 'protocol statements'. Although protocol statements 'refer to the given, and describe directly given experience or phenomena', they do so, Carnap maintains, only in what he designates 'the material mode', that is, the mode of speech in which we refer to facts, phenomena and objects, as distinct from the formal mode of speech in which we refer 'only to linguistic forms'. In the formal mode, protocol statements are described as 'statements needing no justification and serving as the foundation for all the remaining statements of science'.[3] By using it, Carnap does away with all reference to private experiences and makes verifiability a matter of logical relations between statements. Using the formal mode, all one is saying is that certain expressions are used in certain ways within the system.

Within this new conception of verifiability, conclusive verification of any statement requires that there is a logical equivalence between the statement and the set of verifying observation statements. This requirement generates the criticism that **universal** statements, including statements expressing scientific laws, are shown to be meaningless by the verifiability criterion because any statement that refers to an unlimited number of instances cannot be logically equivalent to a limited number of verificational observation statements. To meet this and other related objections Carnap abandoned the require-

ment of mutual entailment between a statement and its relevant observation statements and turned instead to the notion of confirmability. In 1936-7 he wrote two articles called 'Testability and meaning', the first of which started with the following words:

> If by verification is meant a definitive and final establishment of truth, then no (synthetic) sentence is ever verifiable … We can only confirm a sentence more and more. Therefore we shall speak of the problems of *confirmation* rather than of the problem of verification.[4]

He distinguishes between testing and confirming sentences. A sentence is testable if we know an experimental method for testing it and is confirmable if we know under what conditions it would be confirmed. Thus a sentence may be confirmable without being testable since we may know what procedures would confirm it but are unable to carry them out. This did not end the problems connected with verification: every new attempt to refine it had its attendant problems. In the Introduction to the 1967 edition of *Language, truth and logic* A.J. Ayer considers the problems of the several formulations of the criterion of verifiability.[5]

It is sometimes remarked that Carnap's thought is closer than that of any other member of the Vienna Circle to the early thought of Wittgenstein. Wittgenstein's influence on the Circle was profound and his *Tractatus logico-philosophicus* was carefully studied by its members but he never joined the Circle and although many cues for its strategies for rejecting metaphysics were taken from the *Tractatus* his fundamental attitude to metaphysics was very different from that of the Circle. Nevertheless, Carnap's description of philosophy given in his paper 'The elimination of metaphysics' bears close resemblance to Wittgenstein's conclusions in the *Tractatus*. Carnap asks: 'what, then, is left over for *philosophy*, if all statements whatever that assert something are of an empirical nature and belong to factual science?'[6] This is reminiscent of Wittgenstein's remarks at 4.11 and 4.111 in the *Tractatus* where he says that the totality of true propositions is the whole of natural science but that philosophy is not one of the natural sciences.[7] Wittgenstein concludes that philosophy is an activity that results in the clarification of propositions. Carnap concludes that philosophy is 'not statements, nor a theory, nor a system but only a *method* … it serves to clarify meaningful concepts and propositions'.

Carnap's notion of confirmation was a starting point in the 1940s for his work on probability. He gives accounts of two distinct meanings of the term 'probability'. The first relates to degrees of confirmation and concerns the logical relationship between a **hypothesis** and its supporting observation statements; the second meaning concerns the statistical probability derived from calculations of relative frequency. In 1950 Carnap published a major work, *Logical foundations of probability*, in which he explores the possibility of formal similarities between inductive and **deductive** procedures. At the same time he was furthering his work in modal logic, developing Frege's view that meaningful expressions have both reference and sense. The important consequence of this work of Carnap's is that semantics, the study of meanings in language, is now regarded as being of the utmost significance in all branches of logic.

Notes

1. See *Hume* in this book, pp. 81-6.
2. R. Carnap, O. Neurath and H. Hahn, *The Vienna Circle: the scientific conception of the world* in M. Neurath and R.S. Cohen (eds) *Empiricism and sociology: the life and work of Otto Neurath* (Reidel, Dordrecht, 1973).
3. R. Carnap, *The unity of science*, trans. M. Black (Routledge and Kegan Paul, London, 1934), p. 45.
4. R. Carnap, 'Testability and meaning' (1936, 1937) in *Philosophy of Science*, vol. III (1936) pp. 419-71, and vol. IV (1937), pp. 1-40. Reprinted in H. Feigl and M. Brodbeck (eds), *Readings in the philosophy of science* (Appleton, New York, 1953).
5. A.J. Ayer, *Language, Truth and Logic* (Gollancz,

London, 1967), pp. 5-16.
6. R. Carnap, 'The elimination of metaphysics through logical analysis of language' (1932), trans. A. Pap, in A.J. Ayer (ed.), *Logical positivism* (The Free Press, Glencoe, Ill. 1959), pp. 61-81.
7. See *Wittgenstein* in this book, pp. 145-51.

See also in this book

Hume, Bradley, Frege, Schlick, Wittgenstein.

Carnap's major writings

The logical structure of the world (1928), trans. R.A. George (Routledge and Kegan Paul, London, 1967)
'The elimination of metaphysics through logical analysis of language' (1931), *Erkenntnis* II (see note 6 above)
The unity of science (1934), trans. M. Black (Routledge and Kegan Paul, London, 1934)
Philosophy and logical syntax (1935) (Routledge and Kegan Paul, London, 1935)
'Testability and Meaning' (2 papers, 1936 and 1937) (see note 4 above)
Introduction to semantics (1942) (Harvard University Press, Cambridge, Mass., 1942)
Logical foundations of probability (Chicago University Press, Chicago, 1950)

Further reading

Ayer, A.J. (ed.) *Logical positivism* (The Free Press, Glencoe, Ill.; Allen and Unwin, London, 1959)
Feigl, H. and Brodbeck, M. (eds) *Readings in the philosophy of science* (Appleton, New York, 1953)
Hanfling, O. *Logical positivism* (Blackwell, Oxford, 1981)
—— (ed.) *Essential readings in logical positivism* (Blackwell, Oxford, 1981)
Passmore, J. *A hundred years of philosophy* (Penguin, Harmondsworth, 1966), Ch. 16
Schilpp, P.A. (ed.) *The philosophy of Rudolf Carnap*, vol. X in the Library of Living Philosophers (Open Court Publishing Company, La Salle, Ill., 1962)
Urmson, J.O. *Philosophical analysis* (Oxford University Press, Oxford, 1956)
Waismann, F. *The principles of linguistic philosophy*, ed. R. Harré, (Macmillan, London, 1968), Ch. 16

Jean-Paul Sartre   1905-1980

Sartre was a leading exponent of atheistic existentialism. He was a novelist and critic as well as a philosopher. In later life he moved away from existentialism and developed his own style of Marxist sociology.

He was educated at the Ecole Normale Supérieure in Paris and then taught at a number of lycées in Paris and elsewhere.

During World War Two he was a soldier and for nine months was a prisoner of war in Germany. After he was released he worked in the Resistance Movement. When the war ended he became editor of *Les Temps Modernes*, a monthly review devoted to socialist and existentialist concerns. In 1964 he was awarded, but refused, the Nobel Prize for Literature. He became very active politically after the 1968 May Revolt. His last major philosophical work is the *Critique of dialectical reason*, written, he maintained, to reconcile existentialism and Marxism. His trilogy of novels, *Roads to freedom*, is regarded as a classic of twentieth-century literature.

Existentialism, as the '-ism' suggests, is a term used to cover a wide range of views but it is always rooted in the experience of what it is like to exist as a human being. Its investigations are in one sense deeply personal in that they are about personal existence but they are also universal in that they are about the structures and conditions of the personal existence of every human being. Its first concern is to give an account of how an individual consciousness apprehends existence and from this concern flow its main preoccupations: considerations about freedom, choice, personal authenticity, relationships with the world and other people, and about the ways in which meanings and values are generated by individuals, starting only from a consciousness of personal existence.

Sartre's most famous philosophical work, *Being and nothingness*, was first published in 1943. It has become a major document of existentialism. On its title page Sartre describes the book as 'an essay on phenomenological ontology'. Briefly, phenomenology is the study of the way in which things appear or are present to consciousness. It deals with the contents of consciousness just as they are manifested to us without reference to any other status they may have as, for example, physical objects existing independently of our awareness of them. But phenomenology does not simply record the contents of consciousness; it analyses its *structures*. Ontology, in contrast, is specifically concerned to say what there is: what kinds of things actually comprise the universe. Once again, this is not a matter merely of listing items. Ontology works to elucidate the type or types of being of which the universe consists. A phenomenological ontology therefore examines the relationships between the facts of the world and our consciousness of them.

Sartre's primary question is: What is it like to be a human being? He wants to describe what he calls 'human reality' in the most general terms. His answer to the question is already encapsulated in his title *Being and nothingness*; for, he says, human reality consists of two modes of existence, being and nothingness, in both being and not-being. The human being exists both as an In-itself, an object or thing, and as a For-itself, a consciousness which is no-*thing*, but simply *not* that thing of which it is conscious. He describes the existence of the In-itself, of a phenomenon or thing, as 'opaque to itself ... because it is filled with itself'. A thing has no inner and outer aspects, no consciousness of itself; it just *exists*. He says: 'the In-itself has nothing secret; it is solid [massif]' and 'there is not the slightest emptiness in being, not the tiniest crack through which nothingness might slip in'. In contrast the For-itself, or consciousness, has no such fullness of existence, because it is no-thing.

In his novel *Nausea* Sartre forces us to become fully aware of the overwhelming presence and density of things. The hero of the novel, Antoine Roquentin, in a series of curious episodes, becomes fearfully aware of the strangely dislocated nature of his experience. Standing on the seashore, he picks up a pebble and is sickened and horrified by its stubborn and overwhelming existence. Later, in reflecting on the incident, he says:

Objects ought not to *touch*, ... But they touch me, it's unbearable ... Now I see; I remember better what I felt the other day on the sea-shore when I was holding that pebble. It was a sort of sweet disgust. How unpleasant it was! And it came from the pebble, I'm sure of that, it passed from the pebble into my hands ... a sort of nausea in the hands.[2]

In describing Roquentin's numerous experiences of nausea Sartre is trying to make us feel what he calls the contingency of existence. Roquentin has come to a realisation that there is no reason that explains the brute existence of things. If one tried to define 'existence' the essential thing one would have to say is that it means that something just *happens* to be there: there is nothing that precedes existence which is a reason for existence. It so happens that things are there; that is all there is to it and there is no explanation. Contingency is bedrock. When Roquentin reflects and writes about his experience he says, 'The word Absurdity is now born beneath my pen ... I, a little while ago, experienced the absolute, the absolute or the absurd.'[3] The absurdity he has recognised is the absurdity of contingency: the inexplicable existence of each and every thing, the ridiculousness of the world's being there without any meaning at all. And this generates a desire of the For-itself to exist with the fullness of being of an existing thing, but without contingency and without any loss of consciousness. Towards the end of *Nausea* Roquentin says:

I too have wanted to *be*. Indeed I have never wanted anything else; that's what lay at the bottom of my life: behind all these attempts which seemed unconnected, I find the same desire; to drive existence out of me, to empty the moments of their fat, to wring them, to dry them, to purify myself, to harden myself ...[4]

But the desired embodying is never possible. Consciousness can never become a thing *and* remain consciousness. The two regions of being are entirely distinct and the

ideal of fusing them is what Sartre calls, in *Being and nothingness*, 'an unrealisable totality which haunts the For-itself and constitutes its very being as a nothingness of being'. And he says:

It is this ideal which can be called God. Thus the best way to conceive of the fundamental project of human reality is to say that man is the being whose project is to be God ... To be man means to reach toward being God. Or if you prefer, man fundamentally is the desire to be God.[5]

Because it is a nothingness, consciousness desires to be 'effectively involved in a future world' and this, Sartre says, is precisely the situation of our human freedom. Freedom is the nothingness we experience when we are conscious of what we are not, and this makes us aware of the possibility of choosing what we will be in the future. Because our freedom is nothingness the choices we make are made on the basis of no thing, and they are choices of values and meanings. To perform an action we must be able to stand back from our participation in the world of existing things in order to contemplate what does not exist. Into this emptiness we can put an action. According to Sartre, when we choose, the choice of action is also a choice of oneself. But in choosing myself I do not choose to *exist*. Existence is given, and one has to exist in order to choose. What I choose is my **essence**, the particular *way* in which I will exist. I choose myself as I envisage myself. Thus I may, in a particular situation, choose myself as an essentially deliberating self, or an impetuous self, or perhaps as some other self entirely; perhaps as someone who will be submissive to others or perhaps as someone who will resist influences. This is what it is to choose one's essence. If I choose myself as essentially 'someone who will deliberate', it is in *that* choice and not in any particular deliberations which follow it that I make the choice of myself; and because of this Sartre says, 'When I deliberate, the chips are down.'[6] I have already chosen myself as 'one who deliberates' and the content of the actual deliberations is a subsequent matter. From this analysis is derived a famous slogan of existentialism: 'existence precedes and commands essence'.[7]

That is a difficult idea to grasp. I have to think of myself as choosing a meaning or value for myself in the very act of becoming conscious of my existence: the becoming conscious *is* the evaluation. My awareness of myself as a particular kind of being is my choice of myself. Yet there is no reason for choosing myself as I do choose; I could have chosen another meaning for myself and it is because there is no reason for the choice that it is unjustified, groundless. This is the perpetual human reality. We are in the world as beings who are both things and consciousness. The upsurge of consciousness, whenever it occurs, at once makes me into an historical being and, by perceiving what I am not, launches me towards a future which is as yet empty and open. We have continually to choose ourselves by denying what we are, by making it what we were and by choosing ourselves as something else. In the upsurge of consciousness I choose myself afresh as the being who now beholds the being I was and moves towards the being which I am not yet. Sartre calls this 'the radical decision'. He rejects any analysis of the human being as some kind of characterless, basic **substance** which heredity, environment and learned behaviour patterns shape into an individual being. He speaks instead of a 'psychic irreducible' which is undetermined and contingent. The human being is not a substance-with-properties but 'a non-substantial absolute'. Thus he resists any kind of explanation that tries to go further and further beyond or beneath what is open to view and rejects ordinary psychological methods that attempt such explanations. His own method, which he calls existential psychoanalysis, seeks to comprehend a person's fundamental choice. It works to reveal to a person the meaning of his choice so that he can change it if he wishes. The idea of the unconscious is rejected also; for, in existential psychoanalysis, it is a choice which is sought and choice is not found in the unconscious because, for Sartre, choice is identical with consciousness. However, in rejecting the unconscious he is not claiming that we know everything about ourselves but that we are decipherable from those things of which we are aware. There is no need to explain away what is before us by citing a list of unseen causes. A person is a 'mystery in broad daylight'; a totality and not a mere collection of properties; someone who is to be understood rather than conceptualised, for any attempt to conceptualise the fundamental choice must fail and the type of understanding of a person that is possible cannot strictly be described as 'knowledge'. It is more a recognition that someone exists in just the way they are and in no other way, and of there being no ultimate reason for their being as they are other than that they have chosen themselves in that way. A person's life acquires meaning in that the person is wholly responsible for it.

'Bad faith' is probably one of the best-known themes of existentialism. Acting in bad faith is a consequence of turning away from the anguish of realising that one is utterly free and that one does not choose one's being on the basis of this or that matter but out of nothing. Bad faith has many forms. One manifestation of it occurs in the person who lives a role or life style that is a mere stereotype or cliché. Overwhelmed by the responsibility of choosing a meaning and a value for his life, a person may find an escape and a superficial comfort in adopting a ready-made role which provides him with a meaning he does not have to make for himself. Instead of living as a subject who experiences his freedom he treats himself as an object or thing that has a designated function to fulfil. Sartre's most famous example concerns a waiter:

Let us consider this waiter in the cafe. His movement is quick and forward, a little too precise, a little too quick ... his voice, his eyes express an interest a little too solicitous for the order of the customer ... he gives himself the quickness and pitiless rapidity of things ... the waiter in the cafe plays with his condition in order to *realise* it.[8]

Another way to be in bad faith is to deny what one actually is, perhaps by vowing to change one's bad habits or to give up heavy drinking or an idle life and in believing each time one makes the resolution that one will actually hold to it; yet never doing so. In bad faith we deceive ourselves. It is a deception of a particularly complicated kind. In order to deceive at all, one must know the truth, otherwise what one does is not a deception but an error or something done in ignorance. Thus bad faith is a form of lying to oneself. It is difficult to see how it is possible, within the unity of a single consciousness, both to confront a truth and to deceive oneself about it. Yet this is something that human beings commonly engage in: an ignoring of, or fleeing from, something recognised as a truth and a holding fast to an illusion.

For Sartre, to act or live in bad faith is to turn away from one's freedom and from making a meaning for oneself. To live in bad faith is to exist as an object and to be, like an object, determined by laws of nature and convention rather than choosing in freedom. Yet the choice of entering into bad faith is just as free as any other choice. It is a choice of being in the world in a particular way. We get the impression that 'bad faith' is morally bad; that to live in bad faith is to abdicate human responsibility, to deny the freedom that constitutes 'what it is like' to be a human being and to shirk the business of making our own ascriptions of meaning and value. However, Sartre clearly states that his enquiry is intended as a *description* of human existence. His primary concern is not to say what human beings ought to be like but what they are like. He does not, for instance, say that we ought to make free choices but that the

conditions of human existence are such that we cannot avoid making them. He never did write a book on philosophical ethics but in *Being and nothingness,* in a rather enigmatic footnote to his discussion of bad faith, he suggests that there is the possibility of escaping it. He says: 'this supposes a self-recovery of being which was previously corrupted. This self-recovery we shall call authenticity, the description of which has no place here.'[9]

Sartre describes the person who acts in bad faith as living in 'the spirit of seriousness'. Seriousness had two main characteristics. First, it takes values to exist quite independently of human beings. Second, it sees values as somehow embodied in things. It might for instance take 'nourishment' to be an actual element in the constitution of bread. It accepts stereotyped values and meanings, somehow believing them to be objectively there: in short, it takes them seriously. It perceives nothing of the absurd contingency of all things and has no sense of the emptiness that invites us to make meanings. In the presence of works of art, for example, if I am 'serious-minded', I will ignore my freedom to make my own judgements of the works and instead will search assiduously for values I take to be embodied in them.

Sartre maintains that we turn away from freedom because in recognising it we experience anguish. Anguish is felt because where there is nothing to determine choice, *anything* is possible. It is possible that one might choose, in the next moment, something appalling and terrible, from the thought of which one now turns away in horror. He gives the example of negotiating a path that runs along the edge of a precipice. In spite of all the care taken in such a situation, the foresight and calculation of the difficulties and one's cautious and controlled movements, there is still the possibility not simply of the occurrence of mishap or accident, but of one's choosing to be reckless or wild, of choosing to jump over the edge. Although there may be nothing conducive to doing this, although there is no reason for such a choice, although its prospect is horrifying, yet one *might* do it. He says:

> I am in anguish precisely because any conduct on my part is only *possible*, and this means that while constituting a totality of motives *for* pushing away that situation, I at the same moment apprehend these motives as not sufficiently effective. At the very moment when I apprehend my being as *horror* of the precipice, I am conscious of that horror as *not determinant* in relation to my possible conduct. In one sense that horror calls for prudent conduct, and it is in itself a pre-outline of that conduct; in another sense, it posits the final developments of that conduct only as possible, precisely because I do not apprehend it as the *cause* of these final developments.[10]

The notion of anguish, or dread, has become something of a trademark of existentialism; but of course, anguish is by no means the only, or even a necessary, consequence of the realisation of freedom. A sense of total freedom may well generate exhilaration and adventurousness, liberating one from a restless search for meaning *in* things. Existential thought should certainly not be construed as springing solely from despair in the face of absurdity. Sartre himself, in defending his ideas against imputations of pessimism, has said that it cannot be regarded so, 'for no doctrine is more optimistic, — the destiny of man is placed within himself'.[11]

Sartre's political activities after World War Two brought deep disappointment to him and led him to attempt radically to reconstruct his thought. He planned the *Critique of dialectical reason* in two volumes, the first as a theoretical and abstract study, the second as a treatment of history. But the *Critique* was never completed. Sartre abandoned the second volume after writing only a few chapters of it. Volume I was published in 1960 and has been described as 'a monster of unreadability'. In the *Critique* Sartre repudi-

ates many of his earlier views about personal freedom. He says:

> let no one interpret me as saying that man is free in all situations ... I want to say exactly the opposite, namely that all men are slaves in so far as their experience of life takes place in the realm of the *practico-inert* and in the exact measure in which this realm is originally conditioned by scarcity.[12]

The term 'practico-inert' refers to that part of life which is determined by earlier free actions and it is the interaction or, more properly, the **dialectic**, of individual practice and the inherited burden of historical fact that, in the *Critique*, is the predominant concern for Sartre. There is general agreement that the work succeeds neither as sociology, nor anthropology, nor philosophy. Equally, there is general agreement that in this, as in all his abundant and brilliant writing, Sartre articulates and illumines issues that are of the profoundest interest and importance.

Notes

1. J.P. Sartre, *Being and nothingness*, trans. Hazel E. Barnes (Methuen, London, 1969), pp. xlii, 74.
2. J.P. Sartre, *Nausea*, trans. R. Baldick (Penguin, Harmondsworth, 1965), p. 22.
3. Ibid., p. 185.
4. Ibid., p. 248.
5. Sartre, *Being and nothingness*, p. 566.
6. Ibid., p. 451.
7. Ibid., p. 438.
8. Ibid., p. 59.
9. Ibid., p. 70, note.
10. Ibid., p. 31.
11. J.P. Sartre, *Existentialism and humanism*, trans. Philip Mairet (Methuen, London, 1975), p. 44.
12. J.P. Sartre, *Critique of dialectical reason*, quoted in A. Manser, *Sartre* (Oxford University Press, 1966; paperback, 1967), p. 207.

See also in this book

Kierkegaard, Heidegger.

Sartre's major writings

The psychology of the imagination (1940) (Methuen, London, 1983)

Being and nothingness: an essay on phenomenological ontology (1943), trans. H.E. Barnes (Methuen, London, 1958; paperback, 1969)

Existentialism and humanism (1946), trans. P. Mairet (Methuen, London, 1948)

What is literature? (1947), trans. B. Frechtman (Methuen, London, 1950)

Critique of dialectical reason (1960), trans. A. Sheridan-Smith (Verso Books, London, 1982)

War diaries (1939-40), trans. Q. Hoare (Verso Books, London, 1983; paperback, 1985)

Words (autobiography, 1964) trans. I. Clephane (Hamish Hamilton, London, 1964)

Novels

Nausea (1938), trans. R. Baldick (Penguin, Harmondsworth, 1965)

The age of reason (1945), trans. E. Sutton (Penguin, Harmondsworth, 1961)

The reprieve (1945), trans. E. Sutton (Penguin, Harmondsworth, 1963)

Iron in the soul (1949), trans. E. Sutton (Penguin, Harmondsworth, 1963)

Further reading

Blackham, H.J. *Six existentialist thinkers* (Routledge and Kegan Paul, London, 1961)

Cranston, M. *Sartre* (Oliver and Boyd, Edinburgh, 1962)

Danto, A.C. *Sartre* (Viking Press, New York, 1975)

Macquarrie, J. *Existentialism* (Penguin, Harmondsworth, 1972)

Manser, A. *Sartre* (Oxford University Press, New York, 1967)

Meszaros, I. *The work of Sartre* vol. I. (Harvester Press, Hassocks, Sussex, 1979)

Murdoch, I. *Sartre, romantic rationalist* (Bowes and Bowes, Cambridge, 1953)

Warnock, M. *The philosophy of Sartre* (Hutchinson, London, 1972)

Glossary

Abstraction

Abstraction is the process of separating out or abstracting an aspect or quality common to a number of objects, thereby forming an idea of that quality. Abstraction has been put forward as an explanation of how we come to formulate general or universal ideas such as redness, triangularity, sharpness and so on.
See *Universal, Nominalism,* and *Locke, Berkeley.*

Alienation

Karl Marx used the term 'alienation' to describe the depersonalised and purposeless condition of people who have become estranged from vital social and economic elements in their lives. Hegel wrote of a general human condition of estrangement from reality, reality being, for him, a spiritual and rationally coherent whole. Marx translated this conception of estrangement into material terms, thinking of it as an individual's alienation from his or her own productive powers and a loss of control over them.
See *Hegel, Marx.*

Analogy

An analogy compares one thing with another in order to indicate resemblances between them and thereby to increase understanding of the lesser known of the two.
See *Plato, Butler.*

Analytic/Synthetic

An analytic statement is one in which the predicate is contained in the subject. In the statement 'Bachelors are unmarried males' the meaning of the predicate 'unmarried males' is implicit or contained in the subject, 'bachelors'. The negation of an analytic statement is self-contradictory or implies a self-contradiction. Analytic statements are *a priori* in that they are not confirmed or refuted by appeal to experience or observation.

A synthetic statement is one in which the predicate asserts something not contained either implicitly or explicitly in the subject. The statement 'All bachelors ride bicycles' is synthetic because its predicate, 'ride bicycles', purports to give information about, and further to, that contained in the subject, 'all bachelors'. The negations of synthethic statements are not self-contradictory. Philosophers have not been in agreement about whether all synthetic statements are *a posteriori*, that is, confirmable or refutable by reference to experience.
See *a posteriori* and *Kant.*

a priori ('from what is prior')
a posteriori ('from what is posterior')

A priori and *a posteriori* are terms relating to our ways of knowing whether a statement is true. Whether a statement is true or false is known *a priori* if the claim to knowledge is justified without appeal to experience or observation. For example, the claim to know that triangles are three-sided figures is not justified by examining particular examples of triangles (that is, by appealing to experience or observation) but by a consideration of the meanings of the terms 'triangle' and 'three-sided'. Something which is true *a priori* is necessarily true; that is, it cannot be false and its negation is necessarily false (see *Necessary/Contingent* below).

164

A statement's truth-value is known *a posteriori* if the claim to knowledge is justified only by appeal to experience or observation. The claim to know that 'the cat is on the mat' is justified by an inspection (that is, by experience, observation) of the particular cat and mat referred to in the claim. Something which is true *a posteriori* is not necessarily but contingently true; that is, it just happens to be true and it is logically possible for it to be otherwise. Its negation is contingently false.

See *Necessary/Contingent* and *Kant.*

Argument

An argument consists of a statement which is a conclusion standing in relation to one or more statements which are evidence for the conclusion. The statements of evidence are called *premisses*. Premisses are factual statements and may therefore be true or false. Logic is not concerned with the truth or falsity of statements but with the relationships between them and logical correctness or incorrectness is independent of the truth or falsity of premisses. An argument that has a correct logical form is said to be *valid.* To say that an argument is valid is not to say that its premisses are true but that *if* they are (were) true then the conclusion must also be true. There are various patterns of valid arguments and one task of logic is to identify and analyse them.

See *Fallacy, Validity, Deductive/Inductive.*

Behaviourism

The general theory of philosophical behaviourism is that a complete account of all mental states can be given in terms of observable behaviour or tendencies. It runs into difficulties when it tries to give an account of activities such as dreaming, believing, reasoning, which can take place without 'observable behaviour' taking place.

Calculus

A calculus is a system of symbols governed by rules and designed to enable reasoning or calculating to be undertaken. The two most common calculuses used in modern symbolic logic are *propositional calculus* and *predicate calculus.* The *differential calculus* and the *infinitesimal calculus* are mathematical calculuses.

See *Zeno* and *Leibniz.*

Contingent

See *Necessary/Contingent.*

Cosmogony

A cosmogony is a theory or account of the origin of the universe. It may be a scientific, a reasoned, a speculative or mythical account.

See the early Greek philosophers, *Thales* to *Democritus.*

Cosmology

Cosmology is the study of the physical universe. It examines and reasons about such concepts as space, matter, substance, the finite and the infinite. It considers the nature of things and thereby invokes the interaction of the experimental activity of physics with the critical reasoning of philosophy.

See the early Greek philosophers, *Thales* to *Democritus.*

Deductive/Inductive

A deductive argument is one which purports to be valid in the technical sense. In a valid deductive argument the conclusion follows from the premisses. For example:

Every mammal has a heart.
All horses are mammals.
Every horse has a heart.

In a deductive argument all the information in the conclusion is already contained (implicitly) in the premises; and, if all the premises are true, the conclusion must be true.

An inductive argument does not purport to be valid. It draws an inference which does not 'follow from' its premises but which is supported by them. For example:

Every horse that has been observed has a heart.
Every horse has a heart.

In an inductive argument, if all the premises are true, the conclusion is *probably* true but not necessarily true. The conclusion contains information not present, even implicitly, in the premises.
See *Hobbes, Descartes, Spinoza, Leibniz, Mill.*

Dialectic

With Plato, dialectic is a procedure of rational disputation which, by careful consideration and resolution of opposing arguments, works to attain what he regarded as the highest form of knowledge. In the nineteenth century Hegel adopted the view that reality is dialectical in nature: that opposing rational views, a thesis and an antithesis, resolve into a synthesis which then becomes the thesis of a further dialectical process, and so on. Hegel saw this as the activity of pure Spirit. With Marx, dialectic is made material and the dialectical process is seen in terms of a struggle of material and economic forces towards resolution into a better society.
See *Plato, Hegel, Marx, Sartre.*

Dualism

Dualism is the doctrine that reality consists of two basic, distinct substances, one mental and one physical. The doctrine generates questions and theories about what relation-

ship, if any, holds between the two distinct substances. Dualism stands in opposition to monism, the doctrine that reality consists of only one substance.
See *Descartes.*

Empiricism

Empiricism is the view that knowledge of the world is based upon and derived from sense experience. In the history of philosophy the empiricist claim that 'Nothing is in the mind which was not first in the senses' stands against the claim that some of our knowledge of the world is in us in the form of innate ideas. In describing a piece of knowledge as empirical the term 'empirical' refers primarily to how the knowledge is acquired.
See *Locke, Hume, Schlick, Carnap.*

Epistemology

Epistemology is the theory of knowledge. It is a critical enquiry into what is to count as knowledge, what kinds of things are knowable and whether anything at all can be known for certain. Thus it asks what conditions have to be fulfilled if a person may be said to have knowledge, as opposed to mere belief, and examines the different ways in which claims to knowledge may be justified.
See *Plato, Hobbes, Descartes, Spinoza, Locke, Leibniz, Berkeley, Hume.*

Essence

The essence of something may be thought of as its true or essential nature: that without which it would not be what it is. Aristotle held that a correct definition of a thing expressed its essence. Thereafter philosophers have criticised and developed the concept in numerous ways.
See *Aristotle, Aquinas, Locke, Sartre.*

Fallacy

A fallacy is an invalid inference in an argument. If a fallacy occurs in a complex argument it does not follow that the conclusion of the argument is necessarily false or wrong, even though the fallacy impairs the validity (i.e. the formal structure) of the argument.
See *Argument, Validity*.

Form

Plato held that a world of perfect, immaterial Forms exists apart from the world of sensory objects which are imitations or less-than-perfect instantiations of the Forms. Aristotle held that form is that which makes a thing what it is and individuates it from other kinds of things, but he did not share Plato's view that forms exist apart from their instantiations. Medieval philosophers believed that each angel was a distinct Form, different from every other angel. Francis Bacon wrote of the forms of 'simple natures' and thought of those forms as laws governing the fundamental natural structures of the world.
See *Universal* and *Plato, Aristotle, Augustine, Aquinas, Bacon*.

Hypothesis

A hypothesis is a statement which goes beyond any evidence adduced to support it. Once proved the statement no longer counts as a hypothesis.

Idealism

Idealism is a metaphysical doctrine about the nature of the world. It maintains that reality ultimately consists of minds and ideas and that matter has no existence independently of our ideas of it. 'Transcendental idealism' is a term used to describe Kant's view that objects of experience are simply appearances, not existing outside our thoughts. In Kant's view the structures or mental principles through which we formulate our conceptions of the external world are 'transcendental' because they are the basis of experience; and they are 'ideal' because they are 'in the mind': hence 'transcendental idealism'.
See *Berkeley, Kant, Schopenhauer*.

Inductive

See *Deductive/Inductive*.

Intuitive knowledge

Intuitive knowledge is immediate, direct knowledge, attained without intermediary steps or procedures. It may be knowledge of propositions, of sensory objects, or of spiritual objects. Kant describes our acquaintance with sensory objects as 'sensory intuitions'. In Plato, immediate knowledge of a Form is intuitive knowledge but is not sensory.
See *Plato, Spinoza, Locke, Kant*.

Materialism

Materialism is a metaphysical doctrine about the nature of the world. It maintains that everything that exists is matter. Some versions of materialism include mind as a dependency or product of matter.
See *Monism* and *Hobbes*.

Metaphysics

Aristotle described metaphysics as 'the study of Being as Being, and of the properties inherent in it in virtue of its own nature'. It had also been described as 'the study of what is there', meaning that it reflects on the most ultimate and general nature of what exists. Claims such as 'There is fundamentally only

one substance' or 'Every event has a cause' are metaphysical claims in that they assert something about the whole of what is. When metaphysics is confined to the nature of existence, or being, it is called *ontology*. Kant's question 'Is metaphysics possible?' is an epistemological question within metaphysics, since it is a question about whether we can have knowledge of metaphysical principles such as 'Every event has a cause.'
See *Epistemology* and *Spinoza, Kant, Leibniz.*

Monism

Monism is the view that reality consists of only one substance. The one substance may be material or spiritual, or perhaps indefinite, as Anaximander suggested. *Physical monism* is the view that the one substance is matter. It is sometimes called *monistic materialism,* or simply *materialism.* The term *psychical monism* is used to describe the view that the one substance is spiritual, mental, or non-material.
See *Anaximander, Hobbes, Spinoza.*

Monistic materialism

See *Monism.*

Necessary/Contingent

A statement which is necessarily true is true under all conditions. If its truth is *logically* necessary then its denial involves a contradiction. The statement

Either he is here or he is not here

is logically and so necessarily true. It is true in all possible worlds and its denial is self-contradictory. Similarly, a statement which is necessarily false is false under all conditions. If it is logically false, the statement is self-contradictory. The statement

If he is a brother then he is female

is logically and so necessarily false. It is a self-contradictory statement and its falsity obtains in all possible worlds. A statement which is *contingently* true or false is one the truth or falsity of which depends on circumstances; thus it may be *either* true *or* false. The truth or falsity of the statement

Fred is sitting in the dining room

is dependent (contingent) upon circumstances, and may be sometimes true and sometimes false. A statement is contingent if both what it asserts, and its denial, are logically possible. Besides logical necessity, many philosophers speak also of physical or natural necessity. A statement of physical or natural necessity, for instance

Objects heavier than air tend to fall to the ground

differs from a statement of logical necessity in that we can think of a possible world in which objects heavier than air did not tend to fall to the ground.
See *Tautology.*

Neo-Platonism

This term is used to refer to revivals or redeployments of Plato's philosophy. There have been three major revivals. The first took place in the early Christian centuries and culminated in the philosophy of Plotinus in the third century AD. The second major revival had its source in Italy and embraced many other aspects of early Greek thought in addition to Platonism. It was at its peak in the fifteenth century. The third major revival was inaugurated by the Cambridge Platonists in the seventeenth century and was a reaction to the debunking of entrenched Aristotelianism. All three revivals emphasised the mystical elements in Plato's thought.
See *Plato, Plotinus.*

Nominalism

Nominalism is the view that universal or general terms such as 'redness' or 'hardness' are names only and do not refer to any existing thing that is 'redness' or 'hardness'. Thus a nominalist would not allow that Platonic Forms of, for example, Justice or Piety or Courage can exist apart from particular instances of them.
See *Form, Ockham, Hobbes.*

Ontology

See *Metaphysics.*

Pantheism

Pantheism is the doctrine that the natural world is as much part of God as the spiritual world, so that everything is God and God is everything. It has sometimes attracted charges of atheism.
See *Spinoza.*

Paradox

A line of argument results in paradox if it leads to well-supported conclusions which conflict with each other. A well-known example is the Paradox of the Liar. A Cretan states that 'All Cretans are Liars.' Since he is a Cretan, if what he says is true then it is also false, for if all Cretans are liars then the statement 'All Cretans are liars,' when made by a Cretan, is false.

Particular

See *Universal/ Particular.*

Premiss

See *Argument.*

Rationalism

One use of this term is to describe the views of a number of seventeenth-century philosophers, among whom were Descartes, Spinoza and Leibniz, who believed that reason alone can provide knowledge of the existence and nature of things. It is also used to describe the view that reality is a unified, coherent and explicable system.
See *Descartes, Spinoza, Leibniz.*

Scepticism

Philosophical scepticism, in general, is doubt about whether knowledge is possible. It may take various forms. Thus a sceptic may doubt whether sense experience ever yields knowledge, or whether God, the external world and other minds exist. Scepticism is ultimately a debate about what is to count as knowledge.
See *Epistemology* and *Descartes.*

Scholasticism

Scholasticism is the mediaeval philosophy, largely based on Aristotle, which dominated the twelfth and thirteenth centuries. It employed syllogistic reasoning and acquired a reputation for disputing at length over minute points and subtleties. Thomas Aquinas is the greatest of the scholastic philosophers.
See *Aquinas, Duns Scotus, Ockham.*

Sophism/Sophistry

The Greek Sophists, who flourished in the fifth century BC were teachers or 'experts' who taught many subjects, but chiefly rhetoric and debating. They acquired a reputation for scoring points by means of logic-chopping and unsound arguments and these are the traits that are usually invoked when a

person is accused of 'sophistry'; but this is not to say that all Sophists were of shallow intellect.
See *Socrates*.

Substance

Aristotle described substance as 'that which does not depend on anything else for its existence'. Traditionally, it has been thought of as that which supports qualities or properties and which exists independently of them.
See *Aristotle, Descartes, Spinoza, Locke, Leibniz*.

Syllogism

A syllogism is a deductive argument composed of three statements: two premisses and a conclusion. It was first introduced by Aristotle and was the basis of logic until the early twentieth century.
See *Argument, Fallacy, Validity* and *Aristotle*.

Synthetic

See *Analytic/Synthetic*.

Tautology

A tautology is a statement that is obviously or necessarily true in virtue of the repetition in it of a word or symbol. Thus 'a brown dog is a dog' and '4 = 4' are tautologies. In symbolic logic a tautology is a propositional form which yields a proposition that is true whatever the truth-values of its component propositions are. 'Either it is raining or it is not raining' is an example of this kind of tautology; it is true if it is raining and it is true if it is not raining.
See *Truth-value*.

Truth-value

The truth-value of a statement is its truth or falsity. In general, these are the only truth-values but it is possible to have systems of logic with three or more truth-values. A three-valued logic might have 'indeterminate' as its third value. A many-valued logic would include degrees of probability among its truth-values.
See *Tautology*.

Universal/Particular

General terms such as 'dog', 'beauty', 'kindness' and so on are sometimes called 'universals' to distinguish them from 'particulars' such as 'this dog', 'this beautiful object', 'this kind act' etc. The question then arises whether universals have existence apart from particulars: whether 'beauty', for instance, exists apart from particular beautiful things. The philosophical problem here is that of finding a justification for grouping different particulars together and classifying them in the ways we do.
See *Abstraction, Nominalism,* and *Plato, Aristotle, Duns Scotus, Hobbes, Locke, Berkeley*.

Validity

The terms 'valid' and 'invalid' are applicable to arguments, not to statements. An argument is valid when its conclusion follows from the assumptions of its premisses. It is the relationship between the components of the argument that manifest validity or invalidity. Thus an argument may have a valid form even though all or some of its premisses are false and to say that an argument is valid is not to say that its premisses are true but that if they are true then the conclusion must also be true.
See *Argument, Fallacy*.